# TENNIS

## Myth and Method

# Ellsworth Vines
# and Gene Vier

# TENNIS

## Myth and Method

A SEAVER BOOK

THE VIKING PRESS • New York

A Seaver Book/The Viking Press

First published in 1978 by The Viking Press
625 Madison Avenue, New York, N.Y. 10022

Published simultaneously in Canada by
Penguin Books Canada Limited

LIBRARY OF CONGRESS CATALOGING IN PUBLICATION DATA
Vines, Ellsworth, 1911–
Tennis.
"A Seaver book."
1. Tennis players—Biography. 2. Tennis.
I. Vier, Gene, joint author. II. Title.
GV994.A1V56    1978    796.34′2′0922  [B]   77–18544
ISBN 0–670–69665–x

Printed in the United States of America
Set in Videocomp Gael

To my mentor and good friend Perry T. Jones, my coach Mercer Beasley, and to the Southern California Tennis Patrons Association for their encouragement, guidance, and financial help during the formative years of my tennis career. Without their wholehearted assistance I would never have been able to reach the tennis heights. ELLSWORTH VINES

To Robin Willner GENE VIER

# Contents

# PART II  METHOD
Technique, Strategy, and Tactics

# Introduction

Ellsworth Vines in 1936,
when he was professional champion
of the world.

Until the emergence of Don Budge in the latter part of the 1930s,
the most sensational player of that decade was H. Ellsworth Vines,
Jr. It is still the consensus of many experts that on a given day the
greatest player who ever lived was Vines.

After winning the National Clay Courts in 1931 (and thereby dis-
pelling any idea his power wasn't coupled with steadiness), Ellsworth
Vines came out of the West at age 19 and beat Fred Perry in the
Forest Hills semifinals, 4–6, 3–6, 6–4, 6–4, 6–3. It was a fantastic
exhibition of power. Particularly remarkable was that Perry, one of
the strongest, fastest, and fittest athletes in tennis history, had Vines
down two sets to love and *still* lost. In the finals Vines defeated the
formidable George Lott in four sets, to capture the U.S. singles title
of 1931.

The next year Vines won eleven major tournaments. He was the repeat champion at the important Newport Casino Men's Invitational in Rhode Island, and annihilated Bunny Austin and Henri Cochet for the Wimbledon and U.S. titles, respectively. His only important loss was to Jean Borotra of France at Stade Roland Garros in the Davis Cup Challenge Round, in what was considered the most notorious exhibition of bad calls in Cup history.

The level of Vines's performance at Wimbledon that year (1932) has probably never been surpassed. He humiliated the Australian champion Jack Crawford 6–2, 6–1, 6–3 in the semis, and then overwhelmed Bunny Austin 6–4, 6–2, 6–0. Austin confessed afterward that the final ace served by Vines was so fast he didn't know on which side the ball flew by him. Vines's one-sided victory over Jack Crawford was particularly impressive as Crawford had won two Australian titles, and the next year almost achieved the first Grand Slam in tennis history by capturing the Australian, Wimbledon, and French titles.

It is sometimes asked why Vines didn't try for the Grand Slam in 1932. The answer, I suspect, is that like the "big game" myth, the Grand Slam was largely an invention of sportswriters. Until Crawford almost pulled it off in 1933, the Grand Slam was an idea whose time had not yet come. In those preaviation days, Australia was a terribly long boat trip, and until the emergence of such players as Crawford, Viv McGrath, Adrian Quist, and Harry Hopman in the early 1930s, the Australian title did not have the prestige it later acquired.

Nevertheless, Vines journeyed "Down Under" in 1933 only to be upset by Viv McGrath, the first major exponent of the two-hand backhand. (In fact, McGrath's ability to handle Vines's kick second serve with the two-fisted shot was an important factor in the upset.) However, Vines and another Californian, Keith Gledhill, won the 1933 Australian doubles by defeating defending champions Jack Crawford and E. F. Moon in straight sets. Gledhill made it to the finals of the singles, but lost to Crawford.

Vines and Gledhill won several major doubles titles when they were a team. Their most impressive victory was in 1932 over Wilmer Allison and Johnny Van Ryn, 6–4, 6–3, 6–2, for the U.S. doubles crown. Allison and Van Ryn were one of the best tandems that ever played the game. When they faced Vines and Gledhill at the Longwood Cricket Club, they had won Wimbledon the two previous years, the French doubles, and were the U.S. national defending champions at Longwood. When he turned pro a couple of years later, Vines also won several world doubles titles with Bill Tilden.

Vines had a generally disappointing season in 1933. There have been several explanations for it, but I have my own theory. Vines is probably the most unassuming and least egotistical of all the great champions. In 1931, stars such as Fred Perry, Sidney Wood, Johnny Doeg, and George Lott presented a formidable challenge for the youngster, so he could "psych himself up." In his first Wimbledon—which he won in such a devastating manner—the challenge was also obvious, as it was at Forest Hills that year when he faced the great Henri Cochet in the finals. However, after beating the Frenchman 6–4, 6–4, 6–4 for the American title, there suddenly were no more worlds to conquer. Vines had defeated every top amateur in the world, including Francis X. Shields, Sidney Wood, Adrian Quist, Cochet, Clifford Sutter, Johnny Doeg, Wilmer Allison, Baron Gottfried von Cramm, Keith Gledhill, Lester Stofen, George Lott, Bunny Austin, Crawford, and the great Fred Perry. In fact, Perry had lost all four of his matches to Vines in 1932!

In 1933 a letdown was almost inevitable. Athletes constantly set goals for themselves; Vines had achieved his in 1932—he was the world champion. The following year it is possible that Vines unconsciously put himself at a disadvantage early in matches to create artificially the challenge he needed. Further, when a player has the heavy guns of a Vines, there is the constant temptation to feel you can pull out a match at any time. This is a dangerous practice in any sport; in tennis it can be fatal, because you start missing lines by inches on important points and before you know it you've lost the match.

Losing doesn't help your confidence, no matter who you are, and what is more it bolsters the confidence of your future opponents, since the myth of your invincibility has been punctured (much in the same way a psychological barrier is overcome when you defeat an opponent who has always had your number).

There is also a tendency, when you have the minimum ego involvement of a Vines, not to press the advantage with the same ferocity you did when you were coming up. The taste of victory has somewhat paled for you, and in the brotherhood of sport you may unconsciously try to give the other guy that sweet taste for a while.

My assumption, therefore, is that Vines had trouble "psyching" himself up for the 1933 season. The exception was his remarkable match against Jack Crawford in the Wimbledon finals.

Crawford came into Wimbledon with a startling set of victories which rivaled Vines's record of the previous season. He had won Australia for the third year in a row and had just finished off Cochet in straight sets for the French title. In his disappointing Australian tour, Vines had lost in the Victorian finals to Crawford 1–6, 6–4, 6–4, 2–6, 6–4, so the improved Aussie offered Vines more than enough challenge at Wimbledon.

After getting by a tough four-set match with Cochet in the semifinals, Vines met Crawford on the center court in what have been called, by Allison Danzig and other experts, the outstanding finals in the history of Wimbledon. Crawford squeaked through in five sets. British tennis writer Peter Wilson said that throughout the match Crawford's "anticipation was so uncanny it bordered on extrasensory perception." Following Wimbledon, Crawford just missed the Grand Slam at Forest Hills when he lost a cliff-hanger to Fred Perry in five sets. (Vines had earlier been upset by Bitsy Grant.)

Fred Perry said of Vines, "truly a meteoric flash across the sky of amateur lawn tennis. I know his form of 1933 did not match that of the two previous seasons; he had gone stale. But his play as a professional has shown the slump was only temporary."

In spite of Jack Crawford's record in 1933, it was Ellsworth Vines of the famed serve and forehand whom the tennis fans wanted to challenge the world professional champion, Big Bill Tilden. Vines defeated Tilden decisively on their tour. He also won the initial professional world championship at Wembley in 1934 (and every year he competed thereafter). At that time it was a more important tournament than the U.S. pro championship. From 1934 to 1938, Vines reigned over the professional tennis world which, besides Tilden, included Henri Cochet, George Lott, Vinnie Richards, Hans Nusslein, Karl Kozeluh, Bruce Barnes, Dan Maskell, Dick Skeen, Lester Stofen, and, in 1937, Fred Perry. After besting Perry in a close tour in 1937–38, the stage was set for the monumental confrontation: Vines versus Budge. The pro monarch against the king of amateur tennis.

The Tilden-Vines tour established a pattern for professional tennis which lasted into the early 1960s: a tour to find the pro champion, then a move to sign the top amateur into the ranks two years later if it were ascertained he would provide enough box office draw. Vines's electrifying game made him a tremendous draw, especially in his debuts at Madison Square Garden. The Tilden opener in 1934 attracted 14,000, and 15,000 turned out in 1937 for the initial meeting between Vines and Perry.

The opening match between Don Budge and Ellsworth Vines, at the end of 1938, lured 17,000, with tickets as high as $7.70, and scalpers getting three times that amount. Fans recognized the event as something extraordinary. Here was the greatest backhand of all time against the greatest forehand. Both had awesome serves and groundstrokes, both fine net games; when you see this kind of power and control, the game takes on another dimension.

The highly heralded match turned out to be somewhat anticlimactic: Budge won 6–3, 6–4, 6–2, creating the misconception that the tour might be a runaway. The pressure was definitely on Vines, who was several years older than Budge and had put on some weight since his amateur days. Promoter Jack Harris had given Don a $75,000 guarantee, plus a share of the gate; Vines had an equal percentage of the gate but no guarantee. If Budge made the tour a rout, the box office would suffer, which meant little to Budge in financial terms, but a great deal to Vines. Despite the pressure, at the end of 6 matches Elly led 4 to 2. At that point he strained a muscle in his side which affected his serve, and Budge won the next eight matches. After his side mended, Vines, with a remarkable effort, managed to pull within five matches of Budge (it stood at 22–17) by the time their first tour ended. After Budge dismantled Fred Perry in a short tour, the Vines-Budge junket resumed and moved to Europe. The keen competition had made the genial redhead almost unplayable, and Vines took only 5 of their 20 matches. Their overall tour record was 37 to 22, and J. Donald Budge thus became the new world professional champion. They drew large crowds wherever they went and both athletes made over $100,000—a huge sum in those days.

Ellsworth Vines's penultimate net triumph, before he turned to golf, was at the Wembley tournament in England, which he captured for the fourth time. His competitive swan song was at the Beverly Hills Tennis Club in the 1939 U.S. professional championship, when he defeated Fred Perry for the title. (Amazingly, Vines never lost to Perry in a pro tournament.) Because his preeminence would have affected the box office, Budge skipped both tournaments.

When I once asked Elly why he dropped out of professional competition, he replied, "I wasn't going to hang around like Tilden and be second best."

With no more tours on the agenda, Vines became the tennis pro at the Beverly Hills Tennis Club, where he taught movie stars and practiced golf on the side. In 1945 when the war ended, he turned to professional golf and became a leading pro.

Ellsworth Vines is one of the most knowledgeable men tennis has ever known, and he played the game as well as any athlete who ever walked on a court. More important to me, however, was the help that Elly personally gave me at various times in my own tennis career.

Watching Ellsworth Vines playing in a tour match with Bill Tilden on the racetrack at the Los Angeles county fairgrounds in Pomona convinced me that becoming a tennis champion was the greatest thing I could dream of. Till then I was what you might call an athlete for all seasons; I played sandlot baseball, football, basketball, and even did a little pole vaulting. Tennis was just a game to play to have fun with my dad. But after watching Vines play I returned to my hometown, San Bernardino, and gave up all other sports to concentrate on tennis. The very next day, I got my dad to buy me an Ellsworth Vines autographed racquet. That was in 1934 when I was 13. I next saw Ellsworth play Les Stofen on a fast canvas court at the Shrine Auditorium in Los Angeles; he was so tremendous that evening that, more firmly than ever, I made up my mind to do everything possible to play the game the way Vines did.

Fortunately for me, in late 1935 my family moved to Los Angeles, which enabled me to get some good coaching and into the tournament swing. By this time I had copied Vines's walk and thought I had a pretty good imitation of the way he hit his serve and forehand.

My game came along very fast, and in 1936 I won the National Under-15 Championship. My first chance to get to know Ellsworth personally came in the winter of 1937 when he offered Perry T. Jones, the leader of Southern California tennis, a few hours of his time each week to help some deserving kids. Mr. Jones selected me as one of the youngsters.

At that time Vines was starting to pay more attention to his golf than to his tennis, but he still managed to play twice a week with me at the Beverly Hills Tennis Club (he and Fred Perry were co-owners).

It was Vines who stressed to me the importance of developing a much bigger serve, and especially helped me to get good depth on the second serve. He also convinced me that the offensive game was built on control as well as power and that the forehand should be the main weapon. With this kind of inspiration, advice, and competition, I improved to the point where I was no longer just a good young player but a threat in all the men's tournaments played in Southern California. Looking back, I feel that those few months of close association with the world's professional champion improved my game two hundred percent.

The next help from Ellsworth involved two major decisions in my tennis career. The first was a decision about which sporting goods company to join; Elly's advice—from his own personal experience—was to go with Wilson.

Later, when I was weighing three offers from promoters who wanted me to turn professional, Elly convinced me it was best to accept Jack Harris's offer of a lower guarantee but a higher percentage of the gate. Once again the Vines advice paid off as it had when he was my instructor.

The Vines I remember was a 6'2" whipcord who hit a flat forehand that had to be seen to be believed. It was without question the hardest forehand in the history of the game. His backhand lacked the power of his starboard side, but it was still a strong, consistent shot, and he could hit winners off it.

Vines's serve demands special comment. Budge calls it "the hardest I ever faced, and that includes Gonzales." Vines also had a fine American twist for a second delivery with which to take the net; only von Cramm had a better one. But it was his first serve that was awesome. In one match against Bunny Austin—a superb returner—Vines hit 30 clean aces.

Tennis authority Allison Danzig describes Ellsworth's game in these words: "Vines at the peak of his form could probably have beaten any player who ever lived. His lightning-bolt service was regarded by some as the best of all. No one hit a forehand flatter or harder or kept the ball so close to the net. He was murderous overhead and a volleyer of the first rank."

*Tennis: Myth and Method* is excellent in comparing players past and present. I found the central idea original, provacative, and valid; the section on technique insightful and lucid. All in all, this book is a very important contribution to a deeper understanding of how the game was played, is played, and should be played.

JACK KRAMER

# PART I

# MYTH

Reflections on the First Ten since Budge

# Ranking Mystique

For decades "ranked in the First Ten" was the magic phrase in the amateur game. This was true until the watershed year of 1968, when Wimbledon became an "open" tournament, and professional tennis vaulted into its present popularity on the world sports scene.

Before open tennis, all rising stars set their sights on the First Ten goal. The rankings were listed in the Spalding Year Book of Tennis, which carried photographs, physical statistics, the records, and an analysis of the games of the Top Ten. Being listed meant—among other things—that the lucky youngster was assured of playing the Eastern grass circuit, of staying at fine hotels with liberal expense money, and of seeing the world. The circuit tour also meant that a young man could raise the level of his game by competing against the best, for once he made it into the First Ten he would have many more opportunities to get a crack at the more famous players and thus keep his game at a high level. In those days, then, there were the First Ten and beyond that magic circle the "others" fighting to break into it. But few and far between were upsets of the magic circle members.

Since the advent of open tennis in 1968, upsets are the norm rather than the exception. For example, Roger Taylor upset defending champion Rod Laver in the 1970 Wimbledon. Juan Gisbert of Spain beat top-seed Ilie Nastase in the New York Clean-Air tournament in 1972. Nastase was the number-one seed at Wimbledon in 1973 and lost to young Alex Mayer. Colin Dibley ousted John Newcombe in the same year in the $150,000 Las Vegas Tournament at Caesars Palace, and a newcomer, Brian Gottfried, annihilated Arthur Ashe in the finals. Unseeded Roscoe Tanner defeated Stan Smith in the 1974 U.S. nationals. In October of the same year a virtually unknown Polish player upset Ashe 6–3, 6–2. This Iron Curtain entry, Wojtek Fibak, lost in the next round and didn't surface again until he whipped Ilie

Nastase at Stockholm in 1975. In the Louisville pro classic in August of 1975, Nastase defeated Wimbledon champion Ashe 6–3, 6–3 and then was in turn beaten in the finals by Guillermo Vilas. Although the last can't be considered exactly an upset, it certainly shows the inconsistency of performance of the top stars, not only from year to year but even from one day to the next.

In 1976 the upset pattern continued as it has every year since the start of open tennis. Fibak seemed finally to have hit his stride by beating Vilas in the Buckeye tourney in Ohio, and then a couple of weeks later at Boston was trounced 6–1, 6–2 by Paolo Bertulucci of Italy—a player who had never won a major tournament. A week before, Victor Pecci of Paraguay, even less experienced than Bertulucci, had upset the highly ranked Raul Ramirez in the Canadian Open.

Arthur Ashe, who had won 29 out of 31 matches going into 1976, proceeded to lose 6 out of the next 11—one of these, in the *Washington Star* event, to Dick Crealy, a player who hadn't beaten anyone of significance in years. Stan Smith and John Newcombe, the leading luminaries at the start of this decade, have had such a drought of tournament wins that many tennis fans think they've retired.

The usual explanation for the upset phenomenon is that there are so many more great players today. Highly debatable . . . but there is, unquestionably, more money. And there are those who argue that "money talks." Today, players make $1000 for losing in the first round of a tournament; a decade ago Rosewall or Laver got about the same amount for winning one.

The only money in the 1940s, 1950s, and early 1960s was in the pro tours. Jack Kramer, Pancho Gonzales, Frank Sedgman, and Tony Trabert turned professional after winning everything in sight in the amateur ranks and then faced a pro champion who had left the amateurs a couple of years earlier. The former reigning amateur would take on the reigning professional in cities across the country; then the tour would go abroad. A couple of other stars shared second billing.

The tours of yesteryear are gone, as are most of the amateur events; now everybody is a professional. Instead of one-night-stand audiences for a few barnstorming notables, week-long crowds watch scores of athletes play for pay, and often three tournaments go on simultaneously in different cities. The draw is usually restricted to sixty-four competitors, with lesser-known stars attempting to qualify for the open slots.

As tennis became more democratic—and more lucrative—its mass appeal broadened (it is still the fastest growing sport in the country, with an estimated 35 million participants), and this in turn fed its coffers and spread the wealth around. Television, which had long ignored it, began to cover major tournaments the year around. It is a far cry from a decade ago when tennis was in the poverty row of professional athletics.

Today every avid tennis fan has heard of the eighth-ranking American professional, whereas before open tennis the eighth-ranking wrestler was better known. Ten years ago the eighth-ranking tennis pro was the forgotten man of sports; his status among the few newspaper scribes who might have heard of him was nil. If he could afford a wife she was usually as unclear about what her husband did for a living as he was. And if by chance she did know, she had the good taste not to mention it—except in conversation with the wife of the ninth-ranked pro.

In contrast, the eighth-ranked amateur in those days enjoyed a certain amount of prestige, usually made more money, and had a modicum of hope he might someday make *real* money barnstorming in the pros. No such illusion was allowed the eighth-ranking professional. If he did upset one of the "elite four" in the pitifully few tournaments that were held, all it meant was a little more money.

To have a First Ten amateur in a tournament meant box office to the sponsors. The player's reward was not prize money but the travel and other "expenses" he could extract on the basis of his reputation. The magic words were: "I'm in the First Ten." Number Eleven didn't make it; the circuitous hush-hush stipend you could glean if you were tenth was far higher, whereas the difference in "expense" money between Number Nine and Number Ten was slight. This is what we mean by the "ranking mystique." Tennis is a game of tradition, and the First Ten mystique lingers on. The Top Ten of world tennis, chosen by a complex point system, is forging a new mystique.

In this book we have used that tradition as a basis for picking our own All-Time Top Ten—knowing full well the pitfalls of any such selection and the controversy it is bound to engender. As the subtitle clearly indicates we have limited our choices to the post-Tilden era, or, put another way, the era since Budge. Crossing the Rubicon, then, our First Ten, in order of rank, are:

1   Don Budge
2   Jack Kramer
3   Pancho Gonzales
4   Rod Laver
5   Pancho Segura
6   Bobby Riggs
7   Ken Rosewall
8   Lew Hoad
9   Frank Sedgman
10   Tony Trabert

The reader will note that the only two present-day professionals who make the list are Ken Rosewall and Rod Laver.

To explain this, we have to hark back to that magic year of 1968, when the tennis boom really began. The number of good young players increased dramatically—that is unarguable. And yet what is highly debatable a decade later is just how good even the best of this new crop is, at least when compared to the greats of the past. Again we come back to the "upset phenomenon" alluded to earlier. The reason generally advanced for the great increase in upsets is that in the amateur era the top seed only had to figure out how to beat five or six of the next best in any given tournament, whereas since open tennis he has to confront twenty or more players of almost equal caliber. However sound the argument may appear, it is ultimately specious, for, more often than not, the perpetrators of the upsets are not from the elite top twenty.

The real cause of the upsets was the almost religious adherence of most professionals to the "big game" theory, which says: follow in every serve (and if possible the return of serve) to the net. Nobody critically examined the wisdom of this strategy. Among big servers it acquired mythical status. Solid groundstrokes could be dispensed with if you could serve and volley well enough. The "big game" was the touchstone of success, they thought. It often proved just that for unknowns who would suddenly catch fire, with an excess of energy and confidence, would proceed to play over their heads, and knock off a world-class star whose serve was a little off that day. The big star rarely blamed it on his groundstrokes, and the delighted youngster credited his serve and volley for the win. This tended to reinforce the "myth of the 'big game.'"

The only notable who seemed virtually immune to the upset phenomenon during these years was Ken Rosewall, who was admittedly past his peak. Until he tapered off his tournament appearances in 1975 he was the most consistent performer on the circuit—a rather amazing feat for a player approaching middle age. In 1974, when he was almost 40, he was a finalist both at Wimbledon and Forest Hills. In the English tournament he defeated Stan Smith after having lost the first two sets. In both tournaments he bested John Newcombe in four sets. Both victims were younger and stronger than he. And lest it be argued that Ken's game has improved in the last decade, let me go on record as saying that nothing has changed about his game since he was the world professional champion in 1963—except that he's several years older. No, Rosewall *was so rarely upset because his all-around game was so solid.* If some inspired youngster started booming in serves and rushing the net, at some point early in the match Ken would use his return of service to bring the lad down to earth. This is true of Connors and Borg, as it was in earlier eras with Riggs, Trabert, Perry, or Tilden—and particularly with Budge.

The harsh truth is that perfecting groundstrokes is a long hard task, and the "big game" seemed to provide an easy alternative for younger players not willing to knuckle down to it. Ever since that myth became entrenched in the 1950s, young players who should have been out working on their groundstrokes just weren't. They merely kept serving and rushing the net.

Regrettably, most "big game" players today have little alternative to the serve-and-volley strategy. It is too late for the majority to develop a first-rate forehand and backhand mainly because they suffer from the delusion they already have them. Nothing is easier than to deceive yourself into thinking you have perfected a shot when you haven't. Many players don't ask the question that Tilden, Budge, Riggs, and Trabert had to ask themselves very early because they hoped to become champions: "Am I so confident of my strokes that when I'm set I know I won't miss it?" It's the kind of inner dialogue the "big gamers" avoid because they pin all their hopes on the serve and volley. Their service returns indicate that they consider groundstrokes merely a method to get to the net.

In 1975, Marty Riessen surprised the tennis world by capturing the U.S. Professional Indoor title at 33. Riessen, a former Northwestern basketball star, had been around the tennis circuit for over a decade and never won a major professional title before, although he had won tournaments and was considered a tough competitor. In spite of his size (6′ 2″), Marty has always lacked the moves and power to make it into the First Ten in the world. His serve, forehand, backhand, overhead, and net game were all sound but never explosive. Yet his consistency in every department against the in-and-outers of the present day was enough to take this important title.

His victory tells something about the state of tennis. Riessen couldn't have beaten Riggs, Tilden, or Budge his best day ever to walk on a court—he lacks the power and agility. In the Professional Indoor he got by more talented players because he is sure of every shot. But determination, technique, and temperament aren't enough to make a superstar. In addition to those qualities, a star also needs certain native gifts—the kind Riessen was denied but which James Scott Connors and Bjorn Borg have in abundance.

Since Rod Laver's 1969 Grand Slam, no player had been recognized as the universal champion until Jimmy Connors in 1974. Ilie Nastase, Stan Smith, Ken Rosewall, John Newcombe, Bjorn Borg, and Guillermo Vilas were the standouts, but they could rarely sustain their winning ways from one tournament to the next.

The variety of players, big money, and intensity of competition demanded a star of the caliber of Riggs, Kramer, or Budge. All the signs indicate that such a star may finally have emerged in Jimmy Connors. In 1974 when he was barely 22 Connors captured the Australian, Wimbledon, and U.S. titles. If he hadn't been barred from the French championship because of his participation in World Team Tennis he might well have won Roland Garros too and achieved the Grand Slam. In any case, he won practically every tournament he entered in 1974, including the National Indoor, U.S. Clay Courts, and the Pacific Southwest. After a lackluster 1975— highlighted by his humiliation at the hands of Arthur Ashe at Wimbledon and two months later by Manuel Orantes at Forest Hills— Connors came back in 1976 and reaffirmed his brilliance. In 1977 and 1978 Connors still remained close to the top, but both the Swede Bjorn Borg and the Argentinean Guillermo Vilas fought him tooth and nail for the Number One spot.

You'll note that despite this we have not listed Connors in the First Ten. The difficulty is to decide where to place him, for at present no one knows how far he will ultimately go. But this much can be said about him unequivocally: he has the best service return since Budge. It is even better than Rosewall's—harder, more deceptive, and just as consistent. Like his teacher, Pancho Segura, Connors has concentrated on becoming a master of the return of serve.

That it was the other master of the service return, Ken Rosewall, who made it to the 1974 finals at Wimbledon and Forest Hills is no accident. The appearance of these two masters of the service return in the finals of the world's two most important tournaments was a harbinger of the future—the emergence of all-court players in the Don Budge tradition.

Where "big game" practitioners part company with the greats of the past is that the former overemphasize the serve and volley at the expense of their groundstrokes. It is possible the serve is the most overrated weapon in tennis. "Mighty server" Nikki Pilic lost to Frew McMillan in the finals of the Munich International in 1974 even though he aced the unseeded South African 25 times. Nonetheless, all else being equal, if you have a big serve you'll beat someone who hasn't. But as Jan Kodes, the 1973 Wimbledon champion, noted, "If the serve is a vitally important shot . . . the return of serve comes a close second. Yet, important as it is, the return of serve has to be one of the most underestimated strokes in tennis. It's seldom practiced and, as a result, seldom hit as well as it could be by the average players."

Raul Ramirez of Mexico broke Stan Smith's serve seven times on a fast surface in the Davis Cup matches at Palm Springs in 1974. He also broke the even harder delivery of Roscoe Tanner, thus sealing the fate of the United States team. Neither of the Americans was able to break Ramirez' delivery, even though it was much less severe. (Holding serve isn't necessarily a matter of power; often it hinges on what other weapons you have to back it up with.)

The outstanding service returners in the world are Jan Kodes, Ilie Nastase, Jimmy Connors, Raul Ramirez, Bjorn Borg, Guillermo Vilas, Bob Hewitt, Eddie Dibbs, Harold Solomon, Cliff Drysdale, Ray Moore, Vitas Gerulaitis, Tom Okker, Manuel Orantes, Ross Case, Cliff Richey, Ken Rosewall, and Brian Gottfried. None of them is a great server; of that group, Gottfried is the only "big gamer," and he's been faring better since he stopped relying on it.

Present-day exponents of the "big game" are: Roscoe Tanner, Arthur Ashe, John Alexander, Nikki Pilic, John Newcombe, Charles Pasarell, Tony Roche, Dick Crealy, Dick Stockton, Fred Stolle, John Whittinger, Butch Walt, Peter Fleming, Sherwood Stewart, Brian Teacher, Mark Edmondson, Geoff Masters, Alex Mayer, Onny Parun, Jeff Borowiak, Vijay Amritraj, Alan Stone, Andrew Pattison, Erik van

Dillen, Bill Scanlon, Bob Lutz, Haroon Rahim, Colin Dibley, Roger Taylor, Rod Laver, Tom Gorman, and Stan Smith. There are scores of others, but these are the principal disciples of the serve-and-volley strategy.

In the 1975 Washington Star $100,000 Open, Cliff Richey found Stan Smith's serve so formidable he broke it three times in the first set and took the match 6–0, 7–6. There were lots of other "big game" entries, but who were the four to make it to the semifinals? Richey, Vilas, Ramirez, and Solomon—all better known for their ground-strokes than anything else. Vilas, since then, has further improved his all-around game so that, in 1977, he compiled one of the longest winning streaks in modern-day tennis.

For some reason the "big game" exponents rarely seem to win a tournament these days.

I was known for a hard and reliable delivery in my era, but even the best of serves can go off. It most often happens when you place too much reliance on it. When you start counting on your serve to get you out of trouble . . . *you* are in trouble. Don Budge had a big serve, but he didn't have to rely on it because he had everything else too.

Until Laver duplicated the feat in 1962, Budge's famous Grand Slam of 1938 stood as the hallmark of tennis achievement. For 24 years nobody could win the Australian, French, Wimbledon, and U.S. titles in the same year. When Budge turned professional in late 1938, he remained invincible until he entered the service in 1943. He defeated Fred Perry, Bill Tilden, Frank Kovacs, Bobby Riggs—even me—plus a couple of other lesser luminaries, a pretty formidable lineup in any league or era.

When Budge turned pro, I was the dominant name in professional tennis and was just finishing up a tour with Fred Perry. Perry had made an excellent showing. Most older players can't recall who won the Perry-Vines tour of 1937, it was that close. Perry took 29 out of 61 matches. In 1938 I bested him 16 matches to 6, and finally ended up with a 48–35 edge over the two-year span.

Fred Perry came into the pro ranks after overwhelming the ama-teurs. He had won Wimbledon three years running—1934, 1935, and 1936—the U.S. nationals in 1933, 1934, and 1936, and no doubt would have won it in 1935 if he hadn't been injured. In the 1935 Wimbledon Perry defeated the still-improving Budge 6–0, 6–8, 6–3, 6–4. The 1936 Forest Hills finals against Budge was a cliff-hanger,

Perry finally winning 10–8 in the fifth set.

Budge recalls: "Perry was so fast, both afoot and with his racquet, that I came to feel like a street brawler, who, floored, would climb to one knee and then get knocked down again. I could never struggle to my feet." Describing Perry's famed Continental forehand, he said: "He could do so much with the shot, change direction on it so quickly and deceptively. . . . He could put you in trouble, almost in one motion, by flipping his forehand on the rise, on the short hop, and then following it into the net."

Dr. Julius Heldman, the tennis expert, states in Will Grimsley's splendid book, *Tennis: Its History, People and Events,* that Perry was never caught off balance. Like all the leading players of his era, Perry's service return was masterful. Notes Heldman, "His return against a powerful service was small enough to be called a block, yet it was actually a drive." Heldman adds that Perry's backhand would be the envy of every top junior today.

Perry had no weaknesses. He was a peerless net player and half volleyer, his overhead was deadly, and if his serve and backhand can only be called first rate, then his forehand is best described as the finest Continental stroke in tennis history.

Physically Perry was a marvel. About 6' tall, he was extraordinarily quick, and never tired. Along with Lew Hoad (when he was in shape), Perry is probably the only player who could go five sets in sweltering heat without having to pace himself. Perry played a lot of net, but against service returners such as Budge, Jack Crawford, and Baron von Cramm he picked his spots. John Faunce, the 1972 senior champion, has this to say about Perry's chances against most of the present stars. "He'd wear them out; he would run all day. It's discouraging to find yourself against a guy who just keeps pounding. He did everything so fast he was on top of you all the time, and the worst part about it was that he hardly ever made an error." There was only one way to beat Perry: overpower him.

Why isn't Fred Perry listed in the First Ten of this book? Simply because he didn't play competitive singles after World War II. The same goes for Bill Tilden and—with all due modesty—a golfer named Ellsworth Vines. But Don Budge did play competitively after World War II. As late as 1957 he upset Gonzales in the semifinals of a tournament at the Olympic Auditorium in Los Angeles; thus Budge provides a standard of comparison—a line of continuity to the professionals of today. For the purposes of this book, the hiatus of World

War II provides sufficient justification to exclude prewar champions, because Budge defeated them all.

All kinds of lists select Tilden as the greatest player who ever lived. I can't argue with them. His record is amazing. He won the U.S. nationals seven times, Wimbledon three times, the U.S. Clay Court singles six times in a row, the Newport Invitation five times (among others), and was the backbone of the U.S. Davis Cup team which captured the cup seven years in a row (1920–26).

It is often pointed out that the French star Jean-René Lacoste seemed to have the Indian sign on Tilden. Lacoste's big victories over Tilden were in the 1926 Davis Cup in four sets, at Paris with 11–9 in the fifth for the 1927 French title, in the finals of the 1927 Forest Hills with 11–9, 6–3, 11–9, and his 1928 semifinal victory over Tilden at Wimbledon in five sets. What isn't mentioned as often is Tilden's five-set victory over Lacoste, after losing the first two sets, at Philadelphia in the 1925 Davis Cup. Even more neglected is Bill's victory at the age of 35 over Lacoste in five sets in the 1928 Davis Cup Challenge Round near Auteuil racetrack in Paris.

Before going into the comparative merits of the two, I would like to state unequivocally that Lacoste was superb, as his record proves. He won Wimbledon in 1925 and 1928, the U.S. nationals in 1926 and 1927, the French singles three times, and was a stalwart of the famed French Davis Cup team for three years until ill health forced him to retire in 1929 at the age of 25. Lacoste was the baseliner par excellence, with superlative control over all groundstrokes, and he had a fantastic lob. His return of service was unsurpassed, and he could put the ball on a dime. He could also volley, as his Wimbledon and Forest Hills victories on grass demonstrate. He captured the French doubles in 1925 and 1929, teaming with Jean Borotra to defeat Henri Cochet and Jacques Brugnon both times. (These were the famed Four Musketeers who allowed France to capture six straight Davis Cups in the years 1927–32.) Lacoste also won the U.S. Indoor in 1926, another testimonial to his volley.

Lacoste was unquestionably the most studious of all the champions. He kept a notebook in which he carefully recorded the strengths and weaknesses of his contemporaries. His prescription for Tilden: "Play the ball down the center of the court in going to the net." (He had figured out that Tilden's passing shots were even more deadly when he was on the run.) Nevertheless—without discounting Lacoste's greatness—I believe Tilden's ego was the major reason for his defeats at the hands of the Frenchman. Tilden eschewed the net against Lacoste because he was convinced no one could beat him in a backcourt duel. Actually, the reverse was true: no one could beat Lacoste from backcourt; one had to get to the net to have any chance at all. Lacoste was an infallible machine who could handle any amount of pace, power, or spin off the ground. Despite this, it's my firm conviction Tilden would have had the edge if he'd forgotten his backcourt vanity and taken the net more . . . for Tilden could volley (as well as do everything else). He won the U.S. doubles five times, plus Wimbledon with Frank Hunter, so he was no stranger to the net.

From personal experience I can vouch for his all-around game. I played a tour against him in 1934 and was glad to win 47 out of our 73 matches, even though he was 41. In our Madison Square debut, in which he beat me 8–6, 6–3, 6–2, I was not only overawed by him personally but also by his game. I was coming off a rather poor amateur season in 1933 and simply wasn't prepared for a player of his accurate strokes and experience. He had a cannonball serve, heartbreaking length and angles, plus the energy of a junior. I gradually improved on the tour as I became more familiar with the indoor courts; yet I had never played anyone who could do as much off both wings. His return of service was superb; he could blow you off the court with his drives and at the same time was a master of spins. His energy was amazing for his age. I remember one grueling match in Los Angeles which lasted over three hours before I took it in the fifth after losing an earlier set 23–21.

The closest thing he had to a weakness—surprising in such a tremendous server—was his overhead, which he usually placed, instead of smashing.

I agree with tennis writer Allison Danzig that Tilden could have handled the modern "big gamers." Their serve-and-volley strategy would be nothing new to him. I was known for being able to go in on serve, but against Tilden I had to pick my spots. Inveterate server and net-rusher Wilmer Allison says he felt helpless against Tilden in the 1930 Wimbledon finals . . . and that was on grass, and when Tilden was 37.

Danzig asserts:

> The fact is that tennis was played identically in Tilden's time as it is today, except that there were not as many net rushers and the rallies were longer. There was never a more daring game than R. Norris Williams', who went in on his big serve

and made most of his shots on the half-volley or full volley, winning the nationals in 1914 and 1916. Who ever rushed the net more than Borotra or Wilmer Allison?

Tilden was supreme over great volleyers and servers, because of the strength of his groundstrokes. He could return the Big Serve wrathfully and repulsed the volleyer with passing shots from either side. It would be the same today as it was over 40 years ago.

Besides his total mastery of all aspects of the game, Tilden was also a consummate actor; he could wither linesmen with a look. He was also a genius at "psyching" himself up for an important match and a master at "psyching out" an opponent. When he defeated me in the Madison Square Garden debut before 15,000 people he correctly judged that the fast tempo he set in playing the games would shake me up. Perry always rushed his opponents, but I was used to it in his game, whereas Tilden did it to me as a calculated psychological strategy.

In 1950 Tilden was selected as the tennis player of the half century. He had size, speed, brains . . . plus every shot. His already mentioned forehand was textbook perfect . . . a little arc on the backswing, plus flawless footwork and follow-through. He could hit it with all his might, on the run, and almost never missed. His backhand was also devastating, although he wasn't quite as flexible with it. Tilden had a very hard flat first serve and got more of them in than anyone I ever faced. He whipped it in with practically no spin, and because he placed it so well he served a lot of aces. His second serve was a slice or an American twist . . . which allowed him to take the net if he so desired. His service return was unsurpassed until Budge arrived on the scene.

Tilden probably did more to advance the technique of tennis than anybody else. His classic Eastern forehand and backhand were models for everyone, as was his serve. He also could do more with various spins than anyone else, but decided that semiflat strokes were the best, except in special circumstances. Although primarily a backcourt player, Tilden had the reflexes of a Rosewall at the net. (I remember vividly how Bill could grab any unfortunate fly that happened to buzz by.)

William Tatem Tilden—who didn't win his first national title until he was 27 (in 1920)—was a genius at analysis. It took him years to put it all together but he was always learning. No facet of tennis was too small for him to master; he never rationalized a weakness by expecting a strength to compensate for it. For example, when he found out he had to turn his consistent backhand into a more offensive weapon, he figured out how to do it.

In 1931, when Tilden turned professional at 38—an age at which most players are well into retirement—after dominating the amateur circuit for a decade, he held the pro title for three years against such stalwarts as Karl Kozeluh, Bruce Barnes, Vinnie Richards, and Hans Nusslein, until I took the title from him in 1934. In the next five years, an aging Tilden found Perry and me too tough. When he was 57, Tilden defeated Wayne Sabin, a former First Ten star who was 30 years younger.

The only losses Tilden had during his ten-year (1920–30) amateur reign were to Lacoste and Cochet when he was past 30, but he never lost to the third Musketeer, Jean Borotra. (The fourth, Jacques Brugnon, was strictly a doubles specialist.)

Borotra, an apostle of the serve and volley, moved better at net than anyone I've ever seen. The Bounding Basque darted everywhere with his acrobatic feats and was even quicker than Perry. He was twice Wimbledon champion (1924 and 1926), won Australia in 1928, and took the French title twice. He also won every major doubles title in the world at one time or another. He was especially potent indoors, capturing the U.S. Indoor four times and winning the British Covered Court championship 11 times at Queen's Club in London. He was 51 when he took that title for the last time in 1949; to my knowledge nobody else has ever won a national singles title when he was over 50.

My loss to Borotra at Stade Roland Garros in the 1932 Davis Cup was my only major defeat that year, and it is still a sore point with me. Bad calls are hard to take at any time, but when you are representing your country it is especially unpleasant. Besides officiating in a questionable manner, the French had purposely watered down the Roland Garros clay courts to make them slower than usual.

I had beaten Gottfried von Cramm in the Interzone finals and had arrived in Paris in a good frame of mind, confident that I could take both Cochet and Borotra. Terrible is the kindest way I can describe the calls by the French linesman as Borotra beat me 6–4, 6–2, 3–6, 6–4. But the Allison-Borotra officiating was even worse. In the fifth set with Allison leading 5–4, the Texan served an ace for the match. Borotra was already up at the net congratulating Allison when the French linesman called the serve out! Borotra held serve twice and won the crucial set 7–5—which meant the French retained the Davis Cup.

Allison had lost his other match to Cochet in a tough four-setter. But Johnny Van Ryn and Allison had bested Cochet and Jacques Brugnon 6–4 in the fifth, a sensational match in which the American team also had to battle the odds certain noncontestant Frenchmen imposed upon them.

This meant that if Allison's victory over Borotra hadn't been circumvented by the linesman we would have been 2–2, with the deciding match to be played between Cochet and myself. It so happened I did defeat Cochet but it was a meaningless triumph. I must say I was delighted when the French lost the cup the next year to Perry, Austin, and Co. of Great Britain.

I can still see Borotra up at the net—sure that he had been aced, and then having it called back. The thought crossed my mind that the United States should declare war.

By the time I got around to playing world-class tennis, Lacoste had already retired because of his health, but I did play Cochet several times. He was a rare genius at catching the ball early and could half-volley better than anyone I've ever seen. At the net, Cochet compensated for his short stature with tremendous moves, the touch of an artist, and even though he didn't have much of a serve he could crucify an overhead while off the ground.

Cochet's record speaks for itself. In 1926 he administered the first defeat Tilden suffered in the U.S. championship since 1919. He beat Tilden again in the 1927 Wimbledon semifinals and also took the measure of Big Bill in the Davis Cup Challenge Rounds of 1928, 1929, and 1930. Cochet also won Wimbledon twice, Forest Hills once, and the French singles five times. In doubles, he won Wimbledon twice, the U.S. once, and the French title three times.

I never regarded Cochet as that tough. I played him 12 times as an amateur and professional and never lost to him, probably because his game style was made to order for me. I could attack his serve and also take the net on mine. Tilden had trouble with him because he didn't play enough net. To beat Cochet you had to get in or he'd be on top of you with his incredible on-the-rise approach shots. I also believe his penchant for no-man's-land—midcourt—was ill-advised when I was driving well off both sides. Cochet was a master at taking the ball early, that is, on the rise, but the original genius of the half volley was R. Norris Williams. Most of you have probably never heard of him, which is a pity.

In all sports there is a search for fantasy fulfillment, the moment when an athlete transcends what seems the limits of human capability. I once played a set against someone whose performance fit that description—it was Williams. Although I knew R. Norris Williams had been national champion in 1914 and 1916 I was hardly prepared to find a 40 year old who could do what he did to me at Seabright in 1931. I couldn't believe anybody could take my first serve inside the baseline, and by catching it when it was barely off the ground put it away. His own serve was also hard, and he was supreme at the net. Before I knew what hit me I was down 6–0, 3–0. But then, thank God, suddenly the tornado spent itself, and I won the next 12 games and the match.

I wasn't the only champion to experience this eruption of unparalleled brilliance on the part of R. Norris Williams. Bill Tilden had too, seven years earlier in the 1924 Pennsylvania championships at the Merion Cricket Club. Tilden, the premier player of the world, had also lost the first set 6–0. Incredibly, Williams had made only one error and Tilden had won only five points, three of them on serves.

Many years later Tilden told me, "I played my best whenever I could get my racquet on the ball but I could do nothing. No such set of tennis was ever played by anyone else." What had happened to Tilden, me, and a few others, was that we had run into Williams when he was totally inspired. By catching everything on the rise, serves included, Williams's flat shots exceeded even the pace of Budge; fortunately he rarely maintained that speed throughout a whole match.*

In the 1920s Williams frequently had these bursts of brilliance for a set. But the question arises: why didn't his overall record equal his genius? I suspect because Williams really didn't care that much whether he won or not. Once he had captured the U.S. nationals twice (1914 and 1916), his intense commitment to tennis was over. The wealthy cosmopolite—born in Switzerland and educated at Harvard—considered tennis just a pleasant diversion from his other interests. After all, if he had become champion again, it would have

---

*After the incredible first set against Tilden, the 33-year-old Philadelphia millionaire had a letdown—he merely played brilliantly—and Tilden took it in five sets.

messed up his whole life style. Once the flashes waned he never bothered to dig in. He had exercised his genius for a few moments and that was all he cared about.

Sometimes Williams' spark extended for a whole match as it did at Forest Hills against Wimbledon champion Jean Borotra in 1924. Williams wiped him out 6–2, 6–2, 6–2. Then he promptly lost to Tilden in the next round. Williams was the epitome of upper-class Eastern wealth, a group who looked on tennis as a private pastime, certainly not as serious business for a man once he had reached his thirties. As F. Scott Fitzgerald once said: "The rich are different from the rest of us." It was fortunate for other tennis stars of the 1920s that R. Norris Williams hadn't been born poor.

My era was the 1930s—far less money around but I believe even more outstanding tennis players. The best British player next to Perry was Bunny Austin who had an almost perfect all-around game but limited power. Adrian Quist and Harry Hopman were also very tough. The hardest serve I ever faced was Lester Stofen's, although Johnny Doeg's left-hand powerhouse was vicious because of the terrific spin. All you could do was wait until he began to tire. Jack Crawford and Gottfried von Cramm, I'll leave for the chapter on Don Budge, as they were particularly relevant to Budge's amateur career.

As a professional I was Budge's strongest opposition. I've been asked what it was Don could do that I couldn't. Leaving aside a general discussion of the respective merits of our games, I would say the crucial difference boiled down to this: Budge could pass down-the-line off his backhand in a way I couldn't. Beyond that I would say I might have hit harder but I wasn't as consistent.

Bill Tilden, in one of his books, stated that for "controlled power there has never been anything like Budge." He put his finger on it: controlled power. I remember Don in a pro tourney at the Beverly Wilshire Hotel in 1949. Though he was past his peak, he so combined power and consistency that nobody could give him a match. As Carl Earn, the Number Six professional at the time, stated after losing 6–1, 6–2, "I like to play against speed but only up to a point." In the finals Budge wiped out Frank Kovacs 6–1, 6–3.

Kovacs was considered to be the heir apparent to Budge after the war. On a hot streak he could beat everybody else, but if Budge was in the pro tournament Kovacs found himself being toyed with. He beat Riggs several times, but he could never do anything with Budge. It had to do with game styles.

Game style includes the forehand, backhand, volley, overhead, and serve of a given player—and how he uses them. By implication it takes in his size, agility, and speed.

The curious thing about Kovacs was that he didn't use his assets to the fullest. He had size, power, and an excellent serve (about at a level with Budge's); but Frank Kovacs was a groundstroker who for some unfathomable reason eschewed the net. There was no reason he couldn't have developed a fine net game; he had the reflexes, size, and moves. But somewhere along the way he had made the emotional decision that he would rely on his power serve, forehand, and backhand, and stick to the backcourt—the opposite choice of today's youngsters, who ignore groundstrokes and opt for charging the net all the time. Against Don, Kovacs's self-imposed limitation was fatal. Budge was the complete player who always took the net when his stepped-up "pace" forced a weak return.

Pace is the take-off speed of the ball after it strikes the court. On the circuit they call lots of pace "hitting a heavy ball." Pace comes from timing, strength, and proper stroke production. Why certain players have more "pace" than others is as difficult to pin down as why one boxer punches harder than another, although longer arms seem to help (more leverage). Budge obtained his pace through natural power and the fluid rhythm of orthodox strokes.

Unorthodox players can be sensational for short periods, but generally the person with the orthodox strokes lasts longer and plays better. It was true of Budge, just as it has been of the apparently ageless Ken Rosewall.

It is also true of Jimmy Connors. For although he uses a two-hand backhand, it is basically as sound a shot as the two-hand forehand of his teacher, Pancho Segura . . . and Connors' left-handed forehand has the same stroke motion as those of Tilden and Budge.

One of the points of this book is that each player ought to use the strokes and strategy that best fit his or her natural movements and ability, rather than blindly adopting any single method for winning, such as the "big game." It is not that I am against the "big game" per se, for it is a tactic that works very well *at certain times, against certain players*. After all, Jack Kramer, its leading exponent, is ranked Number Two in this book. It is only the Kramer myth—"that groundstrokes are secondary to the serve and volley"—that is under attack, a myth his game style inadvertently fostered. This myth is responsible for the uneven performances of professionals during the past ten years. It is also why only two of the modern players—Rosewall and Laver—are ranked in our First Ten.

# 1

# Don Budge

DINGMAN'S FERRY, PENNSYLVANIA

BIOGRAPHY Born June 13, 1915, at Oakland, California. Height: 6′ 2″. Weight: 178 lb. Right-handed. Member Davis Cup team 1935, 1936 1937, 1938. First player to win Grand Slam by taking the Australian, French, Wimbledon, and United States titles in 1938. Only tennis player ever presented the annual Sullivan Award as the greatest amateur athlete in the world.

DAVIS CUP RECORD Challenge Round 1935, 1936, 1937, 1938, 4–2 in singles; 1–1 in doubles.

STYLE Most famous backhand in history, unmatched for power and freedom of motion. Forehand more mechanical but equally consistent. Eastern grip on semiflat forehand and backhand. Penetrating power on both deliveries, with more spin on second but rarely follows it to the net. Universally acknowledged as having best service return, with knack of catching ball on rise while standing inside baseline. Famed for destroying net rushers. Net game not characterized by great agility but has punishing volley, especially with backhand. Able to change grips at net. Stamina only average, but matches seldom last long. Rarely alters pattern of play or tries to outthink opponent but relies on controlled power and depth backed by amazing steadiness. Nerveless, relaxed temperament, plus forcing shots, allows him to pace himself in longer matches. Shoulder injury hampered serve and overhead after war. Without three-year Army hiatus in World War II doubtful if absolute supremacy would be questioned.

Julius Heldman says that when youngsters start fraternizing for the first time with "name" players on the circuit, the one personality who can still awe them simply by his presence is J. Donald Budge. The legend is fully justified. "Untouchable was the right word to describe Don," Heldman notes. "He never allowed an opponent to get his teeth in the match, and his overwhelming power was not subject to bad streaks." Amen. I played 59 matches against Budge on two pro tours and never saw him when he was "off."

J. Donald Budge was the son of a printer who worked for the San Francisco *Chronicle*. His father was a Scottish emigrant and his mother was also of Scottish ancestry.

In a book written with Frank DeFord, *Don Budge: A Tennis Memoir*,* Don tells how his mother's hair turned from bright flaming red to white in ten days after she was tossed across the room during the 1906 San Francisco earthquake. This wasn't the only strange physical occurrence in the Budge family: until he was 18, Don was short, only

*New York, The Viking Press, 1969.

5′ 6½″. Then, after finishing high school, the skinny lad grew 6 inches in a single year.

Budge is ambidextrous, even down to his feet. He writes with his right hand, but hits a baseball with his left hand and can punt a football farther with his left foot. Yet when he picked up a tennis racquet he used the right hand.

The growth plus a switch in his forehand grip explain why Budge didn't become world champion until he was 22. Don had first adopted a Western-style grip because the asphalt courts in the Oakland area caused the ball to bounce high. This choice of grip was also connected with his size in the early years. The Western is excellent to "kill" a shoulder-level ball. It was the grip his older brother Lloyd used, and was made famous by Billy Johnston, who was also from the Bay area. When Budge was still short, the awkwardness inherent in the Western when switching to an Eastern backhand was compensated for by the number of high-bounding balls he could take with his forehand. But as Don began to sprout up like crabgrass, shoulder-level balls became less frequent, and when he was 20 he made the change to the Eastern forehand. As Heldman says: "From then on it was only a matter of time as to when he would win the world title."

Budge explains that in one sense the fact he was small as a teenager was an advantage.

> It forced me to learn an entirely different game from the one I would have played had I been a big kid who could just get out on the court and huff and puff and blow everybody down. Since that possibility was denied me, I had to find another way to win; or, rather, I had to find a way not to lose. I was really too small to beat anybody. I had to let the big guy across the net beat himself.
>
> The best way to do that was to keep the ball in play. Thus, almost unconsciously, as a matter of survival, I stumbled upon the first major rule for any beginner, of any size or age: Get the ball back into the other person's court.*

Despite his size, Budge played for the University High School basketball team in Oakland and says that basketball "is a sport very complementary to tennis. The movements are quite similar—up and back, cutting, angling, with sharp turns and the need to adjust quickly to a sudden shifting from offense to defense and back again."

*Ibid.

Budge won the 1933 national juniors at the Culver Military Academy, in Indiana, by beating top-seeded Gene Mako 8–6 in the fifth. Once he started growing and adding power to his consistency he became virtually unbeatable—and consistency was to be the hallmark of his game. Budge had said,

> I think a lot of kids are inhibiting their own development by accelerating their pace. Too many youngsters starting in with tennis are really playing handball—they refuse to let the racquet do the work it was designed for. They clobber every ball that comes their way, and follow through with a violent enthusiasm that succeeds in smothering the shot. . . . A good follow-through is like a good handshake, firm but moderate. The bone-rattling handshake is no more pleasing than the flabby paw. Similarly, the roundhouse convoluted follow-through is really no improvement over no follow-through. It destroys accuracy and disturbs balance.

The most underrated shot in the history of tennis was Budge's forehand, because it was overshadowed by his legendary backhand. Just as it is a myth that Jack Kramer invented the "big game," through the years an impression has arisen that Budge's forehand was only one good forehand among many. Dr. Heldman properly lays this myth to rest.

> Technically it was flawless. It was mechanical in that it was not original with him, but although it did not have the personal flair of his backhand, it was a magnificent, forceful weapon. Of all the strokes of the great champions, this was the one that was always hit properly. . . . Budge's forehand was a relentless bludgeon. . . . He gracefully two-stepped into position, pivoting as the wind-up started. His backswing was a compact semicircular motion, the hit was wristless. . . . On return of service (which he hit with an open stance) he was always on balance and his weight was moving forward.
> Don had a slight amount of overspin on the forehand (imparted by the follow-through). The overspin was heavier on the crosscourts and for this reason he was one of the few men capable of hitting a sharp crosscourt with a lot of pace. . . . The racquet head never dropped. . . . He hit so well on a short ball that he seldom had to hit anything but a set-up volley or an overhead.

Could Budge volley? Riggs calls Don's backhand volley the hardest, and John Faunce says, "I never saw Budge miss a volley."

What made his groundstrokes so overwhelming was that combined with the natural power, rhythm, and timing was the heaviest racquet ever used by a top player—16 ounces. (His grip was also peculiar—no leather, just wood.)

Mention of Budge's backhand has already been made; particularly fantastic was the leap he often used because of his flawless timing and confidence in the stroke. It was this leap, supplemented by his natural power and 16-ounce racquet, that made Don's backhand unique.

Budge's backhand was very much like his forehand; but it had an extra flair that made it the envy of every player who ever lived. No matter what you did, he would reply offensively with his backhand.

Yet a player who tried to serve and come in on Budge was in even more trouble if he tried to serve to the forehand. This left the opponent with no choice but to serve to the backhand and stay back. Years later when Don was past his prime, net rushers such as Kramer, Gonzales, and Sedgman still found they couldn't stay on even terms with him if they tried to follow in their serve.

In 1957, at the Olympic Auditorium in Los Angeles, Budge, then almost 42, defeated Gonzales in straight sets—on a fast court which should have favored Gonzales's big serve. In the finals of the tournament, Pancho Segura tossed up lob after lob and eventually edged a tired Budge. In 1953, Budge pushed Gonzales to the limit at the Beverly Wilshire pro tournament by winning the first two sets, but his energy waned in the fifth.

Budge believes there were more players in his era with offensive backhands—Riggs, McNeil, Cooke, Quist, and Kovacs—than in later periods. He singles out Tony Trabert as the one player who had a reliable attacking backhand in the 1950s. He mentions Manuel Santana, Dennis Ralston, Rod Laver, and Arthur Ashe as players in the 1960s who best employed topspin. He puts Rosewall in a special category as the modern player who has terrific power and consistency on the backhand.

One of the other myths that ranks with the "big game" illusion is that the professionals of today have better serves than the greats of the past. Here is Dr. Heldman on Don's delivery, "It was a great serve . . . because the ball was so heavy, deep, and well-placed." He adds that his second serve was almost as hard as the first. "There were no double faults or easing up of the power game." (However, after the war Don developed a slight hitch in the backswing due to a shoulder injury and was never quite able to regain his former freedom of motion.) Says Tony Trabert, "Nobody today serves better than the greats of the past." Jack Kramer concurs, "John Newcombe is the only one who has a second serve with enough kick, pace and depth who would have stood any chance of attaining the net on Budge."

Another one who did, in my era, was Baron von Cramm. He had an American twist that allowed him to take the net with ease. In my opinion it was the best American twist the game has ever seen. Von Cramm is an almost forgotten figure nowadays. Yet Budge says that the German aristocrat, both as a tennis star and as a man, was the most unforgettable person he ever met. In any discussion of Budge as an amateur, the Baron is crucial.

Gottfried von Cramm was easily the greatest player who failed to capture the two big titles of tennis, Forest Hills and Wimbledon, although he won the French title in 1934 and 1936. In 1934 he defeated defending champion Jack Crawford 6–4, 7–9, 3–6, 7–5, 6–3 at Paris for the crown. In the finals the next year he lost in four sets to Fred Perry, but the following year he upset Perry in five sets for the 1936 French championship; it was the only big loss Perry had that year. The clay at Roland Garros was ideal for the long fluid strokes of the Baron. Perry says he could tell the direction von Cramm was hitting because of his long Eastern strokes (this was to a degree true of Budge's shots too, but he hit so hard the information didn't help). Perry always played very quickly; against von Cramm he purposely accelerated the tempo. But the slow clay at Paris kept Perry from hustling von Cramm the way he could on grass.

Besides his serve, von Cramm had a splendid forehand and over-head. His backhand was about on a par with Perry's, consistent and reliable but not a power weapon. His return of serve would be the envy of any pro today. He was a sound, deft volleyer but not as quick as Perry at the net. In short, he had all the stroke equipment of Perry, plus a better serve, and it was only Perry's amazing speed, agility, and endurance which allowed him to best the German.

The middle and late 1930s had the greatest concentration of talent that tennis has ever known (even if you set aside the pros which included Karl Kozeluh, Hans Nusslein, George Lott, Lester Stofen, Bill Tilden, and inevitably me). Standouts among the amateurs were Bunny Austin, Frank Parker, Don McNeil, Jack Tidball, Bobby Riggs, Harry Hopman, Elwood Cooke, Sydney Wood, Welby Van Horn, Jack Bromwich, Gene Mako, and Adrian Quist—plus superstars

Budge, Perry, Crawford, and von Cramm.

Not only were the middle and late 1930s the "golden age" of singles, but in my opinion there have never been two better doubles teams than Budge and Gene Mako, and Adrian Quist and Jack Bromwich. The Aussie pair had a phenomenal record. They won the U.S. doubles in 1939 and defeated Jack Kramer and Joe Hunt in the Davis Cup that same year. Quist and Bromwich won the Australian doubles 8 times in a row starting in 1938.

Quist also won Wimbledon in 1935 with Jack Crawford; and, teamed with D. P. Turnbull, the Aussie doubles in 1936 and 1937, which means he won the Australian 10 times in a row!

Quist and Bromwich also took the 1938 Davis Cup doubles by defeating Budge and Mako, but there were extenuating circumstances. Budge had stomach flu, and even so he and Gene took the first set 6–0 from the Aussies. Budge became so weak he could hardly move, and Quist and Bromwich ran out the next three sets 6–3, 6–4, 6–2. They decided not to say anything, Mako says, "for if Bromwich had known Budge was sick there was no way Don could have beaten him the next day . . . which he did. After the victory over Bromwich Don told me that if it had gone on another five or ten minutes he would have collapsed."

At the U.S. nationals that year, the Americans gained revenge in doubles by crushing the Aussie team 6–3, 6–2, 6–1 to take the crown. "We were both very hot," says Mako. Besides their Davis Cup record, Budge and Mako won Wimbledon in 1937 and 1938, plus the U.S. nationals twice.

As a professional, Budge won every conceivable doubles title with a variety of partners. He was still playing well enough in 1953 to win the Wembley doubles with Frank Sedgman by defeating Segura and Gonzales 6–2, 6–3, 6–2, when both the redoubtable Panchos were at their peak.

Throughout Budge's long career, it was his backhand that gave him the edge, singles or doubles. There have been many fine backhands—Tilden, Trabert, and Rosewall come immediately to mind—but Budge was phenomenal in the way he could hurt you every time you hit to his left side, as I found out on our first tour in 1938–39, which I lost 22 to 17. In comparing our games it is easy to see what I mean. I probably had a harder first serve and a better second one to follow to the net. My forehand was at least as good, and I was, I think, as good at the net. But the backhand was something else.

For one thing, Don could kill a high backhand with his famous leap in a way I couldn't, which also meant he could handle my kick second serve in a way nobody else could. He also caught his backhand earlier than I did, which saved him vital steps, for I was at least as fast as he was. Although I had a good backhand (usually flat), it wasn't my stronger side as it was his. Budge had a flexibility off that wing that was comparable to an outstanding forehand. When you hit to a backhand and that's the strong side, you're in trouble—especially when the other side is a forehand like Budge's.

He also could hit down-the-line off the backhand in a way I couldn't. After our second tour I told him: "Don, it was your damned backhand down-the-line that killed me!"

My first tour with Budge was relatively short—only 39 matches—for he was scheduled to take on his amateur nemesis Fred Perry at Madison Square Garden. Budge had never beaten Perry for a major championship when they were amateurs, and because of Perry's good showing against me—just before Budge turned pro—it is possible that promoter Jack Harris thought Fred would do better than he did.

On March 10, 1939, Budge met Perry in Madison Square Garden. But this time the fans proved shrewder than Harris. They didn't expect Perry, now 30, to stand up to the whirlwind from Oakland. Only 7000 (compared to the 17,000 for the Vines-Budge opener), showed up to watch Budge blast the Englishman 6–1, 6–3, 6–0 in 49 minutes. As Budge said, "The rout removed a lot of drama from the tour from the first." By the summer of 1939, Don was clearly preeminent, as he soundly whipped a slowing Perry, 28 matches to 8. Then Don and I went on our second tour, which he won 15 to 5.

Harris then booked a tour around the world which consisted of Lester Stofen, Bill Tilden, and the world champion. Apparently to get a look at Don was enough, as the fans of Europe, Africa, Asia, and Australia turned out despite his overwhelming superiority. Budge recalls, "Harris was having no trouble in finding dates for us. The balance of power and the interest had, for the moment, definitely switched to professional tennis, and we were in demand." Pro tennis was never again to achieve this popularity until the advent of "open tennis" in 1968. The tour ended in London in September 1939; war had engulfed the world. "Had there been no war to stop what seemed a natural momentum toward accepting the pros," Budge says, "I think it is quite likely that open tennis would have arrived nearly three decades before at last it did."

The war damaged Budge just as it did everybody else. "There is no doubt that the war came just as my game crested," Don says.

A sentimental gate attraction, Bill Tilden, was dredged up by promoter Harris for a head-to-head tour in 1940. Even though he was 47, Tilden had, according to insurance-company tests, the body of a man twenty years younger. (When Tilden was 52 he pressed Bobby Riggs in a 1945 pro tournament.) Nevertheless the tour ended with Budge taking 55 out of 61 matches. The play-for-play junket had screeched to a halt. Budge had run out of opponents.

The lull ended in late 1941 when Bobby Riggs and Frank Kovacs turned professional. A tour was organized with Fred Perry as the fourth member. Riggs, Kovacs, and Perry are three of the top racquet wielders ever to come down the pike, but the round robin became a contest of who would finish second.

In late December of that year Budge went into the Army Air Corps. Typical of the service, it never used him as a physical fitness officer to coach tennis. Althouh never wounded in action, the red-haired lieutenant was in a sense a casualty of the war, for he wrecked his serving arm on an obstacle course while awaiting entry into OCS. Struggling up a rope on a cold bleak day in Wichita Falls, Texas, he tore a muscle in his shoulder. The tear didn't heal, and the scar tissue that formed made the injury more serious. It plagued Budge so all during the war that he played little tennis. Meanwhile, in balmy Hawaii, a sailor named Bobby Riggs was playing every day.

In an interservice match at the end of the war Riggs beat the stale Budge. Don had overcompensated for the arm injury, and he no longer could get the old swing back on his serve or overhead. Riggs, the all-around stroker and consummate lobber, took the first 12 matches on their 1946–47 tour before Budge was able to establish enough of a new style to give him a battle. Because of his weakened serve, Budge ended up trying to outsteady Bobby; he almost succeeded as he won 22 out of the last 34 matches. Budge's early days as a retriever had stood him in good stead, but, despite the adjustment, Riggs emerged as tour champion by a 24 to 22 margin. And yet, Budge managed to beat Riggs for the Wembley professional title at Empire Pool in England that year.

George Toley, pro at the Los Angeles Tennis Club, had helped Don straighten out his serve but it was too late; promoter Harris opted for Jack Kramer as the big new name to oppose Riggs on tour.

However, in the U.S. pro championship on June 22, 1947, at Forest Hills, Budge pushed Riggs to five sets. The following year in the same tournament Budge had pro tour champion Kramer down two sets to one before he was crippled with cramps, and broke Kramer's remarkable serve twice in the fourth set. (Kramer went on to win the title the next day by defeating Riggs in four sets.)

The next year Budge made it to the pro finals again and lost in four sets to a peak-of-condition Riggs who had just finished his tour with Kramer. In 1953, Budge again got to the finals, but lost to Gonzales after taking the first set.

Besides a natural ability and power, to become as great a player as Budge requires insight. Watching a pro match in Chicago between Perry and me in January of 1937, Budge was surprised to see Perry staying even. "I simply could not conceive how Perry could contend with your power," he said later. He had expected to see Perry scurrying all over the court; instead Perry was forcing me to run every bit as much as he did. Then he noticed Perry was taking the ball on the rise, hardly eighteen or twenty-four inches after it bounced, whereas I was waiting in a leisurely fashion and letting the ball get to the top of its bounce before teeing off. Perry was compensating for his lesser power and getting the jump on me.

It occurred to Budge: suppose a man hit as hard as Vines and took it as early as Perry? Who could beat him? (It is these flashes of insight —often occurring when least expected—that have advanced tennis.) Budge went back to California to implement the idea with the help of Tom Stowe.

Don coupled insight with the psychology of convincing himself and others that he was invincible. "I was to keep up the pressure at all times, never let up, so that playing me would be a generally unnerving and unpleasant experience," he says. His 1937 record indicates how well he succeeded. He was undefeated on grass and brought the Davis Cup back to the United States for the first time in eleven years. He was voted the athlete of the year by the American Sportwriters and gained the Sullivan Award. In Davis Cup competition Budge won 8 singles and 4 doubles (with Gene Mako) for a 12–0 record. The next year he made the Grand Slam.

Reflecting on his championship psychology, he says: "Too often I have seen that once an underdog comes to believe he might have a chance, he really does have a chance." He believes a player should never throw an unimportant match, for even a tainted victory increases the confidence of the foe. Players gathering around the draw sheets in Budge's era used to ask, "Who's going to be fed to the Fire Dragon today?"

Jack Kramer's and Tony Trabert's opinion of Budge, in light of the "big game" innovation of recent years, is revealing. Trabert was asked whether he thought the "big game" had qualitatively changed tennis. "It changed it all right," Trabert said, "but whether for the better I seriously question. I was playing during the 'big game' era, but I always picked my spots for charging the net; when you played Hoad and Rosewall you had to. I counted as much on returning serve as serving . . . just as Connors does." Trabert's amateur reign, 1953–55, followed that of Kramer, Gonzales, and Sedgman, names closely associated with the "big game" myth. Yet Trabert saw himself as an all-court player in the tradition of Budge. "I wasn't doing anything different. . . . My objective was to control the third shot, just like Don."

Jack Kramer, the player most identified with the "big game," admits: "It was my ability to spot my second serve that allowed me to go in with impunity." He also grants the "big game" myth has had a certain detrimental effect on tennis in terms of overemphasis on serve and volley. "They tend to forget I relied almost as much on my forehand return as I did on my second serve," he says, adding that Budge could kill you off both sides. "I remember as late as 1955, in Europe when Don was forty, neither Sedgman nor Gonzales could take the net against him in back of their serve . . . and none of the current professionals would have outserved Gonzales."

Budge himself made a comparison between the past and present players over CBS television on the "Living Legends of Sports" program in February 1976. He agreed there are more first-class players now than ever before but doubted whether the top ones are as good. After calling Rod Laver the only great player of the last decade, Budge was reminded by the interviewer that he had split sets with Laver in 1962 when Don was 47 and Laver 24. Then Don was asked about Jimmy Connors. After agreeing that Connors was the standout of the present crop, he said that, in comparison to the stars of both past and present, Connors doesn't have the best serve, backhand, forehand, or net game. His service return is outstanding but "no better than those of Perry, Tilden, or von Cramm."

In his golden years, 1937–42, Budge imparted to the ball with every stroke an average miles-per-hour grand speed that has never been equaled. Yet no one ever saw him make an ugly stroke or mistime the ball. Kramer has called Budge the greatest player who ever lived. When queried about that 1969 quote, he replied: "I stand by it." He explained that what made Budge so tough—even on grass —was that Don usually *didn't* follow in his serve to the net. "A baseliner with a strong serve and great groundstrokes poses a special problem. You cannot attack off his serve and yet he can get to the net with his groundstrokes." Kramer, in his meeting with Budge, was forced into a serve-and-stay-back game style. "Budge returned service so surely and powerfully," Kramer says, "it simply wasn't possible to follow service to the net with any hope of winning."

# 2

# Jack Kramer

LOS ANGELES, CALIFORNIA

**BIOGRAPHY** Born August 5, 1921, at Las Vegas. Height: 6' 1". Weight: 170 lb. Right handed. Member Davis Cup team 1939, 1946, 1947. Won 1947 Wimbledon with loss of only 37 games in 7 matches.

**DAVIS CUP RECORD** Challenge Round 4–0 in singles, 1946, 1947.

**STYLE** Supreme master of all serves, often hits cannonball on second as well as on first delivery. Pinpoint accuracy, amazing depth and consistency on flat, American twist, and slice, which are hit with Continental grip. Uses Eastern for groundstrokes. Usually changes grips at net and on service return. Semiflat forehand best groundstroke, with sidespin on down-the-line attack. Capable of topspin on crosscourt forehand. Deceptive backhand also semiflat but not as forceful and consistent as forehand. Superb volleyer, particularly off forehand. Unerring, deadly, well-placed overhead. Absolute concentration allows him to erase previous point from mind.

Jack Kramer is the only player in the First Ten who can be compared with Budge. He towered over both amateurs and professionals. He was the nonpareil after World War II, just as Budge was before it. Once John Albert Kramer hit his stride, he was indisputably the outstanding player of the world for eight years. He captured the U.S. singles in 1946 and 1947, and was the Wimbledon titleholder in 1947. As the professional champion on tour, he defeated Bobby Riggs, Pancho Gonzales, Pancho Segura, and Frank Sedgman.

It was 1948 when Kramer abandoned his amateur status to challenge world professional champion Robert L. Riggs. It was 13 matches apiece before Jack acquired the savvy to harness his superior power. From then on it was a walkaway, with the tour ending 69–20.

Kramer is 6′ 1″, Riggs 5′ 8″—they formed the classic example of a good big man versus a good little one. It was Kramer's serve that made the difference. Although Gonzales, Johnny Doeg, Les Stofen, Bob Falkenburg, and I hit our first delivery slightly harder, none could match Jack's for pinpoint accuracy. Herbie Flam, 1950 Forest Hills finalist, who played both Kramer and Gonzales several times, gives the nod to Jack over Pancho.

Kramer's first delivery had a perfect relaxed motion, precision, and penetrating power, but his second serve was unequaled. His ability to "spot" it wherever he wanted it with no apparent effort was astounding. For depth, pace, and bounce there has never been anything like it. When he rifled his American twist into the corner, it kicked off like a ricocheting bullet (a deep, hard, kick serve to the backhand is the hardest shot in tennis to handle). Kramer had total command of all serves: flat, slice, or American twist with endless variations. He was as likely to ace you on a second as on a first, then trip you up by using the kicker as his first delivery on the next point.

Don Budge was the only player who neutralized Jack's service. When Kramer defeated him in 100-degree heat in the 1948 semifinals of the U.S. pro championship, it took him five sets. Ahead two sets to one, Budge broke Jack's serve twice in the fourth set but then developed leg cramps, and Big Jake ran out the match.

Kramer admits Budge's return of serve cut his best weapon down to size. It was something that hadn't happened to him since he became dominant at the end of the war. Because of his size, timing, and famous leap off his backhand side, Budge was able to short-circuit Jack's deep kicker. For once Kramer had run into a player who made him fall back on his groundstrokes.

Kramer had a grooved, consistent forehand, at least on a par with Budge's and more deceptive. Jack hit it close to the body with a peculiar rocker-arm style which disguised direction—the unorthodox part of an essentially sound stroke. It was semiflat—sometimes with a slight top crosscourt, sometimes with a slight underslice or sidespin down-the-line; unsurpassed as an effective weapon to force the net against an opponent's backhand. Because of its disguise it was also a superb passing shot.

Kramer's backhand didn't compare with Budge's, although it improved after he turned professional. More unorthodox than his forehand, it was an odd stroke, usually hit with underspin and hardly any backswing. He could get away with it because of his precise timing, footwork, and a fine follow-through. The short backswing made it difficult to "read," so it was devastating to net players. However, it lacked the power of his forehand, and had none of the remarkable consistency and speed of Budge's backhand. Kramer's backhand return of service was superior to his regular backhand. He usually went for an outright winner off it, and because he disguised the stroke so well he often brought it off. As with everything Kramer did, this aspect of his game was well thought out; if he tried to return service safely he was just as likely to make an error as if he hit hard.

Jack's dominance from 1946 to 1954 can best be explained by his ability to force his opponents into playing his game. His unbreakable serve always gave him the edge; if he didn't ace you on the first, the return was generally so weak he would put away the next shot. If a second serve was needed, he would hit the booming kicker and cut off the return at the net. All he had to do was wait for a break in his opponent's serve. He was like a machine on the court—occasionally dull to watch—but he always won. He never let up; he played as hard against a promising junior as he did against Frank Parker. Kramer's methodical style forced opponents into serve-and-volley contests they were bound to lose. He even made Riggs play his game, and Bobby ultimately bowed to the inevitable.

There have been better volleyers than Kramer, but you can count them on your fingers. Ted Schroeder and Frank Sedgman were superior at the net; Sedgman covered it better, and Schroeder's ability to put away a low volley has never been equaled. Roy Emerson, at 5' 10½", was also quicker than "Big Jake" and fully as consistent. A man who is 5' 10" can play net as well as anyone. (There are exceptions: Gonzales didn't volley as decisively as any of the above, but at 6' 3" and with an 81" reach, he was able to cover the net like a blanket.)

Kramer's physical equipment was also an advantage. He had unusually long legs, and in a couple of strides was at the net. He also had a gift for picking higher balls out of the air at midcourt. But Kramer was fortunate he didn't face Budge in his prime; for to beat Budge a player had to get to the net in the first place.

I recall watching Budge and Ted Schroeder square off for three days of practice at the Los Angeles Tennis Club in 1947. They played around 10 sets in three days, and the most games Schroeder could get in a set was 4. Every time Ted tore into the net the ball went sizzling by his ear. The usually composed Schroeder found himself screaming and banging his racquet in fits of frustration. To make matters worse, Budge hadn't even bothered to take off his sweater. Yet Schroeder was the 1942 national champion and in 1947 considered the best amateur in the world next to Kramer.

There were those who believed he had an even chance against Kramer on grass and that he passed up the 1946 and 1947 nationals and Wimbledon to give his best friend a shot at the pro money. Schroeder was from a relatively well-to-do family in La Crescenta, California, whereas Jack's family had little money. He knew Kramer was going to turn professional at the end of 1947 if he won both the U.S. and Wimbledon titles (which he did). But the overriding consideration for passing up Forest Hills—for what to many seemed a curious decision—was that Schroeder knew he had little chance to beat either Riggs or Budge if he did get a professional contract. He rarely beat Riggs, and was always murdered by Budge in practice matches at the Los Angeles Tennis Club. On the pro circuit with Schroeder against either of them, the one-sided matches wouldn't have drawn flies. But he knew his pal Kramer had a good chance because of his serve. Schroeder then would be the natural challenger, provided he could continue his dominance over Gonzales and win both Wimbledon and the U.S. titles.

As mentioned, Kramer whipped Riggs by a big margin in the 1948 barnstorming tour. But when Schroeder won Wimbledon in 1949, no pro offers were forthcoming; it was Gonzales the crowds wanted to see. So promoter Bobby Riggs provided him. Any hopes Schroeder had of receiving an offer were dashed when Gonzales edged him in a heartbreaking five-set match for the U.S. amateur title at Forest Hills. Schroeder got one last chance at Gonzales in the Pacific Southwest of 1949 but an improved, more confident Gonzales again defeated him.

Schroeder knew he was past his peak; he had won his matches on fortitude and endurance. Ted was involved in more five-setters than any big-time star, and at 28 his ability to get to the net diminished daily. His scrambling style depended on a youth he no longer had. Unlike Kramer, he didn't possess an unbreakable serve.

Jack Kramer's childhood was spent in Las Vegas, Nevada. He was unquestionably the most famous person ever born in that garish monument to American greed.

Las Vegas explains a lot about Kramer. A childhood spent in that isolated town, a hundred miles from anywhere, is not easily forgotten. The climate in the summer is inhuman—in Jack's day air-conditioning hardly existed. Vegas was a frontier town, and a damned poor one. Gambling didn't get off the ground until the early thirties, and by that time the country was suffering its worst economic collapse. As a boy, Jack had to endure both Las Vegas and the Depression.

His first appearance on a tennis court was at the site where the largest casino in the world now stands, the Union Plaza Hotel, at the start of Fremont Street (sometimes called "Glitter Gulch"). In those days it was the Union Pacific railway station. At the rear of the depot was a tennis court where his father taught 11-year-old Jackie the rudiments of the game. From Vegas, the family moved to another semidesert town, San Bernardino, California. Finally the Kramers made it to a town on the east side of Los Angeles called Montebello —not much of an improvement, but at least he was out of the desert. In later years, when Kramer became the promoter of world professional tennis tours, he was sometimes accused of being ruthless and money hungry. Perhaps he remembered Vegas in the Depression.

As a youngster in Southern California, Kramer luckily was steered into a class under the aegis of the famous instructor Dick Skeen. Then Perry T. Jones, head of the Southern California Tennis Patrons' Association, sent Jack to me at the Beverly Hills Tennis Club where I was teaching when I wasn't on tour. Kramer looked like a world beater when he won the national boys' singles at 15 and when, two years later, he captured the national interscholastic crown. But it took him a long time to surface as U.S. champion.

His first year at Forest Hills (1939) he lost in an early round after a bout with indigestion. In 1940 he was defeated in the semifinals by Don McNeil. The following year Frank Kovacs, at his superlative best, was too much in the quarterfinals. On the eve of the national championship in 1942 he was forced to withdraw because of the flu, and his friend Ted Schroeder won the title. However he did win the 1940 and 1941 national doubles with Schroeder. Kramer finally made it to the finals of the Forest Hills singles against Joe Hunt in 1943.

Hunt, a Navy lieutenant, prevailed in four sets: 6–3, 6–8, 10–8, 6–0. Joe Hunt—killed in an airplane accident in 1945—approached the game in a manner similar to that of Kramer and Schroeder; he served and went to the net. His serve, although better than Schroeder's, lacked the precision of Jack's delivery, but he was quicker. He also had a fluidity of movement that Kramer lacked.

After leaving the service at the end of the war, Kramer lost to Jaroslav Drobny at the 1946 Wimbledon, but won Forest Hills by whipping Tom Brown 9–7, 6–3, 6–0 the same year. From then on he was invincible as an amateur, although Frank Parker took the first two sets against him in 1947 in the finals of the U.S. nationals. When he turned pro at the end of that year he was already 26.

Kramer is an example of what practice, self-discipline, and perseverance can accomplish. Dr. Julius Heldman goes so far as to say, "Kramer was not a great natural athlete—too heavy on his feet." Heldman tells how Kramer became influenced by a Detroit automotive engineer, Cliff Roche, who convinced Jack that winning tennis should be played in set patterns called "percentage tennis."

Actually, Kramer was more an acolyte of percentage tennis than an adherent of the "big game," but he served so masterfully that the "big game" put the percentage in his favor. What is percentage tennis? It means hitting the shot that yields the maximum chance of winning the point, either immediately or later in the exchange, and that minimizes the likelihood of losing the point. This may sound obvious and simplistic, yet the ramifications of this strategy are complicated.

The percentage tennis idea is an extension of the "zoning" theory taught by my coach Mercer Beasley; for example, when hitting a ball from behind the baseline you have only a small chance for an outright winner. The area between the baseline and service line allows for more aggressive hitting—depending on the score, your opponent's return, and your own court position. The zone between the service line and the net offers the greatest opportunity for an all-out attack; the angles of placement are wider, your opponent has less time to get set, and you are already en route to the net.

Roche expanded on the "zoning" theory. He geometrically figured out a theory of angles for Kramer which maximized his chances of maintaining superior court position in every rally, irrespective of the angle of the return. Because of Kramer's potent serve, Roche helped Jack develop a sequence which fully utilized this extraordinary weapon. The sequence was related to the point. At 30–0 Jack would attempt an ace down the middle, but at 40–30 or 30–40 he seldom did because the percentage was less favorable.

It is a sound strategy, provided a player has the serve, strokes, and concentration to carry it out. Kramer had one of those computerlike minds which allowed him to mix up the sequences and still keep everything in order. The serve-and-volley tactics of the "big game" were an essential ingredient of the Roche technique—but only part of the strategy.

The few times Kramer played Don Budge illustrate the "percentage" play approach and contradict the belief that Kramer was totally committed to the "big game." When questioned by *Lawn Tennis,* the official British publication, Kramer had this to say about Budge, "He returned service so surely and powerfully it simply wasn't possible to follow service to the net with any hope of winning." In other words, there was no percentage in charging the net on serve.

The percentage pattern which Kramer employed became oversimplified by the "big game" fanatics of the past twenty years because it was the most dramatic aspect of the Roche principles. It is far easier to go to the net behind every serve, and whenever possible behind every return than get involved in the intricacies of percentage tennis. The "big game" became a household term in the tennis world as percentage tennis receded into the background.

Kramer, of course, did fit the prototype of the "big gamer"; he had the serve and the volley. The same can be said for Pancho Gonzales and Frank Sedgman, his successors as amateur kings. Because these three champions used serve-and-volley tactics, the "big game" has had a tremendous influence, much of it detrimental. Too often overlooked is the fact that it was a style perfectly suited to all three.

Kramer because of both serves; Gonzales because of his serve, moves, and reach; and Sedgman because of his astonishing reflexes.

Also overlooked is the fact that Joe Hunt defeated Kramer with the "big game," in the 1943 finals at Forest Hills, and Ted Schroeder, the 1942 national champion, did nothing but rush the net at every opportunity. Will Grimsley says that "Kramer was credited with introducing the modern game of big serve and volley," but adds, "He didn't actually introduce these tactics, but, according to Bill Talbert, he utilized them better than anyone before."

Nevertheless it was the Kramer mystique that created the "big game" myth. Although never precisely stated, the three main points implied were: (1) that the "big game" was something "new," (2) that the serve-and-volley strategy could overcome the best groundstroker, (3) that the serve and volley were more important than the forehand and backhand. Kramer's record reinforced this myth.

Jack Kramer's reign spanned the eight-year period from 1946–1954. His only losses as an amateur after World War II were to Jaroslav Drobny of Czechoslovakia at Wimbledon in 1946, and to Gayle Kellogg the same year in a minor tournament at the Town House Hotel in Los Angeles. In 1947 he went undefeated, although he didn't play Australia and wouldn't risk his unblemished record on the slow clay at Roland Garros for the French title. Kramer also ducked the National Clay Courts in 1947 as well as the "Hot-cha" winter circuit, also clay, in Florida. But he did make an appearance at the River Oaks Invitational at Houston to prove he could win an important title on clay. (He did.)

Kramer wasn't a particularly active amateur champion in 1947. He passed up both the Eastern Grass Court championships and the prestigious Newport Casino Invitational, both won by his friend Ted Schroeder. Schroeder's prowess on grass has already been mentioned, as has his absence from the U.S. nationals and Wimbledon to allow a clear field for his buddy. However, Kramer clearly demonstrated his superiority over Schroeder on cement by beating him in the Pacific Southwest twice. (They teamed up to wrest the Davis Cup back from Australia in 1946 and won it again in 1947.)

At the end of 1947 Kramer turned professional. Between 1948 and 1954 Riggs, Gonzales, Segura, Sedgman—and everybody else—suffered the same fate at his hands.

After Kramer took control of the professional tours, "he became the game's most prosperous and controversial promoter. . . . He could wreck a nation's Davis Cup team with a stroke of a pen," says Will Grimsley, "and he frequently did. . . . For close to a decade they called tennis, 'the big, green world of Jack Kramer.' "

But Grimsley adds: "More than any other man, he was responsible for the removal of barriers to open tennis."

Open tennis was not to Kramer's advantage. It automatically meant no more tours, the basis of his fortune. But in 1968, he knew that tour tennis had had its day. By this time Kramer was a millionaire, and with his diversified business interests he was no longer dependent on the game. He knew the only way tennis could compete with golf in sports coverage was by offering big money tournaments. As a legend in the game's circles, Kramer's voice carried weight in the highest tennis councils. He pushed hard for "open tennis."

Contrary to what the old guard believe, the professional circuit since 1968 is what has given tennis its present dignity. The under-the-table "shamateurism" of earlier days forced players to be extra nice to USLTA officials, who were more interested in self-perpetuation in office and gate receipts than in easing the financial troubles of promising youngsters on the circuit.

Teaching professionals also suffered from the game's general lack of status in this country. Making money was something people didn't associate with tennis. Presumably, if you played the game you already had it—which was nonsense. It is true that it was largely the upper classes who supported the game, but practically all the champions from 1930 on had come from the lower economic strata. Nobody understood that better than Jack Kramer.

In spite of his hard-line business reputation, Kramer's integrity on the many tours in which he was involved—as a performer or promoter—is incontestable. No tour participant has ever hinted that there was at any time even a veiled suggestion by Kramer to ease up for box office purposes.

This integrity underwent its severest test during a match with Hoad in 1957 in the first round of the Wembley tournament in London. This tournament, the U.S. professional championship, and to some extent the tournament in Paris were the major professional tournaments prior to 1968.

Promoter Kramer had guaranteed Hoad $125,000 for the Gonzales tour, and the name of the handsome, blond Aussie had been built up to the sky. For his 1957 debut as a professional it sounded like a good idea for Hoad to play the great Kramer himself. The arthritically inclined Kramer was given two chances at Wembley: slim and none. The fiercely competitive 36-year-old went all out (as always) and beat the 23-year-old Hoad.

Kramer walked off the court speechless with rage; his promotional scheme had backfired . . . and he was the cause of it. When he finally calmed down he told a tennis writer he couldn't "possibly estimate how much the victory would cost him." As it turned out, his upset of Hoad didn't put a crimp in the box office. People always expected Kramer to be a winner.

# 3

# Pancho Gonzales

LAS VEGAS, NEVADA

**BIOGRAPHY** Born May 9, 1928, at Los Angeles. Height: 6′ 3″. Weight: 190 lb. Right-handed. Member Davis Cup team 1949. At age 41 won record 112-game singles at Wimbledon in 1969 against Charles Pasarell.

**DAVIS CUP RECORD** Challenge Round 2–0 in singles, did not play doubles as United States retained cup over Australia.

**STYLE** Powerful flat first serve with little effort and great control, plus fine kicker on second delivery. Rarely makes double-faults. Amazingly graceful and quick for a big man, one of the outstanding half volleyers of all time. Excellent Eastern forehand with peculiar hammer grip. Backhand less consistent. Groundstrokes more effective in exchanges than on returning serve. All-around player capable of great defense as well as offense. Has delicate touch and is master of changing speeds. Can slow game down when advantageous and lob adroitly. Net game more consistent than forceful, but reach and lightning reflexes make him overwhelming in forecourt. Extremely difficult to lob, and buries overheads. A ferocious competitor, who is at his best under pressure.

Based on his domination of professional tennis from 1954 to 1962, Richard Alonso Gonzales is regarded by a great many tennis experts as the greatest player who ever lived. During those years he decisively defeated on tour five of this book's First Ten: Frank Sedgman, Pancho Segura, Tony Trabert, Ken Rosewall, and Lew Hoad—plus everybody else. Even as late as 1968, when he was pushing 40, he managed to take Rod Laver in two tournaments. It is not without misgivings that I have ranked him third in this book, for it's difficult to rank him behind anybody. Nevertheless there was a basic—though minor—flaw in his game for most of his career, which explains why Budge and Kramer are ranked ahead of him.

This flaw, in my opinion, is why Jack Kramer was able to defeat Pancho so decisively on their midcentury tour. When their long nightly odyssey had ended, Kramer had demolished Gonzales 96 matches to 27—a surprisingly one-sided score, for these two great power servers appeared evenly matched. But Kramer had spotted something: a weakness in Pancho's backhand—not in the swing or footwork, but in the grip.

Gonzales used a peculiar type of modified Eastern forehand grip on all shots; he held the racket like a hammer. This Eastern "hammer" grip had advantages on the backhand: it meant he didn't have to change grips, and could hit the ball very late. It made his backhand deceptive, and also allowed him to lob at the last moment. Pancho usually hit his backhand semiflat, but the odd grip imparted a peculiar underspin that caused it to skid, which proved especially effective on grass. But there is a basic drawback to hitting a backhand with an Eastern forehand grip: it forces a player to "hit up" on a deep forcing shot and allows the opponent to cut off the return at the net.

Kramer was able to exploit this because of his piercing down-the-line forehand; his serve also kept constant pressure on Pancho's faulty side. It wasn't that Pancho didn't hit superb shots off his backhand—he did; but when he was forced he could only push it back, because of the way he held the racquet, and Kramer would pulverize the defensive return.

Kramer's backhand was also his weakest side. Why therefore couldn't Gonzales pull a turnabout? Because Kramer held the racquet correctly (standard Eastern backhand grip). He would either net it or hit an offensive shot; it wasn't inevitable that his backhand would "push up" if forced in a certain way. Actually, in the ordinary exchange of groundstrokes, Kramer was as likely to make an error off the backhand as was Gonzales. But one could never tell, whereas with Gonzales you could predict a pushed-up backhand if enough pressure was put on it.

Why didn't other players do the same thing to Pancho? Because they lacked the weapons. In order to exploit Gonzales's unsound grip he had to be pressed in back of the baseline, a tall order as Pancho's serve, forehand, and net game allowed him to stay on top of opponents most of the time. Only Kramer could put him on the defensive to the point where a relatively minor fault became a major weakness.

Despite the panegyrics to Pancho's greatness, his game is probably the most misunderstood of the net champions. The misconception is that Pancho was a power player in the tradition of Kramer, Budge, and Hoad. He had big shots, but they were almost incidental to the overall composition of his game. To properly assess his prowess on the court, one has to analyze him completely. First he was a superb competitor, never choked, and was a clever tactician. Also at 6' 3" and 190 pounds, Gonzales was tremendously strong. How well he moved has frequently been commented upon. He had a "freedom of motion" that was extraordinary, much as Budge had on his backhand, only he had it on all shots. But rarely mentioned is another physical asset, his reach of 81". Whenever he got into trouble he would "windmill" the net. His long right arm, plus his reflexes, allowed him to volley, or smash, everything within reach—and that reach was really something!

Gonzales's smoothness of movement and reach allowed him "to saunter" on the court in a unique way. The saunter was a weaving motion in which he swayed on his toes from side to side while gradually moving on the net. Although he had quick acceleration, Gonzales was never really fast, so he developed a saunter which allowed him to maximize his agility, reach, power, and still conserve his energy. It is the principal reason he lasted so long. No other player was ever as good at 40—not Rosewall, not even Tilden. The saunter suggested a stalking tiger as he journeyed into "no-man's-land."

Play in this area around midcourt is usually disastrous but, like Henri Cochet, Frank Sedgman, and Fred Perry, Gonzales's reflexes and half volleys were such that he was a master in this normally taboo area. His anticipation, grace, and superb half volleying were coupled with a rare ability to move sideways. From no-man's-land he would blanket the net with his next move.

Gonzales never seemed to be lunging or dashing around. One got the impression that this overpowering presence was never really extending itself, and that he always had "big guns" in reserve . . . which in fact he did. A blasting forehand, tricky backhand, and mighty serve, and above all that awesome reach, seemed to allow him to cover everything, whether in the forecourt, midcourt, or backcourt.

However, against Kramer sauntering spelled calamity. Jack hit for winners in returning serves; there was rarely a second shot. When Kramer served it was worse yet; little chance for Pancho to saunter and blanket the net. He found his latent "big guns" rendered ineffective by the preemptive strike of Jack's artillery. Like everybody else, Pancho was forced into playing Kramer's game; and he experienced the futility of trying to outserve and outvolley a relentless machine. Whenever he defeated Kramer, it was because Jack's return of service was off.

Against Budge in his prime, Gonzales would have discovered a return of service that was never off. He would have also found himself facing a very good serve; but it is doubtful whether Budge would have rushed the net as consistently against him as Kramer did. The Oakland redhead would have relied on his usual technique of "controlling the third shot," which Pancho would have found just as devastating as Kramer's serve-and-volley tactics.

Nonetheless, Gonzales's game style was better suited than Kramer's to neutralizing Budge's power. Pancho mixed up his shots more and was a master of chips, deep junk, and not giving his opponent anything to hit. Kramer never soft-balled an opponent. Budge was the only player who could handle Kramer's service with consistency. Jack would have been forced into a ground game by Don, and he never liked stroking duels. He either attacked the net or went for winners. Gonzales, contrary to popular belief, wasn't averse to groundstroke exchanges. It gave him a chance to saunter and maneuver his opponent until he could force the net.

Although Pancho would have made it to the net more often than Kramer, it wouldn't have been often enough to have defeated Budge in his prime . . . for Pancho had trouble when the big redhead was over-the-hill. Budge, like Kramer, exploited Pancho's backhand grip. Gonzales also found that relying on his lightning reflexes in no-man's-land didn't work against Budge, although it made better sense than rushing the net on every serve.

Pancho rarely won a first set against Budge. He would manage to eke out the match because of his serve, youth, and quick moves, but it was obvious to spectators that the aging Budge had the better all-around game. When they played at Cleveland on June 21, 1953, for the United States professional title, Gonzales was 25, Budge 38. Gonzales won 4–6, 6–4, 7–5, 6–2. It was no walkaway, even against a Budge who had little in the way of legs left. Nonetheless, Gonzales is assuredly one of the five or six greatest players ever to pick up a racquet. Pancho Segura says he was the one big man who could also defend brilliantly. There was no clumsiness, and he retrieved as well as any big man who ever lived.

The most satisfying triumph of Pancho's career was at the professional championships at Wembley, England, in October of 1952. He outlasted the 31-year-old Kramer in five sets. Says Jack, "I wanted to win that match badly, as I'd just signed Sedgman as a tour opponent. In fact, I played well but Pancho wouldn't be denied. His kick second serve had become too penetrating."

Richard Alonso Gonzales, the eldest son of a middle-class Mexican-American family, first startled the tennis world in the 1947 Pacific Southwest by defeating Herb Flam, Bob Falkenburg, Jaroslav Drobny, and Frank Parker on successive days at the Los Angeles Tennis Club. The victory over Parker amazed everyone. The former national champion had pushed Jack Kramer to the limit at Forest Hills the week before by winning the first two sets. Ted Schroeder finally stopped Pancho's Pacific Southwest string in the semifinals in four sets (but lost to Kramer in the finals).

Gonzales easily whipped Parker for the National Clay Court title the next year. Parker's strategy, depth of stroke, and sneaky passing shots were to no avail against the quick moves and awesome reach of Gonzales.

But in 1948 Schroeder usually proved too much for Pancho when they played each other on the West Coast (even though Gonzales took the national title at Forest Hills). However the next year Pancho finally got to the net-rushing stalwart by defeating Schroeder in five sets at Forest Hills to win his second national title, and then beat him again in the finals of the Pacific Southwest.

Gonzales also captured the National Clay Court again in 1949, thus dismissing the unfounded assumption that he had no groundstrokes. He also won the National Indoor as well as the Pacific Southwest (he was upset by Geoff Brown at Wimbledon). That year he became the first player to capture all four major tournaments of the four American surfaces: grass, clay, indoor, and hard court (Pacific Southwest). He was also the first public parks player to ever achieve such eminence.

The fundamentals for Gonzales's achievements were laid at the Exposition Park courts in the shadow of the Los Angeles Coliseum (the courts were removed near the end of the 1950s to make room for the Sports Arena).

Talent is never sufficient to make a tennis champion; technique is also required. It is doubtful that Gonzales would have risen above the public parks level if he hadn't run into an older player named Chuck Pate, who laid the foundation for his serve and forehand. Pate showed the gangly boy the easiest way to achieve the maximum power with the minimum of effort by having the youngster imitate his own movement on the serve. To this day it is hard to distinguish between Pate's delivery and that of his famous pupil of over thirty-five years ago whom he taught so patiently at the Exposition courts.

Exposition Park was the center of public parks tennis in Los Angeles from 1940 to 1950, and the technique plus the feel of competition Gonzales learned there, were the foundation of his future greatness. An indication of the quality of tennis at Exposition after the war is that in 1947, the year before he captured the national champion-

ship the first time, Gonzales lost in the semifinals in the local Exposition tournament to Fernando Isais. Isais was one of a group of "Expo" players liable to upset an international star. Phil O'Connell was another spoiler of big reputations. He defeated Gayle Kellogg after Kellogg had upset Jack Kramer in the 1946 Town House Hotel tournament. In April 1948, Gonzales won the club tournament by beating O'Connell in the finals. A few months later he was the national champion.

In addition to O'Connell (now a pro in Hollywood) fine players who came out of Exposition Park include: Carl Earn, the sixth ranking professional in 1947; Bobby Perez, a star at USC, and now one of the outstanding seniors in the country; Bob Rodgers, who beat both

Wayne Sabin and Frank Kovacs in a pro tournament in 1950; Jimmy McDaniels, seven-times National Negro champion; Pancho Delgado, Santa Barbara champion; and Willis Anderson, who was acknowledged as the best of the lot until Gonzales burst into national prominence.

It so happened that Isais didn't even win the 1947 tournament in which he upset Gonzales. Isais lost to the three-times National Public Parks champion, Willis Anderson. Nowadays with tennis so popular, it is doubtful if the public parks will turn out players of this caliber; it's too difficult to get on a court. Gonzales was lucky to be living in a decade (1940–50) when players were around who could teach him . . . and did.

In the tours of 1954–60 he defeated Frank Sedgman, Pancho Segura, Tony Trabert, Ken Rosewall, Lew Hoad, Alex Olmedo, Butch Buchholz, Barry MacKay, Mal Anderson, Ashley Cooper, and Rex Hartwig. His greatest tour was against Lew Hoad. Gonzales was behind 21 matches to 9 on their 1957–58 tour, even though he was at his peak and playing a less experienced Hoad. The Australian was getting to his backhand. Says Hoad: "Gonzales was not a top-class backhand shotmaker, but he could control his backhand. It couldn't hurt you, but he could set up the ball for forehand winners with it, and he had a tremendous forehand."

He adds that because of Pancho's hammer grip he could hit backhands only "up the sideline." Hoad would force this side and just cut it off at the net. It looked like the tour was going to be a runaway as Hoad was getting stronger match by match. Once a player gets that far behind on a pro tour it is difficult to catch up; the leader has the psychological momentum.

At 21 to 9 Gonzales did an amazing thing—he changed his backhand grip. A grip is so fundamental to a tennis player that a change of this sort in the middle of a tour is unheard of; yet Gonzales did it. He knew he would have to hit crosscourt off the backhand or he'd never close the gap. Almost overnight he moved his hand to the back of the handle in the approved Eastern backhand fashion and started hitting crosscourt too.

His greatest match against Hoad was on May 5, 1958, in the U.S. Professional tournament. After losing the first two sets, 3–6, 4–6, Pancho—a few days away from his thirtieth birthday—managed to call on all his experience to edge the much younger Australian powerhouse in a fantastic 14–12 third set. This was the turning point of the match and eventually the tour; Pancho ran out the next two sets 6–1, 6–4. The tour ended with Gonzales ahead 51 matches to 37.

The grip shift was only on groundstroke exchanges; on returning service he stuck to his hammer grip on both sides. The automatic reflex for the backhand switch on a service return has to be acquired early. A weird psychology is at work here; the grip change takes only a split second, but to the unaccustomed it seems an eternity. Budge, Riggs, Tilden, Schroeder, Patty, Kramer, and Trabert did it effortlessly; it was second nature from boyhood. As an astute student of the game, Gonzales realized it was too late in his career unconsciously to change grips on returning serve; however, the baseline duels allowed time for the adjustment. Also his old-style backhand was well-suited for handling kick second serves because it was a shorter, more deceptive stroke than a regular Eastern backhand.

Hoad's impression of Gonzales was that he had been provided by nature with the ideal physical equipment for a tennis player. "A man with vast physical toughness and unwavering mental strength who had reduced the percentage of errors lower than any player had ever done." He took advantage of the slightest lapse, Hoad says, and nothing shook his sullen confidence. Initially, Pancho's ability to apply pressure made Hoad feel like he was trying to "force apart the jaws of a vice which was crushing him." In their first two meetings —pro tournaments at Forest Hills and Los Angeles—Gonzales downed him easily.

Later Lew adapted to the advanced professional level, even led the series, but found that Pancho was eminently capable of adaptations himself—as evidenced by the backhand grip alteration.

In 1959—the year following their marathon five-set battle for the U.S. professional title—Gonzales again met Hoad in the finals of the pro championship. This time Pancho won easily in straight sets.

In 1960 Gonzales began his semiretirement saga, which meant he came out of retirement at almost yearly intervals, that is, whenever he needed money. In 1961 he came out of "retirement" to whip Frank Sedgman 6–3, 7–5 and win the U.S. professional championship for the eighth time. In May 1964, having played only one tournament in the previous three years, he won the U.S. Professional Indoor championship by defeating Rod Laver, Lew Hoad, and Ken Rosewall, on successive days. At Forest Hills in 1964 he lost to Laver in the finals of the pro championship in a close match. But the tennis world had not heard the last of the old lion.

Two years later, defying age and lack of competition, he launched another comeback at Wembley. After disposing of Rosewall, he beat the supposedly invincible Laver. Why didn't he rest on his laurels? The obvious answer is the correct one: with ex-wives and lots of growing children he needed the money.

The Gonzales of 1966 knew he no longer had the energy of youth, that he couldn't use the big serve as frequently because it took too much out of him, and that if he was going to beat anyone he had to exercise more self-discipline and be cagier than ever.

When he launched his "comeback" in 1967, his once coal-black hair was graying; he was lean, almost gaunt looking. At 39, his weight of 184 pounds was the lowest it had ever been in his career. "If I'm four pounds over that weight I know I'm going to lose," he told a journalist at Queen's Club in London.

Considering the layoff and his age, Gonzales gave a surprising account of himself that year. He pushed Rod Laver, who was at his peak, in the finals of the New York pro to 7–5, 14–16, 7–5, 6–2. Then he teamed up with Dennis Ralston to defeat Laver and Fred Stolle in the doubles. At Orlando, Florida, the same year he played Laver again and won the second set 6–2.

But it was the following year that he astonished the tennis world. In 1968, at the age of 40, he won the Birmingham, Alabama, pro classic and then captured the Midland, Texas, tournament by whipping Roy Emerson in straight sets. Near the end of the year he defeated the Wimbledon Open champion, Laver, in two tournaments.

In 1969 he took the Howard Hughes Open in Las Vegas by annihilating the 1968 U.S. champion, Arthur Ashe, 6–0, 6–3, 6–4 and gave Cliff Richey a lesson in the Pacific Southwest finals with scores of 6–0, 7–5. For good measure he also won the doubles.

In 1970, he won the Howard Hughes Open again by beating Rod Laver 6–1, 7–5, 5–7, 6–3, and in 1971 the old lion, at the age of 43, kept a young tiger named Jimmy Connors at bay to win the Pacific Southwest again. Even in 1972, at 44, he was still the ninth ranking professional in America. He is still a living legend, and still picking up the marbles at Grand Masters Tournaments (45 and over) where opponents Frank Sedgman, Hugh Stewart, Torben Ulrich, Sven Davidson, Vic Seixas, and Pancho Segura wish he had stayed in retirement.

# 4

# Rod Laver

NEWPORT BEACH, CALIFORNIA

BIOGRAPHY   Born August 9, 1938, at Rockhampton, Queensland, Australia. Height: 5′ 9″. Weight: 154 lb. Left-handed. Member Davis Cup team of Australia 1959, 1960, 1961, 1962. Only player to win the Grand Slam twice; in 1962 as an amateur and in 1969 as a pro.

DAVIS CUP RECORD   Challenge Round 6–2 in singles, 1959, 1960, 1961, 1962; 1–0 in doubles, 1962.

STYLE   The ultimate wizard of passing shots. Made more effective use of spins and angles than any other champion. Master of peculiar "Ping-Pong" groundstrokes, with excessive top for "dip" shots in which he utilized oxlike wrist. Continental grip on forehand, with Australian for backhand and net. Most unorthodox of First Ten, except for serve which is consistent and unexceptional. Very quick at net and pulverizes overheads. Tough fighter, extraordinary coordination, and great scrambler. Indisputably the outstanding left-hander of all time.

In his own way, Rod Laver has modified tennis as much as has Kramer. His use of excessive topspin for dip shots to force an opponent to volley up has become standard practice with most professionals, just as Kramer's "big game" had an enormous influence in an earlier period. Pancho Gonzales—the most famous champion between Kramer and Laver—was not an innovator; that is, nothing in his style could be said to have radically changed the game to the extent that Kramer and Laver did.

With orthodox, grooved players such as Budge and Riggs, tennis appeared to have reached a plateau of excellence. Most of the bugs in technique had been ironed out with the emergence of these superb craftsmen; all a talented youngster had to do was to follow the model of these champions. They had perfected technique to a point where erratic tennis could be eliminated and consistent power maximized. Tony Trabert is a classic example of a player who followed in their mold.

But in the universe of a game, just as it appears all contingencies have been reduced to order, a new contingency appears, then another. The paradigms here are Jack Kramer and Rodney Laver. First came Kramer with his "big game," second Laver with his variety of spins. Whether either innovation improved the quality of tennis is questionable; but both assuredly altered the way it is played.

Rodney George Laver was introduced to tennis when he was 10 years old, after his father had built a tennis court in the backyard of their home in Queensland. Lights were strung up in back, and one night Rod met tennis coach Charlie Hollis who was hitting balls with Rod's father and brothers. It was to have a lasting impact on his career, as Hollis took the red-haired youngster under his wing. Besides teaching Rod, Hollis drilled into him the importance of a winning temperament. A champion should never get upset over mistakes and never give an inch, Hollis told Rod.

When he was 16, Rod and his coach drove five hundred miles to meet Davis Cup coach Harry Hopman in Brisbane, the capital of Queensland. Hopman was impressed. Laver lived up to his promise, and when he was 18 Hopman arranged for an Australian millionaire to finance a five-month world tour for Rod which started in Paris and ended in California. In the Junior World Championship at Wimbledon, Rod lost in the finals to America's Ron Holmberg. Holmberg was a classic stroker in the Budge-Riggs-Trabert tradition, which allowed him to neutralize the flashes of brilliance from the unorthodox Aussie. (Holmberg made it into the First Ten of the men's division a few years later, but his brilliant strokes could not compensate for a tendency to weight and slowness afoot.) After losing to Holmberg at Wimbledon, Laver crossed the Atlantic and won the Canadian and American junior crowns.

Despite this auspicious beginning, Laver had a long struggle before he made it to the top. He lost his first two Davis Cup matches in 1959 to Alex Olmedo and Barry MacKay. He also lost to Olmedo twice in big tournaments that year—in the semis at Forest Hills and the finals at Wimbledon. Olmedo had the one thing that has always spelled trouble for Laver: a superb return of serve; he also had an excellent serve and steady groundstrokes. In this he was similar to Holmberg. He managed to keep the constantly attacking Laver off the net. Alex also made sure that his own net approaches were always in back of a forcing shot, for even in those days Rod had the best passing weapons in the game.

Fellow Aussie Neale Fraser took the measure of Laver in the Wimbledon finals the following year (1960). He dropped straight-set matches to Fraser and Roy Emerson, respectively, in the U.S. finals in 1960 and 1961. But Rod captured Wimbledon in 1961 and again in 1962, the year he finally peaked with the Grand Slam.

He began his first Grand Slam by beating Roy Emerson in the

Australian finals at Sydney. At Rome, Laver again defeated Emerson in the Italian championships. The Italian crown is the most important next to the Big Four (Australia, France, Wimbledon, and Forest Hills). At Paris, Laver clearly demonstrated that he had gained the decisive edge over his former nemesis by besting Emerson for the French title. It was the third time in a row he had whipped his fellow Davis Cupper in the finals of major tournaments; all were close—five sets at both Rome and Paris. These contests followed a pattern. The magnificently conditioned Emerson would finally run out of gas in the fifth, while slow-starter Laver would find his passing shot getting sharper and more consistent as the match progressed. Emerson lacked the penetrating deep second serve to neutralize Laver's exploding returns. Yet he had to attack the net; otherwise Rod would force his forehand. Ordinarily Emerson was very much at home at the net but in Laver he was facing a man with the most deceptive collection of passing shots in the game's history. Coping with the physical and psychological pressure of handling an endless variety of disguised blockbusters proved too much even for this great competitive athlete. It was a pattern repeated again and again in Laver's career. Any player who had to rely on the "big game" was in trouble against Laver's passing wizardry. Only a great serve and consistent forcing groundstrokes could reverse the process. Emmo's serve and forehand just weren't good enough once The Rocket hit his stride.

In the 1962 Wimbledon, the gifted Spaniard Manuel Santana was the only player to give him trouble. Laver defeated Fraser at Wimbledon and Emerson again at Forest Hills to complete the first Grand Slam (Australia, France, Wimbledon, Forest Hills) since Budge. On January 4, 1963, Laver turned professional for a $100,000 guarantee. In his debut, the Rockhampton Rocket found out how tough the pros were; Lew Hoad defeated him 8–6 in the fourth at Sydney. During the rest of 1963, Hoad and Rosewall had an edge on him. Rosewall continued his dominance over him until 1964. But that year the tide turned, as Rosewall only occasionally beat Laver. Until the middle of 1967, Laver won the major pro tournaments; I believe this time was the greatest Laver.

Besides strength, speed, and reactions, his shots were uncanny—maximum disguise, maximum angle, maximum power. One thing is certain, he made shots on a court that had never been made before and are unlikely to be made again. In this period (1964–67) he had passing shots that can only be called unique. I recall watching him

against Gonzales in 1965 at the Sports Arena in Los Angeles. Pancho intentionally would carry a ball in his left hand whenever he took the net, for if his approach shot were only adequate he knew he'd be passed. Then he would toss the ball onto Laver's court with an ironic smile . . . bowing to the inevitable. In effect he was saying that this was the only way you'd ever get the ball back if your approach didn't put Rod on the defensive.

Dennis Ralston was the only professional to give Rod trouble in 1967. Strangely enough, groundstroker Ralston had finally developed a big serve just as he left the amateur ranks. When he first hit the pro circuit he beat everybody for a short period—Rosewall, Mal Anderson, Butch Buchholz, Barry MacKay, Andrés Gimeno, Mike Davies, Pierre Barthes, and even Laver . . . once in a while. Unfortunately, the interest in the pros had lapsed and nobody noticed Dennis's feats. There was no big money in 1967, and the traveling circuit received scant coverage in the press. Dennis's serve suffered a relapse, and he never attained this form again.

It took the British to give tennis the much needed shot in the arm. They "opened" Wimbledon to professionals and amateurs alike in

1968. As expected, Laver took it by beating fellow Aussie Tony Roche in straight-set finals. Despite this impressive victory, cracks were beginning to appear in the indomitable redhead's game. Cliff Drysdale upset him at Forest Hills; Tony Roche beat him a couple of times; and even the aging lion, Pancho Gonzales, defeated him in two pro tourneys that year.

Although Laver pulled off his second Grand Slam in 1969, Cliff Richey upset him in the 1969 Madison Square Garden Open, and in other tournaments the pros were starting to get him. In both 1971 and 1972, Laver lost to Rosewall in finals of the World Championship of Tennis tournament at Dallas. This history leads me to believe that Laver's game crested in 1964–67 and not at the time of the second Grand Slam. For in those middle-sixties years Laver could beat Rosewall—or anybody else—any time he felt like it. The later losses to Ken were not because the aging Rosewall had improved but because Rod had slipped. Nevertheless in 1970 and 1971, Rod managed to be the point leader on the WCT circuit.

During 1972, Rod was plagued by a tennis elbow and back injury, and many people thought that at 34 he was through. In 1973, Rod made somewhat of a comeback but he ended up being ranked only eighth in the world. In 1974 he started off well by winning the National Indoors in January, but after his sensational Davis Cup play he simmered down. In one tournament final in the middle of that year, he dropped a match to Cliff Richey after winning the first set 6–0. Richey is a fine all-court player of the old school who returns serve well. He has no big shots but no weaknesses either. By hanging in there, Cliff pulled out the match. In the mid-sixties Richey would have been lucky to have won three games a set. Because of age and the peculiar makeup of his game, Rod often is unable to sustain his form even in a match in which he starts out as the "Laver of old." It is true he hits streaks, as in his brilliant Davis Cup performance in 1974 and in capturing the $35,000 first prize in the Vegas tournament at Caesar's Palace that year, but such wins are becoming less frequent.

Laver is considered by many experts as the finest player of all time. I rank him fourth, but I have to agree that on a given day during his peak years (1964–67) he may well have been unbeatable. But then the same could be said of Lew Hoad. Yet in 1968 he lost to Gonzales in two major pro tournaments. It is extremely doubtful if Budge, Kramer, and Gonzales—the three players ranked ahead of Laver—

could have lost to any 40-year-old at the prime of their careers, especially when big money was on the line. The answer lies in Laver's game style. He is the most unorthodox stroker of all the champions.

Describing his game is difficult. Jack Kramer says, "Despite his marvelous timing, speed and reactions . . . Laver always had Ping-Pong strokes." Kramer is not being derogatory. What he was referring to is the extremely high finish Rod used off both sides—particularly the forehand. This excessive top is similar to the forehand and backhand drives in table tennis.

Here is the way Laver describes his own game in *Rod Laver's Digest*.

> My forehand is not the conventional shot, I hit it with quite a lot of wrist and, frequently, with a great deal of topspin. It gradually grew from an Eastern forehand into a Continental wrist flick. It can hardly be called a safe shot since I sometimes close the hitting surface just as I make contact with the ball. Therefore, if my timing isn't exactly right, I don't have good control. With the Eastern grip you can get a much flatter hitting surface and, consequently, a safer stroke.

Laver explains that 1957 U.S. singles champion Mal Anderson is one of the few Australians with an Eastern forehand. Starting with Frank Sedgman, nearly all Aussie players have used a composite grip (between the Eastern and Continental forehand). Laver's forehand is closer to a Continental. The composite has become so common Down Under that the grip is now dubbed "the Australian." He says he likes the topspin because

> I can hit the ball very hard and still keep it in play, the ball doesn't sail over the baseline, and if it falls short it dips and is tough to volley.
>
> I never hit the same shot twice. "On my regular forehand from the baseline in a groundstroke exchange, I try to flatten my shot, hit through the ball and keep my follow-through lower to avoid excessive topspin and to get better length. On approach forehands, I sometimes try a little slice (it is too long a stroke to be called a chip). However, if the ball is slow and sits up I will topspin the return. . . .

Laver points out that his heavy topspin shot, hit with a wrist snap, allowed him to make better shots from bad positions, adding that it required perfect timing and confidence—there was no margin of safety.

He felt it was important to experiment with spins. "It was easy for me to obtain spin. It was my natural game. Lefties as a rule seem to take better to spin, and had I been a right-hander I might have had an Eastern forehand. The only way I could *never* hit the ball was to take the racket straight back, wait and hit. My forehand always had to be in motion and the circular backswing seemed very natural."

Laver is noted for his roundhouse swing. He adds that his backhand is more accurate, but that none of the pros serve to his forehand regularly. (Laver calls Segura's forehand the best, but also mentions Lew Hoad's "tough forehand.") Laver's backhand is more orthodox, except for the excessive use of wrist and his very high finish when he topspins it. His usual backhand is an underspin. He uses an arch on the backswing and rarely makes the mistake of crowding it. But on high backhand he sometimes snaps his wrist and turns the racquet head over completely—he is one of the few players able to get away with this.

The above description of Laver's strokes suggests how difficult Laver is to imitate. Unfortunately, all kinds of players have tried, but very few of them have succeeded. As John Faunce, former U.S. pro doubles champion, says, "Laver has a forearm that resembles most guy's thighs—and a wrist like the average guy's forearm. His wrist allows him to change the direction of a shot at the last second. This was true of Hoad and is true of Nastase today."

At the net, Laver is decisive, but is subject to missing setups at times and occasionally nets low forehand volleys. But he is very quick, and remarkable in the way he can step in and volley away an opponent's volley (called taking the volley on the volley). His overhead is murderous.

In the January 1975 issue of *World Tennis*, Billie Jean King says,

> Rod is so unpredictable. His game has very little margin for error. If he's hot, he's hot; if he's not, he's not. He's that type of player—hit or miss. I've seen Rod play badly one day and the very next day he will play out of his mind. . . . He's trying to play the same as he has always played, but he is 36 now. He is appreciated more by the public now than he was in 1968 and '69 when I used to see him play unbelievable matches, but he doesn't play as well as he used to.

Laver's game style requires a conditioning and timing that also requires youth. The relative brevity of his greatness was inherent in his stroke production. This is not a criticism of Rod's approach to tennis. At 5′9″, the great Aussie would have never reached the heights he did if he hadn't followed the bent of his highly individual style. It isn't even a criticism of the excessive wrist he uses, for he takes advantage of a unique physical asset when he utilizes his powerful wrist to kill high backhands in returning serve—a shot normal players (including Rosewall) are content to return with depth.

To help explain our ranking of Laver as the fourth best since Budge, it has been pointed out that Gonzales defeated Rod in two major tournaments when Pancho was around 40 and Rod was at his peak. Enough said. The big Mexican-American has to be rated higher. Pancho had fewer losses when he ruled the pros and lasted far longer. Above all, he had a much better serve. The same applies to Kramer and to Budge.

Laver is the first to admit his game lacked the built-in consistency of more orthodox strokers, whereas those masters of orthodox consistency, Budge, Riggs, Trabert, and Rosewall, could almost predict where their game level was and how well they would play.

Kramer is given the nod over Laver, and again the serve makes the difference. Rod never possessed a good enough second serve to have forced Jack consistently . . . and his first delivery was never in the same league. Nevertheless I believe Kramer would have had more trouble with Laver than he had with Gonzales—Laver returned serve better and had better passing shots. But in the long run Laver's inability to break Jack's serve would have spelled the difference. Budge is another matter. He not only had a stronger serve than Rod, but sounder groundstrokes—although he could never make the sensational trick shots that were Laver's trademark. But these wondrous passing shots were only effective against those who were forced to come to the net against Rod (in the modern era of poor service returns, this was the only way an opponent had any chance against the phenomenon from Outback).

Don would not have worried about the net; his serve and return of serve would have kept Laver at bay. Only when he had Rod out of position would Don have forced the net with a majestic forehand or backhand. Laver would have been forced into a groundstroke exchange because he could not have consistently pressed Don with his serve. He would have pulled off sensational shots now and then, but Budge's steady, controlled power would have ground him down. The perpetual-motion Laver has always counted on his facility for moving his opponent around—directing the action—and then pulling out of his repertoire the amazing spins, power, and angles that left his opponent floundering. He could not have dictated the game style to the Budge of 1937 to 1942.

Did Laver have any assets that were superior to Budge's? Laver aficionados say: much faster, quicker reactions, more endurance, but above all infinitely more deception on his strokes. True—but not enough. For Budge ran into several players who fit this description (Perry, for instance), and his consistent power neutralized them all.

Was Laver better than Segura? Rod gets the nod in the ranking over Segura because of his serve. (The main reason, as mentioned, that Gonzales, Kramer, and Budge get the nod over Rod.) Segura's big windup delivery could only be described as average when talking about first-class tennis, whereas Laver has always been able to hit aces on his first delivery. However, Rod's second serve wasn't much better than Segura's. Dr. Heldman says of Rod, "He never had a heavy, deep spin second ball (despite being a left-hander)." Still, Laver's second serve was smoother than Segura's; that is, it took less out of him. If Laver could have developed the service of a Tony Roche he might have wound up Number One on our list. At that, he is the most phenomenal player of all time—if not the greatest.

Considering the peculiarity of his strokes, the amazing thing about Rod Laver is that he managed to be as consistent as he was. When he was dominating tennis he rarely had the bad losses that Hoad and I had when we were off. He managed—through conditioning, dedication, and concentration—to keep his unorthodox shots honed to perfection. This made him the most startling performer ever to walk on a court.

With Budge, Tilden, Gonzales, Kramer, and others in the pantheon of giants, experts could at least discern how they did it. But Rocket Rod was the ultimate magician; there is no way of explaining in rational terms the incredible angles he achieved.

Jerry Teeguarden, president of the Master Tennis Coaches Guild in Los Angeles, credits Laver with producing more changes in the game than anyone else. Teeguarden talks about such talents as "hitting off the hesitation," taking "the volley-on-the-volley," and "the sink factor of spins." Teeguarden is right; the effect of Laver's excessive use of topspin on the game can't be questioned. He turned the game around just as he did the record books. Yet this supreme master of spins began losing his precision as far back as 1970, and it has been on the wane ever since.

In 1976 Ken Rosewall easily defeated him in the $10,000 all-or-nothing contest in the Hawaii WCT. Rosewall beat his erstwhile conqueror every time he played him—even though he is four years older—because he has the kind of strokes that last and Laver doesn't. The television audience watching the Hawaii match saw only a shadow of the Laver of old. The exquisite timing isn't there any more for those unorthodox strokes. Nor is his once famed passing shot, the dreaded bullet of yore.

It is undeniable that Laver was the most effective player who ever lived when it came to the use of spins. No one ever played the game like Rod did in his heyday, and no one will again. Unfortunately what those who have tried to copy his style fail to realize is that Rod is one of a kind.

# 5

# Pancho Segura

LA COSTA, CALIFORNIA

BIOGRAPHY  Born June 20, 1921, at Guayaquil, Ecuador. Height: 5′ 7″. Weight: 147 lb. Right-handed. Won U.S. pro title three times in a row.

STYLE  Two-fisted forehand is most outstanding stroke in game's history; unbeatable unless opponent could avoid it. Improved as professional by taking advantage of volleying ability he rarely used as amateur. Backhand also better later in career. Returns serve brilliantly, particularly off right side where quicksilver moves give him unusual positioning talent. Serve only average for his class of player but well placed, as is overhead. Very deft volleyer, particularly off forehand. Lob and dropshot unsurpassed. Superb passing shots, change of pace, and absolute consistency make him greatest "little man" to ever play the game.

To rank Francisco (Pancho) Segura Number Five seems excessive; he is the only one of the First Ten who failed to win either Wimbledon or Forest Hills as an amateur. True, he was three times National Intercollegiate champion as well as Forest Hills semifinalist three times in a row (Kramer beat him in four sets in 1943); he also won the National Clay Court in 1944 and the National Indoor in 1946. As an amateur, Segura seemed to have a lock on the Number Three ranking, but never rose above it.

In 1947, at the age of 26, Segura became a professional. Most people thought he had reached his peak, but it was as a pro that he came into his own. He resoundingly defeated ex-Australian champion Dinny Pails on the Riggs-Kramer tour. Then in 1949 he faced his old nemesis Frank Parker in the preliminary to the Gonzales-Kramer confrontation (which was to be the longest tour in the history of the game).

Segura literally toyed with Parker in the nightly odyssey where formerly he had rarely beaten the man from Milwaukee. What was Segura doing as a professional that he hadn't done as an amateur? The explanation for the form reversal in the Parker-Segura tour is simple: as an amateur Segura was reluctant to take the net in singles.

His tendency to avoid the net was based on an erroneous assessment; at 5' 7", Segura believed he was too short. Pancho owes a deep debt of gratitude to whoever straightened him out, because as a pro his net game supplemented his magnificent forehand, and turned him into a phenomenon.

Segura could do much more with a forehand than any other player. His two-hand technique (developed in Ecuador as a child because he had rickets) allowed Segura to pull the ball across a net opponent at the last second, drive it down the line, hit a surprise lob, or knock it through him. He had tremendous power, remarkable deception, and he never seemed to miss. Segura also improved his backhand as a pro; it became as consistent as his forehand, though without the same pulverizing effect.

In a 1953 pro tournament against Sammy Match at the Beverly Wilshire, Match—a former First Ten amateur—didn't make an unforced error. Yet he lost 6–1, 6–3, meaning Pancho didn't make any errors either and hit one outright winner after another.

By 1953 he had worked out all the kinks in his game and had forged a chain of shots of astounding certainty . . . all built around the unique forehand. In his six years as a professional he had improved enormously, particularly his volleying. He had faced the pro crucible of Riggs, Parker, Kovacs, Kramer, Gonzales, and Sedgman.

Other superlative forehands have been mentioned: Tilden's perfectly executed stroke, Perry's flashing Continental, Budge's relentless bludgeon, and Kramer's slasher. But Tilden had less power and deception, Perry had deception but the force couldn't compare, Budge lacked the flexibility and deception. Kramer's forehand had disguise but not the force. (My own forehand was possibly even harder than Segura's, but the deception and total consistency weren't there.)

Midcentury was a time when professional tennis was at a low ebb. Kramer was routing Gonzales on their tour, and ended up winning 96 out of 123 matches. A disgusted Gonzales—temporarily dead as a drawing card—returned to his tennis shop at Exposition Park in Los Angeles. Riggs had taken his lumps from Kramer before that, so he was also a dud at the box office.

With the nightly junket undergoing a lull, the only exciting professional tennis event in the latter half of 1950 was the U.S. pro championships at Forest Hills. Kramer was a heavy favorite, but Segura upset him. In the other half of the draw Riggs went down before Frank Kovacs in an unbelievable exhibition of power. Mixing cunning with savage forehands, Segura beat Kovacs to win the 1950 U.S. pro title at the Westside Tennis Club.

This showing was enough for Kramer to sign the colorful little Ecuadorian for the next tour. (A year earlier Segura had also stunned Kramer in the U.S. professional championship before losing in the semifinals 6–4, 8–10, 1–6, 6–4, 6–3.)

In the opening match of the tour, Segura crushed Kramer 6–1, 6–2, 6–1 at Madison Square Garden, a stunningly one-sided match. It

couldn't have been because Kramer was overconfident; after all, he had lost to Segura in the professional championship at Forest Hills.

How was Segura able so decisively to whip Kramer in this important opening match and on the fast surface? Return of serve. Kramer at his best couldn't return like Segura.

Big Jake was also dumbfounded by "Segoo's" agility and consistency at the net. He didn't expect the former backcourt artist to be so devastating in the forecourt, even though he knew Segura had become more daring at the net. Kramer suddenly found himself being forced on serve, and all too often on return of serve. This, coupled with Segura's attacking weapons off both wings, allowed Pancho to hold serve, and his return of serve neutralized Kramer's net attack. An incredible performance.

Segura "was up" for the Madison Square Garden debut. He was serving "over his head" that night and his delivery was never quite that potent again. It was inevitable that because of his overall prowess Jack would eventually grind down the smaller, spindly-legged marvel. Segura's big windup on his serve always took a lot out of him (he was giving away a half-foot height advantage to Big Jake on serve). Pancho had to put everything into his delivery to press Jack's backhand. On a night-after-night basis it proved physically too taxing for a player of Segura's size. Before long, Kramer led 10 matches to 4.

After the opening-night disaster, Kramer had figured out that serving his big one against Segura all too often meant it would be coming back at 150 mph. Kramer had to alter his strategy. Instead of serving hard he temporized on his power while still keeping his delivery deep. He resorted more to his modified American twist delivery with its kick topspin or his sidespin forehand for the net attack—and the attack was almost always against Segura's backhand.

Segura used two hands on the backhand, but unlike his forehand he switched to a one-handed grip just as he made contact with the ball. If he'd perfected the two-handed backhand to include the follow-through, in the manner of Cliff Drysdale, Bjorn Borg, or Jimmy Connors, he might have been able offensively to handle Kramer's kicking second delivery. As it was, he was too small to keep Kramer consistently off the net.

When the tour finally ended Kramer had won 64 out of the 92 matches. Nevertheless, Pancho had won a larger percentage of his matches than Gonzales had—and with a far weaker serve. After the conclusion of the tour, Kramer passed up the pro championship tournament, largely for box office reasons. He was so dominant there would have been little interest in the U.S. professional championship if he had entered it.

Richard Gonzales came out of retirement to challenge the other Pancho for the crown. Fittingly, the two Panchos met in the finals on July 4, 1951, at Forest Hills. The 30-year-old Segura wiped out the 23-year-old Gonzales in straight sets 6–3, 6–4, 6–2. Another stunning performance! The following year Kramer ran out of opponents; Jack was waiting for the reigning amateur rage, Frank Sedgman, to turn professional. Nonetheless, a 1952 pro championship was held. Gonzales, who wanted revenge against the smaller Pancho, made it to the finals again. He had practiced more this time, but lost 6–0 in the fifth set on June 21, 1952, at Lakewood Park, Cleveland. Segura had won the U.S. pro title for the third year in a row, after breaking Gonzales's serve three times in the last set!

In 1954 Gonzales defeated both Segura and Sedgman in a round robin tour, with Sedgman and Segura evening off. Segura pushed Gonzales to the limit in 1955 and 1956 in the U.S. pro tournament finals. In the mid-fifties it nearly always took Big Pancho five sets to win against Small Pancho. By the fifth set the Ecuadorian's delivery —with its excessive windup—would weaken. Gonzales never ran out of steam because his serve—with its easy motion—took so little out of him. Eventually Big Pancho would break Little Pancho. The pattern repeated itself again and again. But if Gonzales was the least bit out of shape, he was sure to lose to his smaller namesake. Against the other stalwarts of the 1950s, Segura had the edge; these included Sedgman, Trabert, Rosewall, and Ken McGregor. When Rosewall turned pro in 1956, Gonzales recalls: "What I did to Rosewall, Segura did even worse. He demoralized him."

Even at 36 in 1957, Segura proved he hadn't slowed down by making Lew Hoad look like a novice in a round robin tournament at the Los Angeles Tennis Club. The final score: 6–3, 6–0. Later that year he managed to upset Gonzales at Wembley before losing in the finals to Ken Rosewall. Year after year in the 1950s it was always the same in pro tournaments; it wasn't just a question of having a hot day and upsetting Gonzales—you had to get by Segura first. And he was still going strong after he turned 40.

To the surprise of everyone, Segura made it to the finals of the U.S. pro championship in 1962 (one of the years in which Gonzales went into temporary retirement). His opponent was Butch Buchholz who was at his peak after five years on the professional circuit (but who had lost numerous times to Segura at the close of the 1950s). This time Butch's youth and familiarity with Segura's game stood him in good stead, as he took the U.S. pro title in four sets against the 41-year-old graying warrior.

I once asked Ken Rosewall who he thought was the greatest small man of the modern era, Riggs, Segura, or himself. He quickly replied: "Segura. No doubt about it. When I joined the pros he beat me for over a year. As for Riggs . . . Segura simply hit too hard."

Pancho had the big shot, and this is why he is a notch above Riggs in the First Ten. This leads to the apocryphal battle between the higher-ranked Laver and Segura. Laver is two inches taller, which gave him a little more reach on serve, net game, and overhead. Rod's service was harder, made with less effort, and he was a lefty (always an advantage). In concentration, speed, and reflexes they were close, with a slight nod to the Rocket for speed. Off the ground he could do things that even a Segura couldn't, with the backhand in particular. At the net the edge goes to Segura. Next to Rosewall, Segura had the finest net game of the smaller champions. Gonzales calls Segura's forehand volley the best. If Segura had a weakness as a pro it was on the serve, which was only weak in comparison to Kramer's or Gonzales's. He maintained consistent depth, and his second delivery allowed him to take the net, but, as mentioned, his big windup was exhausting in a long match.

But in one aspect of tennis Segura was unparalleled. On every shot there is the transition point when the weight shifts from the rear to the front foot. The "summing up of forces" (be it serve, overhead, volley, forehand, or backhand) takes place before the forward weight shift. How well a player can coordinate all aspects of his body before the forward movement will determine the maximization of his power.

Segura's ability to "sum up his forces" is to a certain extent related to his famous coaching dictum: "Always move on the ball; never let the ball move on you." It might also be related to his size. Shorter players often have a total command over their bodies (Riggs, Bitsy Grant, Frank Parker, and, of course, Ken Rosewall) which taller ones can't duplicate. But Segura's remarkable "body flow" aptitude undoubtedly goes beyond size or technique. The lightning coordination was a God-given gift, which hard work refined into a form of genius.

He could do it on every shot, but his two-hand forehand was the nonpareil—with every sinew of his body being utilized. It was this ability that so dumbfounded players a half-foot taller when they found themselves being outpowered.

"Segura is the most underrated of professional champions," Bobby Riggs said.

> Everybody forgets he won the U.S. pro tournament three years in a row (1950–51–52). I played the 1950 tournament at Forest Hills and lost in the semis to Kovacs, who was in fantastic form, and believe it or not, Segura put out Kramer in the other semis and proceeded to beat Kovacs, too, for the title.
>
> Segura's two-hand forehand is the best single shot in tennis history, even superior to Budge's backhand . . . he could do even more with it because of the deception. Segura also had the most deceptive dropshot in the game's history.

Riggs explained that Kramer and Gonzales had to resort to an explicit strategy to defeat Segura on their respective tours. "At all cost they had to keep the ball away from that forehand. This gives you an idea of just how good it was because both Kramer and Gonzales could usually match forehands with anyone. Kramer handled Segura on tour by literally neutralizing this big shot.

"Jack could do anything with a serve," said Riggs, "so he didn't give Pancho a chance to run around his backhand and return serve with the two-hander." He explained that Segura couldn't count on all deliveries to the backhand, for often Kramer would hit so wide that Segura had to revert to a one-hand forehand. "It was the same serving strategy Gonzales used. It took a tremendously powerful and skillful server to do this to Segura. His backhand return of serve wasn't weak, and against the average good serve, Pancho was a master at turning his two-hand forehand into an offensive weapon."

Segura was also one of the toughest competitors ever to walk on a court. He never choked, never lost concentration, and never quit. As a clever player he ranks with Riggs, Rosewall, and Gonzales. He was also a consummate actor and tremendously colorful. His winning smile, coupled with his peculiar pigeon-toed walk, and his shouts of "Pancho" will be remembered whenever luminaries of the past are discussed. Segura is also proof of how much one can improve after the age of 30; he was at his peak between 31 and 36. Unfortunately, Pancho hit his peak when pro tennis was in the doldrums, and thus is the most underrated star who ever lived.

# 6

# Bobby Riggs

NEWPORT BEACH, CALIFORNIA

BIOGRAPHY   Born February 25, 1918, at Los Angeles. Height:
5′ 8¼″. Weight: 155 lb. Right-handed. Member Davis Cup
team 1938, 1939. Captured triple crown at Wimbledon in
1939. Competed in most publicized tennis match in history
against Billie Jean King in 1973.

DAVIS CUP RECORD   Challenge Round 2–2 in singles, 1938,
1939.

STYLE   Absolute master of all aspects of orthodox tennis from
serve to lob. Eastern groundstrokes with wristless control;

74

forehand strongest shot but backhand is also impenetrable. Excellent serve for relatively small man; can hit flat, American twist, or slice. Overhead well placed, but lacks decisiveness of serve. Fine touch at net. Changes grips both at net and back-court without effort. Returns serve beautifully. Game charac-terized by errorless deep shots and ability to vary pace, which allow him to maneuver opponent.

When some people think of Bobby Riggs they immediately remem-ber the 1973 show business travesty with Billie Jean King. Yet, in his prime (which, by the way, lasted a long time) Robert Lorimer Riggs was remarkable, beautiful to watch, a classic stylist who did every-thing right.

From 1936 until the United States' entry into the war, Riggs had the best record of any American, except Budge. A versatile, active competitor, he was equally gifted on any surface. He took the East-ern Grass Courts four straight years, the National Clay Court, U.S. Indoor, Newport Invitational, River Oaks, and Pacific Southwest, among others. After losing in the finals to Don McNeil at Paris in 1939, he captured the triple crown (singles, doubles, and mixed doubles) in his first try at Wimbledon that year. He was also U.S. national champion in 1939, lost in a five-set final to McNeil the next year, but regained the Forest Hills crown in 1941 against Frank Kovacs.

Riggs reached his peak after the war when he edged Don Budge 24–22 in their 1946–47 pro tour, and also won the U.S. professional championship at Forest Hills three times.

What did Riggs have? It wasn't so much what he had as that he lacked nothing. He was an almost errorless tennis player, with noth-ing that approximated a weakness. A little over 5' 8", he isn't as small as sportswriters often imply; an inch taller than Ken Rosewall, Pan-cho Segura, Adrian Quist, and only three fourths of an inch shorter than Rod Laver. He had shrewdness, anticipation, and speed; he was as quick as Segura although not quite up to Rosewall or Laver. (Like Segura he had a funny walk. Bobby walked like a duck, whereas

Pancho was pigeon-toed, but both accelerated like sprinters.) And he was always in perfect condition.

"The best founded strokes in the tennis game belonged to Bobby Riggs," says Julius Heldman. "Riggs's forehand was absolutely correct in every particular. It had the least wrist of all big forehands. Because of the lack of wrist his accuracy was fantastic in depth and direction. . . . He had a rather short backswing, which helped his disguise, and he got his accuracy from perfect timing. He did not flick his wrist for change of direction but instead hit the ball slightly earlier or later. . . . When his opponent attacked he could skim the net on a passing shot, and that locked wrist and very slight overspin would put the ball just where he wanted it. With the same action he could lift lobs, which were just deep forehands to him." Heldman says that Riggs was "primarily a parrier off his opponents thrusts," which gives a brilliant description of his groundstrokes—in short, Riggs was a counterpuncher who could use his opponent's speed against him.

It was this talent that allowed him to defeat Budge after the war. Riggs's backhand was as sound as Don's; it had to be, for only a perfectly produced stroke could withstand Budge's blockbusters. In watching the Budge-Riggs matches of those days, I was constantly amazed. The greatest backhand of all time was being neutralized by a backhand that appeared on the surface to be just as good. Actually, Riggs never possessed the freedom of motion or power on his backhand that Budge did, but his great reflexes and soundness were able to turn Don's pace against him. The slower Budge often found himself unable to get set. He had become a victim of his own power.

The reversal of form on their serves was almost as striking. Stale from lack of competition during the war and beset by injury, Don was not serving well. Riggs, on the other hand, had played constantly. He had developed a first serve that appeared to be going long, then would dip and catch the service line. This tricky delivery allowed Riggs to outace Budge, Kramer, and Gonzales after the war.

Commenting on their 1946 tour, Budge noted,

> Everything went right except my serve, and, for the same reasons, my overhead. Bobby was a great lobber, and he kept throwing them up and I kept missing with my overheads. [Budge doesn't mention his shoulder was troubling him.] Riggs took the first twelve matches from me and then led 13–1 before I was finally able to establish enough of a

new style to give him a fight. . . . In the end I was really trying to outsteady Bobby. I was just trying to beat him at his own game. . . . But the tour was not quite long enough for me, and I was never able to catch him [even though Budge won 21 out of the last 32 matches].

In 1946 when I was still struggling with my serve, Riggs beat me in the finals of the United States Professional Championship at Forest Hills in three quick and easy sets. By the next year, though, I was able to carry him to five sets in the finals.

If Riggs managed to hold his own with Budge in the forties, one may wonder why we have ranked him only Number Six. The answer is simply that by the end of World War II, Budge was past his prime.

In his book *Court Hustler,* Bobby admits as much. "He took a lot more chances in those days [prewar] but he made them all," is the way Riggs puts it. Budge had trounced Riggs (along with Kovacs and Perry) on the 1942 pro tour, and at Forest Hills the same year, Don massacred him 6–2, 6–2, 6–2 for the United States professional title. Says Riggs, "In those days the hardest thing for us to get over was that he was invincible."

At the end of the war Riggs defeated a slowed-down, out-of-practice Budge in an interservice match. "It was then I knew he was no longer invincible," he recalls. The word got out that Budge had slipped—and, in fact, he had. The 28-year-old Riggs caught a slightly over-the-hill legend, and in this caliber of tennis the loss of a single step can spell the difference.

Despite Budge's soundness and power, he probably would have also lost on tour after the war to a Laver, Gonzales, Kramer, or Segura, although it would have been close. Budge's stamina—never his strong point—was less, and his ailing shoulder hampered his serve and overhead. He had also added weight, and even in his prime he wasn't as quick as any of the above, with the possible exception of Kramer.

Riggs confesses, "Even after the war Don hit the ball better than I did, but I was faster and lasted longer."

How would a contest between Robert Lorimer Riggs and Laver have gone? Very close. But the redheaded Australian would have had a slight edge in his prime (1964–69). Bobby's deep shots off serve and ground—enough to force anyone else—were not enough to have forced Laver, because of the Rocket's unique ability to pass. And Rod was too daring an attacker to be beaten from backcourt; he was always on top of the foe. Even Riggs's lobbing ability would have proved ineffectual, for Laver's overhead was fearsome; if an opponent did manage to lob him he'd turn around and pull off one of his magical passing shots.

Riggs played Gonzales several times—mostly practice matches—and the service-return artist found Pancho's delivery easier to handle than Kramer's. He actually handled Gonzales's serve as well as Gonzales handled his. But I believe Gonzales would have squeaked through if they had met in their primes and for the same reason that Gonzales beat Segura: he would have outlasted him. Riggs would have had to expend too much energy to compensate for Gonzales's superior serve and reach.

Even though Riggs had a better serve and backhand than Segura, Pancho is ranked higher, because Segura had something Riggs never had: the "big shot" of his unique forehand. Riggs had dropped out of competition by the time Segura hit his stride in the professionals. They split matches the two times they did meet before 1950. Of all the rankings in this book Riggs and Segura are the closest; I give a slight edge to Segura because I don't think Bobby was big enough to have covered Pancho's passing shots.

When I speak of the superior power of Laver or Segura, I do not wish to give the impression that Riggs was simply steady. Players such as Seymour Greenberg, Tut Bartzen, and Bitsy Grant could hit the ball back all day long. Bobby hit harder than any of these when he wanted to. He could hit as hard as Rosewall, although he tended to vary his shots more. To defeat the stars that he did, Riggs had to be able to "hit out" with depth and power. He was noted for putting away the big forehand after forcing an opponent out of position.

There probably has never been a player who could manipulate an opponent better than Riggs. But even more important than the cageyness was the absolute confidence Riggs possessed on every shot. If he was set he knew he wouldn't miss, whether in backcourt or at net.

His balanced, penetrating groundstrokes on both sides were at least the equal of Rosewall's, including return of serve. Speed never disturbed him, not even a big serve. Budge had a harder delivery, yet Bobby's service was probably more effective because he had more varieties. He could hit a cannonball, slice, or American twist. The only server that gave Riggs real trouble was Kramer, because of Jack's unique ability to spot and mix up deliveries.

Because of his technical mastery, Riggs is the ideal player with whom to discuss tennis greats of the past and present. He was active on the Eastern circuit from 1935 to the end of 1941 as an amateur, and in the pro ranks from 1942 to 1950 as both a player and promoter.

This self-acknowledged hustler, who managed to publicize tennis more than any other individual via the media-hype matches with Margaret Court and Billie Jean King, is remarkably straightforward when analyzing the game historically or technically. When he discusses tennis seriously, even his vaunted ego recedes into the background (albeit temporarily). His sobriety on the subject stems from the pride of expertise; rare is the man who talks nonsense about a subject he totally understands. Evidence of Riggs's objectivity when discussing tennis in a serious vein is his acceptance that Segura is ranked above him in our First Ten.

Riggs refused, at first, to be pinned down on who he thought was the greatest player of all time. But it soon became obvious Jack Kramer was his choice.

> Kramer beat me because I couldn't get set for his serve, and serves hardly ever bothered me. I grew up against net rushers and learned to catch kick serves early off the backhand. I defeated Welby Van Horn in the finals in the 1939 nationals, and Welby was superb at serving a kicker and rushing the net. But with Kramer you never could tell what he would do . . . and he could do anything. For one thing, he'd hit his second serve as hard as the first. Then he'd hook it to the forehand corner on the first serve. And the worst of it was that every one was within six inches of the line.
>
> I beat Jack in our Madison Square Garden debut because I was reasonably able to handle his usual kicker to the backhand. It was 12 matches apiece before he figured out the right way to serve against me and he pulled away. [The tour ended with a 69–20 margin in Kramer's favor.] He kept getting better as I kept getting tireder; he even learned how to lob like an expert.
>
> Speaking of lobs, I've always considered myself the best lobber around, but Kramer never missed an overhead . . . and he placed it beautifully. Whereas Budge—even in his prime—hit down the middle. Gonzales was another outstanding smasher who could back-pedal better than anyone, but at least I recall him missing a few. Kramer not only had the best overhead but the best first volley off return of serve—especially on the forehand.

Gonzales was the supreme artist on the half-volley and in his ability to engulf the net. He could scramble better than either Budge or Kramer and was able to crowd the net more; reminded me of Fred Perry. Both had the agility to cover almost any lob.

Riggs was impressed by Perry. "The most ruthless player who ever walked on a court," he says. "An inexorable determination which even outdid Kramer's, or Gonzales's. Not only did Perry have the ultimate in competitive spirit but a stamina which was a constant source of awe to opponents. Such a big edge it's unbelievable."

This prompted Riggs to comment on another champion who had an endurance comparable to Perry's—Lew Hoad. "Hoad's physique and talents were undeniable, but frankly, I didn't like his tennis head or heart. He never played smart or hung as tough as he could have." Riggs added that Ken McGregor was another star with unique physical gifts who never realized his potential because of temperament. On the other hand Riggs considers four other Australians paragons of the championship temperament: Laver, Emerson, Sedgman, and Rosewall.

Now Trabert was another case. When he was amateur champion he was a good competitor but I felt as a professional he threw in the towel too early after being waxed by Gonzales on their tour. He didn't hang around the scene . . . and he should have. He was the one player who hit as hard and almost as consistently as Budge, and his serve was even harder. I've told Tony he was a disappointment to me in this regard . . . and he simply said: "I realized all my goals. . . . I could make as much money running tennis camps."

Then Riggs dropped an odd aside, "Maybe Trabert was too intelligent . . . or you might say rational, for there is an emotional element beyond the mind if you're going to be a great champion."

Bobby then reminisced about other stars: "Kovacs had incredible groundstrokes. I recall—I can't remember the tournament except that it was on clay—a match around 1950 in which he blanked Frank Parker 6–0, 6–0, 6–0 . . . simply not to be believed. It gives you the heights Kovacs could reach when he was hot. I'm certain no one else who ever played the game could have beaten Parker that badly." In 1941, Riggs won his second U.S. nationals title by defeating Kovacs.

Don McNeil had defeated Riggs in 1940 for the U.S. title in four sets, and in straight sets for the French title in 1939 on the clay at Roland Garros.

> He put out Kramer in the semifinals at Forest Hills in 1940. More of an all-court player than Hunt; hit hard, very good backhand. When he was hot he was murder. . . . But Kovacs beat him in straight sets in 1941 and then I beat Kovacs . . . Elwood Cooke was another gritty, tenacious player who got in the finals against me at Wimbledon in '39. Elwood had a textbook game; in fact, he copied Budge's strokes down to the last detail. A very similar player to Quist. [Quist defeated Riggs in the 1939 Davis Cup.] Both Quist and Cooke were an inch shorter than me, only about 5' 7", or they'd have been even tougher.
> I never had much trouble with either Schroeder or Joe Hunt. Schroeder was a great scrambler and fighter, with a crushing net game. Hunt had a better serve and was somewhat better off the ground, another net rusher, but for some reason I never lost to him. I think it was my return of serve.

A peculiarity of Riggs, usually thought of as a baseliner, is that he considers grass his best surface. This is borne out by his record in Eastern Seaboard tournaments.

> On grass I became more offensive-minded. I seized every possible chance to take the initiative . . . any kind of a short ball and I was at the net. My serve was also more effective on grass . . . as it is with most players. [Ordinary contestants get more games off champions on grass than on any other surface.] Yes, grass was my best surface. On other surfaces I would sometimes be tentative about taking the net, but on grass I had no choice, because if I wasn't up at the net I knew the other guy would be. [On grass the net game is primary because of the low, uneven bounce, and volleys and overheads tend "to die," giving your opponent less chance to pass or lob.] I also preferred grass because my overhead was more effective there. My overhead was consistent, well-placed, but not particularly decisive. But on grass it was as good as a crusher.
> Strange as it might seem, I preferred to play Budge on grass rather than clay. Budge could groove on clay better than on grass. Of course, before the war he could beat me or anybody else on *any* surface—but after the war, he had put on weight and had less stamina. Anyway, stamina was never Budge's strong point.

In the Riggs-Budge crosscountry tour in 1946–47, as mentioned, stamina did play a major part, even though Don's serve and overhead had deteriorated. "I concentrated on staying with him," Bobby said. "Power never bothered me much, and I counterpunched by borrowing his speed and waited for a break." The break usually came when Don would tire after Riggs threw up lob after lob. Riggs claims Perry beat Budge 10–8 in the fifth for the U.S. title in 1936 because of the Englishman's superior endurance.

It never occurred to me that Don had low stamina when I played him on our tour. Of course, I played a slimmer and younger Budge than Riggs did. And big men have to use more energy than small ones to make the same moves.

Riggs emphasized that the myth of Budge's invincibility was a major hurdle he had to transcend after the war. "The best hitter of the ball," Riggs calls Budge. "Although he wasn't a scrambler at the net in the sense of Gonzales or Perry, his volleys were more severe than either, especially off the backhand. And in his prime he had a strong serve, although he couldn't spot or mix it like Kramer."

What about the present-day game and players? "It's gone back to the backcourters," Riggs commented.

> Connors was always an exponent of airtight tennis, and Jimmy is balanced off both sides. He also is a punishing volleyer and fine competitor.
>
> Nastase is also an outstanding talent, except for his antics on the court. Something I wouldn't tolerate if I were running a tournament. He was raised in a Communist country where he never really had to scrape for a buck, so if he's fined $5000 he just bitches and keeps on pulling the same shenanigans. What they ought to do is threaten to suspend him for a year. When it comes to dropping well over a hundred and fifty grand, he'll think twice.
>
> I saw Nastase play Vilas at La Costa in 1975. They're always talking about Budge's topspin backhand, but both of them—Vilas in particular—have far more top on their backhand than Budge. Budge's backhand was mostly flat, and I must say a lot more penetrating than either of these guys, although they are both very steady. I was amazed how many backcourt exchanges they had, sometimes thirty on a point. I can't imagine Budge or Perry letting a rally go on that long without doing something with the ball.

When asked to volunteer his All-Time First Ten, Riggs replied, "I'd put Kramer, one; Budge, two; Vines (a nod), three; Tilden, four; Gonzales, five; Perry, six; Laver, seven; Segura, eight; Sedgman, nine. . . ." Then he paused. "Ten is rough—probably Rosewall. He's been winning major tournaments for over twenty years." Then a pause . . . followed by a smile. "But I agree with you, I was better than Rosewall. Better serve. Better balance off both sides . . . his forehand was always a little suspect."

# 7

# Ken Rosewall

SYDNEY, AUSTRALIA

BIOGRAPHY  Born November 2, 1934, in Sydney. Height: 5′ 7″. Weight: 145 lb. Right-handed. Member of Australian Davis Cup team 1953, 1954, 1955, 1956. Won U.S. nationals in 1956 as amateur and again in 1970 as professional. Longest competitive career of any player.

DAVIS CUP RECORD  Challenge Round 1953, 1954, 1955, 1956; 6–2 in singles, 2–1 in doubles.

STYLE Remarkably durable athlete, rarely injured in career of over twenty-three years. Orthodox stroker, best backhand of any short player. Uses Australian grip (halfway between Eastern and Continental) for all strokes. Forehand also semiflat but less sensational than backhand. Serve weakest part of game. Compensates for serve by outstanding service return. Best small man of all time at net; overhead first class. Wily player with rocklike consistency and concentration who never beats himself.

In terms of sheer longevity of brilliance, Kenneth R. Rosewall is in a class by himself among the First Ten. He has been one of the best players in the world for over twenty years. Of the modern players only Gonzales compares in durability, but Pancho dropped out of major competition for a couple of years in the early sixties. Rosewall, year in and year out, has been the major hurdle for other stars of the game. If you got by him "you were home."

Seventh appears a bit far down the list, considering Rosewall's amazing record. Alex Olmedo, former Wimbledon winner and U.S. pro tournament champion in 1960, considers Rosewall the finest player he ever played . . . and he confronted Laver and Gonzales many times. "The other two are great, but Rosewall's groundstrokes are like nothing I ever faced," he says. Few would dispute him. There simply has never been a more consistent performer off the ground than Kenny. But tennis is made up of more than groundstrokes; Rosewall lacked size, and his serve was never more than adequate.

Olmedo's assessment is related to his own game style. Alex had a fine serve, good groundstrokes and net game, plus great moves. But his serve wasn't the blast that Gonzales or Kramer possessed; his passing shots were never those of Laver or Segura, and his groundstrokes never those of a Rosewall, Riggs, or Budge. At the net he volleyed consistently and accurately, but, at 6', he never had the reach to pull off Gonzales's "windmill" tactics. In short, Olmedo didn't have anything to bother Rosewall.

Olmedo's serve, which he could usually hold, was relatively in-effective against Kenny's ability to return it. If he charged the net he was passed. And if he stayed back he was outrallied by master strokes. But Rosewall facing a serve like Gonzales's was another matter. Pan-cho would put that extra something on his big one and would also "blanket" the net in a way Olmedo couldn't. Also Gonzales was a much headier player than Olmedo.

Off the ground it took the power of a Budge, Segura, or Laver to upset Ken's methodical depth and brilliance. The importance of power in tennis is that even flawless strokers like Rosewall and Riggs occasionally find themselves unable to get set against big hitters.

Unless Rosewall was out of position he rarely missed a shot, because of his phenomenal concentration. Any error in tennis is a minor psychological blow. No player is immune to missing a shot—even a first service. Ken's delivery was relatively slow but he usually managed to get the first one in and rarely double-faulted. This, com-bined with his groundstrokes and net game, allowed him a concen-tration that was unparalleled. A man who plays errorless tennis is awfully hard to beat, for he doesn't beat himself.

Why Riggs above Rosewall? Because he was an inch and a quarter taller, could do everything Rosewall could do, and had a better serve. The last point is central. The last-second surprise dip on Riggs's first serve gave him ace after ace. Rosewall rarely aced anybody. He served deeply, so only a few players could take advantage of the lack of power; but he had to rely on groundstrokes to win the point. He never had a crusher to turn to when he was in danger of dropping his serve.

Outside the serve, Bobby Riggs's form and tactics bore a remark-able similarity to Rosewall's. In fact, in *Court Hustler*, Riggs com-pares his game style with Rosewall's and argues for what he calls "defensive" tennis. Actually the adjective "defensive" is somewhat ill-advised and misleading. What Riggs is talking about is "counterhit-ting"—allowing the opponent to initiate the power and the misses.

> My theory, that the defense is more important than the offense, has never been endorsed by the so-called experts. Gonzales is primarily a defensive player. The public doesn't realize this. Gonzales has a catchy volley, not a punchy put-away shot . . . Pancho looks impressive as he pounds his serve and overheads. But the thing that made him great, in my opinion, was his ability to use defensive tactics. He could run

and stretch and reach and make incredible gets and saves.

The best defensive players are usually short men—Pancho Segura, Ken Rosewall, Art Larsen, and me. All of us had basically sound groundstrokes and were originally backcourt players . . . Ken has become as good a net-rusher as anybody in the game, but basically he is a defensive player with a truly great return of service.

Rosewall was and is an absolute master at the net. Curiously enough, he "went in" very little as an amateur, which is probably why he didn't win Wimbledon. As a pro he became the finest 5′ 7″ net player who ever lived—even better than Segura.

After he turned professional, Rosewall observed that Segura wasn't afraid to take the net gainst Gonzales, even though the Ecuadorian's serve was only slightly better than his own. But Ken found it difficult to do the same. He didn't feel his serve was good enough to allow him to attack consistently, so he compromised. On any relatively short ball he "went in" in back of a forcing approach shot. When he was serving well, he intermittently followed it in . . . depending on how well Gonzales was returning. Nevertheless, the deficiency in his serve lost Rosewall the 1957 tour against Gonzales, 50 matches to 26.

Segura at 36 also had a decided edge on Ken for over a year. Rosewall himself admits Segura was better. "He hit too hard," said Kenny. Segura also had the magnificent disguise that two-hands provide in passing shots, and despite his groundstrokes, Rosewall found it hard to pass Segura.

But in the 1960s Rosewall was the top pro in the world. He began getting to Gonzales around 1959, defeating him in four tournaments. Starting in 1960 he captured the professional title at Wembley four times in a row, defeating Lew Hoad the last three years in the finals. He won this important tournament eight times. He also won the Paris tournament in 1960, 1961, and 1962, defeating Sedgman, Gonzales, and Hoad at various times in those three years. He beat Laver for a year after Rod turned professional at the start of 1963. He has defeated nearly all the present crop of pros with regularity. From late 1964 to 1969 Laver was the only player who dominated him; Laver slipped and then there were none.

In 1970 Rosewall captured the U.S. nationals (called the U.S. Open after 1968) championship. Ken's opponent in the finals was Tony Roche, another Australian, who had gained the final round against Rod Laver in the first Wimbledon Open in 1968.

Rosewall's victory over Roche at Forest Hills in that final is central to the major argument of this book, for Tony was a "big game" player. Before his tennis arm went bad, Roche had one of the wickedest left-hand serves in the game's history. He also had good groundstrokes (very hard), return of service, and excellent passing shots. He was strong as an ox, and also a first-class volleyer.

What was amazing about the 35-year-old Rosewall's victory was that it was played on grass, a fast surface which is the best possible arena for powerful servers with net games. Ken defeated Roche because he returned serve better, moved more quickly than the stocky Roche, and had more depth on the groundstrokes. Tony's looping lefty forehand is similar to Vilas' . . . lots of pace, fine passing shot, but often short because of the extreme topspin. It gives fits to lots of players, but a really sound stroker can handle it and even attack the net off it.

Rosewall captured the World Championship of Tennis tournament at Dallas in 1971 and 1972 when he was past 35 by defeating Laver in the finals both times. In the past seven years Rosewall has evened off with Arthur Ashe and Stan Smith, won 4 out of 6 matches from Nastase and has the edge on John Newcombe. He whipped Newcombe in the 1968 and 1969 finals of the Wembley professional championship in London on a fast court, and did it again in December of 1975 in the finals of a pro tournament in Tokyo. He also defeated net-rushing Vijay Amritraj in the finals of a 1975 WCT tourney at Tucson after beating both Nastase and Newcombe. He took Rod Laver in straight sets in Hawaii, and in 1973 won the WCT tourney at Jackson, Mississippi, over Ramirez.

Rosewall's career over the past decade illustrates his unparalleled ability to deliver under pressure year in and year out despite the encroachment of age.

In 1967 he won the hard court professional title over Andrés Gimeno 6–3, 6–4. The tall, aristocratic-looking Spaniard was a very tough player on the pro circuit during the sixties. He managed to defeat Gonzales, Olmedo, Laver—everybody except Rosewall, who lost to him only once on a fluke. In 1969 Gimeno won the Madison Square Garden pro tourney by upsetting Arthur Ashe in five sets . . . and as late as 1971 he was still playing well enough to capture the German singles and doubles crowns. Yet Rosewall always "owned" him, as he had Alex Olmedo—and for the same reasons.

Both Olmedo and Gimeno were sound in all departments of their game. But to give Rosewall real trouble, consistency was not enough —an opponent had to have at least one "big shot." Olmedo's and Gimeno's only "big shot" was their serve, but their cannonball became a firecracker when Kenny was returning it. Neither had the blockbuster of a Newcombe, Kramer, or Gonzales. In lieu of a mighty serve, an opponent needed a great forehand or backhand to stay in a match with Ken, and neither Olmedo nor Gimeno had that "big shot" off the ground.

But Laver was another matter. From 1964 to 1966 he was Rosewall's nemesis (as he would have been for almost any player who ever lived during those years). Still, in 1967 Rosewall defeated The Rocket three times for titles: in the Los Angeles pro tournament, the International Cup at Newport in Southern California (6–3, 6–3), and in the Pacific pro tournament at Berkeley. However, in the big money Madison Square Garden and Wembley events, Laver emerged victorious.

In 1968 Rosewall defeated Laver in four sets at Roland Garros for the French title (the same year Laver won the first open Wimbledon). It is symbolic that Rosewall in 1968 captured the first open tournament ever played by winning Bournemouth, for he would be "the player to beat" on the circuit for the next several years. That same year he also took the London Professional Indoor Championship (formerly called the Professional World Championship) at Wembley by defeating Newcombe.

In 1969 tennis was inundated with "overnight" young pros from the amateur ranks, all eager to get caught in the flood of big money. Wisely, Rosewall kept his competition to a minimum. He knew they would all be after him, and on a "hot day" they would have him. Ken did manage to get to the finals of the French Open at Roland Garros, but this was the year of Rod Laver's second Grand Slam. Besides Laver, John Newcombe, Fred Stolle, Tom Okker, Bob Hewitt, Roy Emerson, and Tony Roche were all on the rampage that year. Although he had his share of wins, Rosewall at 34 was highly selective in his tournaments. His major victory in 1969 was over John Newcombe at Wembley . . . the sixth time he had captured that title.

The relative inactivity of 1969 paid off. In 1970 Rosewall defeated Tony Roche in the professional championship finals at Boston, and, as has already been mentioned, took the national championship at Forest Hills by beating Roche again. At Wimbledon that year Kenny carried Newcombe to five sets in the finals and a couple of weeks later beat Newcombe 6–3, 6–4 to win the Welsh Open. Earlier Rosewall annihilated the beautifully stroking Bob Hewitt 6–2, 6–2 in the South of England championships at Eastbourne. The Number One American player in 1970 was the unheralded Cliff Richey, who had the edge that year on Stan Smith, Arthur Ashe, Rod Laver, and John Newcombe, but it was the phenomenal Ken Rosewall who was the Number One player in the world.

In 1971, Kenny didn't slacken off as he captured the U.S. pro tourney at Boston again. He beat Laver for the important WCT title at Dallas, took the Welsh Open again, and whipped Fred Stolle 6–4, 6–0, 6–4 to win South Africa. He also won the Australian title for the third time. In 1972 Ken played fewer tournaments, but he did win the World Championship of Tennis tournaments again at Dallas by repeating his victory over Rod Laver. In 1973 the 38-year-old Rosewall eased off again. His remarkable 1974 record has already been discussed (finalist at both Forest Hills and Wimbledon) as has his 1975 victory over Newcombe at Tokyo.

Why has Rosewall lasted so long? Because his errorless tennis expresses a concentration others cannot equal. His groundstrokes were virtually perfect. "Muscles," as he is sometimes affectionately called, is always in shape and rarely bothered by injuries. But when all his amazing qualities and durability are added up, his 5' 7" height and lack of a strong serve are still limitations no amount of skill can overcome if a player is faced by the power of Budge, Kramer, Hoad, Gonzales, or Connors. Jimmy Connors, in particular, can move in on Ken's serve, as he did in 1974 in the Wimbledon and Forest Hills finals.

However Rosewall is so sound that power is not enough to beat him. Like Riggs, his perfect form allows him to counterhit hard shots. (Players have often commented that they'd rather face Rosewall's serve than his returns.) The Australian has been taking the net for twenty years, but relies primarily on the service return, or "control of the third shot" to do it. But when Connors attacks on his serve and return of serve, then Rosewall can't get to the net at all—which explains the massacres in the 1974 Wimbledon and Forest Hills finals. Nonetheless even though Rosewall was serving poorly, it took a groundstroker of the stature of Connors to press his advantage. On Ken's part it wasn't any reluctance to take the net; he just couldn't.

As pointed out in the first chapter, it was Frank Kovacs's refusal to follow his fine serve into the net that limited his greatness. (Although 6' 3½", Kovacs followed his serve in less than Rosewall.) Jan-Erik Lundquist, the great Swedish star of over a decade ago, was, like Frank Kovacs, a big man who could have been the best if he'd "gone in" more. Like Kovacs, he was one of those peculiar players who would rather hit groundstrokes than win. At that he was the best European player for a couple of years. Yet in the 1962 U.S. nationals he lost to 39-year-old Vic Seixas. A 39-year-old Rosewall would also have taken the measure of Lundquist because he would always take the net when it was "expedient." Budge did it, I did it, Perry did it, von Cramm did it, Segura did it, Riggs did it . . . and Connors does it.

Expedient is the operative word. It is inexpedient to go rushing to the net when the service return is by a Tilden, Budge, von Cramm, Trabert, Riggs, Rosewall, Borg, Vilas, or Connors. When Rod Laver was returning well it was absolute suicide.

Assaulting the net recklessly is a violation of the first principle of aggressive tennis: only take the net when you've really forced the opponent (then it is imperative to do so). What big servers forget is that a serve isn't necessarily a forcing shot . . . For example, when a Rosewall or Connors is on the other side of the net.

Offensive tennis is still the name of the game, just as in the Budge era. A rule-of-thumb definition of offense is: press your opponent so he can't get set. This, of course, incorporates the net game as well as the approach shot (serve included) that leads up to it. But rushing the net on every serve can be a specious offense. Rosewall—despite his well-deserved fame as a retriever—plays offensive tennis. It's just that he picks his spots.

8

# Lew Hoad

TENNIS RANCH, SPAIN

**BIOGRAPHY**  Born November 23, 1934, in Glebe, New South Wales, Australia. Height: 5' 10½". Weight: 176 lb. Right-handed. Member Davis Cup team 1953, 1954, 1955, 1956.

**DAVIS CUP RECORD**  Challenge Round 1953, 1954, 1955, 1956; 6–1 in singles, 2–2 in doubles.

**STYLE**  Overwhelming, sometimes erratic court dynamo, whose career was cut short by back injury. Uses Australian grip on all shots. Crushing first serve. Wrist of steel lets him hit shots beyond the capacity of the normal human being. Forehand steadiest side, but backhand equally severe. Amazing strength, acceleration, and moves. Rarely varies pace and given to lapses

94

of concentration. Pulverizingly consistent net game and overhead. On best days invincible.

It is difficult for anyone who has never been subjected to them to comprehend the pressures that an outstanding youngster in the amateur tennis of bygone days had to cope with. I speak from first-hand experience.

After winning Wimbledon and Forest Hills in 1932 I had a miserable season in 1933, largely because of an ill-fated decision to compete on the Australian circuit. I was only 21, yet expected to walk through every tournament I entered. My first jolt was being upset in an early round by a 17-year-old Viv McGrath, who put on a fantastic display of form—particularly with his two-hand backhand. The Australian doubles crown, which I won with Keith Gledhill, consoled me but failed to satisfy the sportswriters. Also, being called to account by the United States Lawn Tennis Association for considering a professional offer by Bill Tilden didn't help, nor did the threat of removal from the Davis Cup team. (As it turned out I hurt my ankle in the fifth set of the 1933 Davis Cup against Perry and lost the key match.)

Without going into the vicissitudes of my 1933 season or trying to justify the defeats (partly erased by my showing against Crawford in the five-set Wimbledon finals), I only wish to say it is not easy to be very young and have too much expected of you.

It is worse when you are not in control of your own life, and in the amateur ranks you never were, even if you were a champion. The purse strings were in other hands, and to this extent so was your destiny. An untimely serious injury—which can happen in any sport at any time—meant a return to the humdrum world of earning a modest living, usually without a skill, after the glamor of international travel and fame.

Nowadays there is enough money around the circuit so a youngster can put aside a nest egg; nobody, except himself, really cares much if he is upset, especially since upsets have become an almost everyday occurrence. But when amateurs were predominant and the box office depended on the performance of the First Ten—particularly the top two or three—there were all sorts of subtle rejections by officialdom when you failed to live up to your billing.

But my travail with official committees and the ever-eager-for-a-story press pales in comparison with what Lew Hoad endured. In analyzing the game and career of our Number Eight "great," then, I'd like to dwell a little on his early years.

In Australia tennis is a major sport and major news. Compared to the United States where tennis was a minor sport until the recent professional circuit phenomena, Australia is a backwater, sports-crazy nation where the biggest event of the year until recently was the Davis Cup Challenge Round.

Lew Hoad was even younger than I—around 18—when he had to face the pressures of tennis fame. He was also of a more flamboyant nature than I and plagued by far more injuries, most of them of the nagging type, invisible to onlookers. The irony here is that Hoad was physically the strongest, and one of the fastest, of all the champions. And he had more endurance than any of the others, with the possible exception of Fred Perry.

Lewis Alan Hoad was born to working-class parents in Glebe, a suburb of Sydney, and was blessed with a strong father, devoted mother, and cheerful family life. He was also blessed at an early age (around 10) with a skilled instructor, Joe Harris, the best player for miles around.

With champions there is always a guiding influence that lays the foundation for their strokes. With Budge it was his brother Lloyd and Tom Stowe; with Kramer, Dick Skeen and myself; with Riggs, Dr. Gerald and Esther Bartosh; with Gonzales, Frank Poulain and Chuck Pate; with Jimmy Connors, his mother, and grandmother (whom he nicknamed Two Moms); with me it was Mercer Beasley.

When Hoad was 12 he dashed into the house and exclaimed, "Hey Dad, I can serve hard." He rushed out to a nearby court and showed his parents the service swing which was almost identical to the one he used as champion.* At 14, he entered the Balmain district championship and his showing prompted a call to Adrian Quist, who was a director with Dunlop Sports and also the reigning Australian champion. Lew, an indifferent student, dropped out of school and took a job as a combination racquet stringer and office boy at Dunlop's. In addition to the job, Dunlop gave Hoad free tennis gear and two

*It is pointed out in the chapter "Shortcuts to Technique" that of all strokes the service is the most vital to acquire early.

afternoons off a week for practice. He received coaching from both Quist and Dinny Pails, and Quist also arranged for Lew to play in exhibitions with Jack Crawford, Jaroslav Drobny, and Eric Sturgess. In the New South Wales junior championship, the unseeded Hoad upset Ken Rosewall 6–3, 6–2. This was a complete reversal of form, as Rosewall had easily beaten Hoad in previous meetings. In 1950, the 16-year-old Hoad captured the Australian junior title, but lost to Harry Hopman in four sets in the National Hard Court Men's tournament. (He got revenge over Hopman in the Victorian championship.) The following year he defeated Ham Richardson for the national junior title of Australia.

In 1952, Rosewall took the junior championship from Hoad 10–8, 6–2, a match in which Lew inexplicably folded toward the end. To Hoad's amazement, he was among the Australian players chosen to go overseas in 1952. Being three weeks younger than Rosewall made the 17-year-old Hoad the youngest Australian ever to represent his country abroad. Both he and Rosewall were being groomed as possible replacements for Frank Sedgman and Ken McGregor (who were flirting with offers from Jack Kramer to turn professional).

At this critical time Hoad suffered his first major clash with officialdom. He was accused by Harry Pitt, the first Life Member of the Lawn Tennis Association of Australia, of not trying in a match at King's Park in western Australia. Pitt, then in his late seventies, was joined in the condemnation by the influential Sir Norman Brookes, president of the Lawn Tennis Association of Australia (L.T.A.A.).

The press jumped on the story, and for several days the affair was hot news. Along with the manners of their son, Lew's parents were subject to close scrutiny. The seven days Hoad had to wait for the special meeting of the L.T.A.A. were open season for the sports columnists.

The local New South Wales Lawn Tennis Association gave Hoad their full backing, and one member castigated the L.T.A.A. in these terms: "Here is a boy of seventeen summoned before a jury of grandfathers. I don't think Mr. Pitt and some of the others could see what is happening on the court even if they were looking at it."

Adrian Quist sent a letter to the L.T.A.A. with Lew's reply to charges, and then instructed him to "apologize" in order to safeguard his trip overseas. He apologized and the storm blew over.

At the National Hard Court, Hoad defeated Rosewall 2–6, 6–1, 1–6, 6–2, 11–9 for the open title when the slighter, smaller teenager tired in the fifth. (Hoad's future wife, Jenny Staley, won the junior title in the same tourney.)

Both Hoad and Rosewall made good showings at Paris and in the London Grass Court championships at Queen's Club, previous to Wimbledon. In the famed All-England Club tournament, Rosewall lost to Gardner Mulloy 9–7, 6–3, 8–6, and Hoad lost to Drobny in the semifinals after acing the Czech star fourteen times.

Curiously enough, it was not Hoad and Rosewall's singles but a doubles match in the 1952 Wimbledon that captured the imagination of the tennis world. The two 17-year-olds defeated Gardner Mulloy—one of the best doubles players of the period—and Dick Savitt, who had won the Wimbledon singles the previous year. The Americans were seeded Number Two.

After a shaky start, word spread that two Aussie boys were making a fight of it, and a huge crowd gathered at center court. Over 11,000 miles away, thousands of Down Under fans glued themselves to the shortwave radio as the excitement built. In the tenth game of the fifth set, the Americans—playing equally brilliant doubles—had match point. Then Rosewall hit two fabulous backhand passing shots, and Mulloy lost his serve. Hoad held his, and the Whiz Kids changed from promising juniors into players everyone wanted to watch.

The London press went wild. Trumpeted the *Sunday Graphic,* "Frenzied spectators see Australian boys, barely out of school, blast second-seeded pair." The more sedate *Times* of London commented, "The defeat of two of the world's best players by seventeen-year-olds has never happened at Wimbledon before." Fan mail flooded in, and the youngsters were presented to Clement Attlee, Field Marshal Montgomery, and the Duchess of Kent. The crowd cheered the boys frantically when they faced the formidable Vic Seixas-Eric Sturgess team in the Wimbledon semifinals but the more experienced world-class stars won in a close match.

The Aussie squad flew to New York, and Hoad bested ex-American champion Art Larsen in straight sets at Forest Hills while Rosewall upset Vic Seixas. However, Mulloy edged Rosewall in the next round, and Hoad decisively lost to Sedgman. (Sedgman captured the 1952 U.S. singles without the loss of a set.)

When Hoad returned to Australia he was a public figure, although he wasn't quite 18. Quist remarked at the time: "Hoad's innate shyness is almost an embarrassment to him. At times big crowds have mistaken this for superciliousness."

On his return Lew hit a slump; still, he was selected for the first time to the Australian Davis Cup team a month after turning 18. Hoad didn't get to play, as Sedgman and McGregor retained the 1952 cup for the Aussies.

As 1953 got underway Hoad didn't improve much on his disappointing performance at the close of 1952. His best tournament was the Australian Hard Court in which he beat Rosewall after being down 5–2 in the fifth (as usual Hoad's strength gave him the edge). When the Aussie team left for overseas, the two 18-year-olds were considered senior players as they stepped into the breach left by

McGregor and Sedgman, who had succumbed to Kramer's pro offers. Mervyn Rose was the Number One singles; another member was Clive Wilderspin, who had beaten Hoad in the Western Australian before the team's departure.

At Rome, Drobny whipped Lew in straight sets for the Italian championship. Then at Roland Garros Hoad lost in the semifinals of the French championship to Vic Seixas. (Seixas developed into Hoad's nemesis that season. Hoad claims Seixas always gave him trouble because of his jerky style of play—never sending the ball over in a regular pattern, but returning it at varying heights and speeds which made him completely unpredictable. Seixas was also one of the first players to effectively use the offensive topspin lob.) Seixas lost in the finals at Paris to Rosewall, who, unlike Hoad, practically always had Vic's number. Why? Because his return of service was more consistent. In the doubles at Stade Roland Garros, Hoad and Rosewall added the French title to their Australian and Italian doubles crowns.

In the warmup for Wimbledon, Hoad beat Rosewall 8–6, 10–8 in the London Grass Court at Queen's. In the Wimbledon quarterfinals, number-one seed Rosewall was upset in five sets by a hard-serving Dane, Kurt Neilsen, and thus the 18-year-old little dynamo's hopes for a Grand Slam were destroyed (Kenny had already won France and Australia). Hoad had a grim tussle with Seixas on a very hot day while playing with an upset stomach. Seixas won the match 9–7 in the fifth and went on to capture Wimbledon by whipping Neilsen.

The Aussie team then journeyed to America, where Rex Hartwig, in one of his unpredictable brilliant flashes of form, drubbed Wimbledon champ Seixas in straight sets in the Eastern Grass Court championships at South Orange. Then Hoad downed Hartwig in the finals, which scotched the Australian press's theorizing that the 18-year-old was "overtennised." But it was at this period that Hoad's chronic back trouble first appeared, and the sensational youngsters from Down Under, who were after a doubles Grand Slam, were upset in the quarterfinals of the American doubles by two relatively unknown players, Hal Burrows and Straight Clark. This shocking defeat of Hoad and Rosewall started the "overtennised" argument all over again in the press. Nevertheless, Hoad was favored to take the U.S. nationals.

Forest Hills that year was a furnace. Hoad, despite his strength,

was never at his best in extreme heat, and he lost to Seixas on the 118°
center court. Trabert won the U.S. title the next day. In the Pacific
Southwest, Hoad, unaccustomed to concrete, lost to Seixas again.

Back in Australia, Lew's game picked up as the Davis Cup team
prepared for the invasion of the Americans. Despite an indifferent
season abroad, his groundstrokes—backhand in particular—had improved. But both he and Rosewall were underdogs, and the experienced Trabert and Seixas were Number One and Three in the
world, respectively.

At Melbourne in the Davis Cup, Hoad disposed of Seixas in straight
sets. However Rosewall made a poor showing in a straight-set loss to
Trabert. Then the brand new partnership of Hoad and Hartwig fell
before Seixas and Trabert, and the Aussies lagged 2-1. In the key
singles matches, Hoad defeated Trabert 13–11, 6–3, 2–6, 3–6, 7–5
before 17,000, and Rosewall took Seixas in four sets. Australia had
retained the cup 3–2. Hoad was now a national hero and received
over a thousand letters from Aussie fans. Shortly afterward, Lew was
drafted into the infantry for the obligatory military service.

In May 1954 Hoad was mustered out, and, with only six days to
prepare for the overseas tour, left for Paris with the Aussie squad. He
was seeded Number One at the French championship but lost in the
quarterfinals to Gardner Mulloy on the slow clay.

In the Queen's Club tournament before Wimbledon, Hoad regained his form for the first time after his army tour and defeated
Mervyn Rose in the finals in straight sets. At Wimbledon, Hoad
gained revenge over Mulloy. But Drobny defeated both Hoad and
Rosewall to become the 1954 champion.

In America, Hoad retained his Eastern Grass Court title by defeating Mulloy and Rosewall in straight sets. But at Newport he was upset
by a 17-year-old fellow countryman named Roy Emerson. Hoad
called it "one of the really bad matches I seem to get half a dozen
times a year." Nevertheless, Hoad was favored to win the U.S. nationals. He lost to Ham Richardson in five sets in the quarterfinals.

The Australian newspapers came down hard on Hoad when he
returned from the 1954 tour. With all the hullabaloo about him, he
had still not won one of the four major singles titles. Although Hoad
was unaware of it, his mannerisms on the court often showed annoy-
ance, pained expressions, and other theatrics. This behavior, coupled
with the slump, occasioned such articles as "Is Hoad a Hoax?" and
other bad publicity. Lew managed to capture Queensland but lost to

an aging Jack Bromwich in the quarters of the New South Wales grass tourney at Sydney. This was followed by a loss to Vic Seixas in the important Victorian championship—and Hoad knocked the ball over the grandstand.

Reporters surrounded him after the match. Lew told them he hit the ball over the stand "because I felt like it! I'm sick of everybody getting on my back." The same critics who had been so ecstatic after his victory over Trabert in the 1953 Davis Cup began to express doubts about whether Australia could afford to gamble on him in the 1954 Cup Challenge Round.

Quist defended him and said Lew "is not a tennis automaton and I hope he never becomes one," admitting that the husky blond always had trouble maintaining concentration for lengthy periods.

Hoad said years later that he considers himself an easygoing person, but that the constant adverse publicity really got to him. A Melbourne paper expressed it succinctly in one of the few sympathetic comments: "Lew is not a racehorse nor is he a sophisticated star of twice his age. The sooner people realize this, the sooner the danger of us losing the greatest tennis player we have ever had will pass." But even this friendly support suggested the Australian lack of objectivity when it came to their major sport.

On what basis could Hoad—who hadn't won a major world title—be called Australia's greatest player when Frank Sedgman had won everything in sight just a couple of years before? (Down Under there has always been a national tendency to overearnestness and exaggeration about big sports which borders on the ridiculous; the raucous fans are a reflection of this.)

Over 25,000 people jammed the enlarged stadium at Sydney to watch Hoad go down in defeat to Trabert in four sets in the Davis Cup. To make matters worse Rosewall (also under great pressure) lost to Seixas in four sets; it was only his second loss to Seixas in nine matches. Then playing with extraordinary momentum and confidence, Trabert and Seixas took the doubles from the young Aussies, and America regained the cup for the first time since 1948. On top of everything, Hoad pulled a groin muscle during the doubles. As usual, the press came down hard on him, so hard that Melbourne journalist Clive Turnbull wrote: "Probably no Australian has ever been submitted to such a barrage of bunkum."

When the Australians made the annual trip overseas in 1955, Hoad and Jenny Staley were secretly married in London. The marriage triggered an uproar from Australian tennis brass. It was ironed out but indicates the subservience of amateurs to officialdom in those days.

In the quarterfinals of Wimbledon, Hoad lost to Budge Patty. Lew was jolted when Hopman dropped him from the singles against Mexico. Against Brazil, Lew was defeated by an unknown, but defeated Bob Falkenburg (who had moved to South America). During the match one of Falkenburg's cannonball deliveries hit Lew in the groin, and caused a reinjury which kept him from reaching top form. Hoad was again dropped from the singles in the matches against Japan. (A ridiculous report said Hoad had refused to play in the final singles after the Aussies had crushed Japan 4–0.) Against the Italian team, Lew was back in form and the Australians won 5–0 which bolstered Hoad's morale to face the American team.

The Australians regained the cup only eight months after they lost it. Trabert, troubled by blisters on his hand, lost in four sets to Hoad and was replaced in the final rubber by Ham Richardson. Rosewall took the net-rushing Seixas, and Hartwig and Hoad won the doubles. Then Hoad beat Seixas in four sets for a 5–0 Aussie triumph. Possibly Hoad's excellent showing was because the Challenge Round was played in the United States instead of Australia.

The American and Australian stars returned to Forest Hills shortly afterward for the U.S. nationals. Fully recovered from his blisters, Trabert took Hoad in straight sets in the semifinals and then polished off Rosewall in the finals. There was no outcry against Hoad this time; losing to Trabert in 1955 was almost a foregone conclusion.

With Trabert out of the way (he turned pro at the end of 1955) Hoad had his greatest amateur year in 1956. Though his back occasionally plagued him, the press had finally eased off. Hoad was allowed to travel privately accompanied by his wife, and his expansive nature enjoyed the new freedom after so many years under the tight rein of Harry Hopman. His horizons broadened as he began investigating a world that had formerly been restricted to tennis.

Hoad's marvelous play in 1956 has been recounted many times . . . and most people agree that marriage appears to have been a contributing factor. It had happened before. Vic Seixas at 29 was transformed from an erratic star into the Wimbledon titleholder in 1953 and the U.S. champion in 1954. John Newcombe was at his best after he tied the knot, and (however hard to believe) Nastase was even crazier *before* he got married. More recently, marriage seems to have had a settling effect on Adriano Panatta's game. In any case, Lew Hoad was certainly a steadier performer in 1956 than he had been before. That year he almost duplicated Budge's Grand Slam by capturing the Australian, French, and Wimbledon titles. Only his loss to Rosewall in the U.S. finals at Forest Hills prevented him from joining the magic circle. That final was a match to remember.

Playing with the customary brilliance he exhibited that season, Lew polished off Kenny easily in the first set. Then Rosewall changed his tactics and began taking the net whenever possible. Instead of mixing up his shots and trying a few lobs against his short friend, Lew just blasted away and lost his chance at the Grand Slam.

The husky blond Aussie had all the talent in the world, but he was never a smart player as an amateur; for that reason he continually lost to Budge Patty even though he had a better serve, forehand, backhand, and net game. Lew once confessed to me, "I never knew anything about tennis until I turned pro." He got away with this in the amateurs because of his overwhelming talent; he would find the professional ranks another story.

Hoad agreed to turn professional after winning his second Wimbledon in 1957 in which he annihilated Ashley Cooper—the singles winner himself a year later—with the loss of only five games. After the match Cooper said, "I've practiced a lot with Sedgman and even he can't touch that play." Hoad received a $125,000 guarantee from promoter Jack Kramer, but at first it looked like Kramer had made a mistake.

In his first outings Hoad lost to almost every professional on the circuit, including Kramer. Earl Buchholz, Rex Hartwig, Dinny Pails were some of the lesser stars to dim the luster of the amateur king. Keener competition, television shows, and too much tennis had made him temporarily listless and sluggish. But before long, after recognizing the pros were a different ball game, he snapped out of it. The pros meant facing a star every night with no warmup matches.

Hoad started off strong on the Gonzales tour, but Pancho was eventually able to neutralize Lew's big guns and win 51 to 37. On their European junket Gonzales actually lost to Hoad in Ampol points, but Pancho's record was superior against the other players so he won out on a day-to-day basis. In 1959 Ashley Cooper and Mal Anderson joined the tour, and as usual Lew lost several matches he should have won.

One fantastic sideline of the European junket was Lew's training habits. Because it was one of the hottest European summers on record, Hoad drank so much beer he became dehydrated in the sun and lost 18 pounds. Yet he still beat Gonzales and made mincemeat of an over-the-hill Jack Kramer. What he couldn't defeat was a bad hand dealt him by fate.

It is one of the ironies of tennis history that at the age of 25, while he was in his prime, one of the finest physical specimens ever to play the game should fall victim to an ailing back. Although the ache had been annoying him off and on for almost five years, by 1960 it had gotten substantially worse.

Hoad had temporarily licked his back problem by 1963 and spoiled the debut of Rod Laver as a professional by taking him in four sets at Sydney. He also had Laver's number in several other matches until the chronic back trouble returned and forced him out of competition. Lew's superiority over Laver was attributable to the serve; that is, he could handle Rod's delivery easier than Rod could handle his. This supports the claim that Hoad at his best was as good as anybody. (However, it should be kept in mind that Rosewall also defeated Laver at this stage.) Although he was only 29 at the time of the Laver series, Hoad never again reached top form—physically or on the court.

Because he was subject to "off days" and had a career that was cut short, Lew Hoad is ranked only eighth. Injuries are part of life, and it is the track record that counts; nevertheless Hoad was nonpareil when he was "on." If he hadn't hurt his back he probably would be winning yet.

He wasn't tall as tennis players go, but his serve was certainly the most severe delivery of any player under 6' in the game's history. He hit the ball at the acme of his stretch (which often took him off the ground) with a crackling snap of his bull-like wrist. Art Larsen claims it was swifter than Gonzales's (however, it took more effort for Lew because of his height). His second serve was also fine, but not quite up to Pancho's kicker.

In contrast to Gonzales, however, Hoad didn't know what defense was. He never temporized. Lew went for winners even when out of position, and although this resulted in sensational shots it also meant unnecessary errors. He rarely varied his game and would hit a hard shot when an ordinary one would do. But in his prime his forehand

and backhand were as solid as a rock. At his peak, Hoad was capable of taking Gonzales's first serve inside the baseline. His reflexes were that good! None of Pancho's other opponents could stand in that close and handle his delivery. This, coupled with his serve, speed, stamina, and outstanding volleying ability, made Hoad literally unbeatable on a "given day." He was even superior to Budge, although he would never have defeated Don on tour because Don didn't have "off days." Differentiating between Hoad and Budge concerns game styles.

Hoad would blast on his first groundstroke, whereas Don worked up to his maximum power through the rhythm of the exchange; on the third trade of groundstrokes nobody in history had Budge's controlled speed. But if he had been playing Hoad on one of the muscular Aussie's "on days" no third exchange would have been likely.

Lew at his best was a genius at getting on top of his opponent with his tremendous speed afoot and ability to catch the ball early. He also had trickier passing shots than Don had because of the natural disguise in his stroke production, plus quicker reflexes and more stamina. For once Budge would have found a player who initiated the power before he did; and he would have found himself a step late.

Hoad had the better serve; Budge the better return of serve. Their forehands were on a par, with Don's a shade more consistent. On the backhand Don was stronger and more consistent. At the net Lew was quicker, but no more consistent. Thus in the long haul Budge's consistency would have spelled the difference . . . except on certain days.

# 9

# Frank Sedgman

SYDNEY, AUSTRALIA

BIOGRAPHY  Born October 29, 1927, at Mont Albert, Victoria, Australia. Height: 5' 11". Weight: 168 lb. Right-handed. Member Davis Cup team 1949, 1950, 1951, 1952. Didn't lose a singles or doubles match from 1950 to 1952 in Davis Cup play.

DAVIS CUP RECORD  Challenge Round 1949, 1950, 1951, 1952, 6–2 in singles; 1950, 1951, 1952, 3–0 in doubles.

STYLE  Uncanny anticipation and ability to get in position in forecourt make him possibly finest net player of all time. Game ideally suited to grass where he has won greatest victories.

Australian grip on all shots. Service first class but not outstanding. Good groundstrokes, with forehand best side. Very difficult to keep off net; strong serve essential to keep him at bay. Preeminent at positioning himself at net and unsurpassed at volleying from service line. Little variation in tactics but difficult to put on defensive. Aggressive play supplemented by superb conditioning and speed.

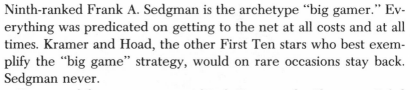

Ninth-ranked Frank A. Sedgman is the archetype "big gamer." Everything was predicated on getting to the net at all costs and at all times. Kramer and Hoad, the other First Ten stars who best exemplify the "big game" strategy, would on rare occasions stay back. Sedgman never.

Because of the preeminence of Jack Kramer, the "big game" fad was at the zenith of its popularity when Frank was coming up; there never was a player whose physical gifts so fitted the demands of the net-attack principle. As an amateur they carried him to the heights, but when he turned professional and faced Kramer, Gonzales, Segura, Rosewall, and Hoad, it was another matter.

Jack Kramer signed Sedgman in December 1952 for a guarantee of $75,000 or 35 percent of the gate. The Aussie had spearheaded his nation's Davis Cup team to victory for four straight years (1949–52). He had won the Australian title in 1949 and 1950. In 1951 he captured all four of the world's major doubles titles with countryman Ken McGregor and took the Forest Hills singles for the first time. After losing to Jaroslav Drobny in the finals of the French championships in 1952 (although he retained his doubles title with McGregor), Sedgman gained revenge over Drobny in the Wimbledon finals by whipping the Czech in four sets. He also retained his doubles crown with McGregor and won the mixed doubles with Doris Hart to become the second triple crown winner in Wimbledon history (Riggs was the first). Also in 1952 he won the U.S. nationals for the second time by wiping out Gardner Mulloy.

McGregor, the other half of the victorious Australian Davis Cup team, was also signed by tour promoter Kramer. This power-serving friend had upset Sedgman for the 1952 Australian title in four sets. In the 1953–54 tour, world pro king Kramer took on the miraculous mover from Down Under, while McGregor faced Pancho Segura on the second half of the bill.

Sedgman made an excellent showing by winning 41 matches from Kramer, though Jack managed to hold onto his professional tour crown by taking 54.

As usual, Kramer's serve proved too potent; his return of service was also better. It was dogged determination, superb conditioning, and a fantastic facility at the net that allowed Sedge to do as well as he did. Also Kramer was 32 and physically not what he had once been.

The other half of the tour was more one-sided. Despite advantages in size, strength, and serve, the lanky McGregor was carved to pieces by Segura. Pancho handled Ken's cannonball first serve with amazing ease (after Kramer and Gonzales he was used to serves). It was a startling example of how superb groundstrokes can cut a big net rusher down to size. At 6′ 3″, McGregor was the same height as Gonzales, faster, moved as well, and could jump higher, and once he got to the net he was as difficult to pass because of his amazing reach.

McGregor had the most extraordinary overhead of all time. His quickness and the spring in his legs made him invulnerable to lobs. Even Segura, who lobbed as well as Riggs, soon gave up this tactic against the handsome Australian. Under competitive conditions against Segura, McGregor hit 67 in a row without a miss, most of them putaways.

Yet all McGregor's net ability was to no avail against Segura. Tennis as a sport is a great equalizer. Size doesn't count that much—less so in any case than in football, basketball, or even baseball. As important as height and a big serve are, they have to be backed by other expertise. Riggs, Rosewall, and Segura prove how in tennis Davids can down Goliaths. McGregor faced the same dilemma net rushers experienced against Budge: the volley and overhead are useless unless you can get to the net in the first place. Segura returned serve almost as well as Budge, and his passing shots were superior because of the two-hand deception. In order to reach the net against Segura a serve wasn't enough; it had to be reinforced by strong approach shots. McGregor also had a flaw common to most big men: trouble with balls driven directly at them. Ken never mastered the art of getting out of his own way when he was at net; something Sedgman and Gonzales accomplished with consummate grace.

In the 1954–55 round robin tour with Segura, McGregor and Gonzales, Sedgman had the same problem with the Ecuadorian buzz saw that McGregor encountered, although Sedgman made the contest much closer. (Segura also did better against Big Pancho than did either of the Australians.)

Like Gonzales, Sedgman had the unusual ability to take an ordinary serve (and Segoo's serve was just that) with a half-volley-type chip or block and then force the net. Also, Sedgman could move sideways in midcourt like a dancer and scoop up half volleys with the facility of a Gonzales.

The chip-and-block technique Sedgman employed to attack serves greatly influenced the "big game," especially during the period when he was reigning supreme as an amateur. This style is most effective on grass where Frank achieved his greatest victories. What the younger players watching him didn't realize (and still don't realize today) is that the Sedgman style of going to the net on everything takes remarkable stamina, and entails handling a plethora of balls at your feet. Because of his reflexes Frank was exceptionally adroit at hitting half volleys even when out of position. He also had a unique knack of always being in the right place at the right time for a volley. Moves, anticipation, and dexterity like his can only be learned up to a point; the rest requires the sheer talent of a natural; it was that special genius that transformed him from a very good player into a great one. Sedgman's most impressive victory as a professional was over Gonzales at Wembley in 1953. In 1956 he gained the finals again against Gonzales in London and lost in a sensational match. However, in 1958 he captured this important British tournament for the second time by defeating Tony Trabert.

Sedgman never made quite the mark as a professional that he did as an amateur. He reached the U.S. pro final round only twice, the first time in 1954 and again in 1961. Unfortunately, Gonzales was on the other side of the net both times.

Riggs was too old and Laver too young to be included in the Sedgman era. Riggs would have blunted his net attack with his service return. Laver also returned serve better than Sedgman, and his passing shots would have been too much.

Sedgman had a serve roughly comparable to Laver's—plenty good, but not outstanding. Good enough to go in on, unless he was

facing a returner like Rosewall, Segura, Riggs, or Laver. If he'd had a better serve he might have edged Gonzales. He returned serve as well, had better anticipation, and was equal as a competitor. In terms of implacable determination Sedgman can be compared to another Australian of more recent times—Roy Emerson.

Emerson is not one of the First Ten listed here, but he would surely be Number Eleven. He won nineteen major titles in the sixties, including Forest Hills, and Wimbledon twice. (Roy defeated Laver in 1961 for the American title.) He was Australian doubles champion six times; and every other world-class doubles crown is on his mantelpiece. Both Sedge and Emmo had outstanding Davis Cup records, and neither lost to anyone he should have beaten. They had in common what can be called "the heart of a champion," an ability to hang tough when things were going badly and to press their advantage when given the least opening.

Both were extremely fast and around the same size. Emmo was 5' 10½" and weighed around 170 pounds; Sedge was a half inch taller and weighed a couple of pounds less. Besides heart, concentration, and coolness, their sturdy physiques furnished the endurance to pull out five-set matches. Both were always in perfect mental and physical shape. However, Sedgman had a little more going for him; his serve and forehand were better; Emerson had the better backhand, which was especially good on returning service.

But it was at the net—as with most Australians—where they stood out. Emerson rarely missed a volley he could get his racquet on. Sedgman also rarely missed . . . with the difference that he got his racquet on almost anything. Once at the net he was unpassable with an anticipation never equaled, except possibly by Borotra. Sedgman always seemed to be there. In 1952 he defeated Linn Rockwood 6–0, 6–0 in the Pacific Southwest at the Los Angeles Tennis Club. Rockwood was twice National Public Parks champion and steady as a rock. He didn't make a single unforced error, yet he couldn't get a game. He didn't have the power to keep Frank off the net, and he didn't have the serve or volley to take the net away from him. These drawbacks spelled certain defeat for any player in the two years (1951–52) Sedgman dominated the amateurs.

In spite of his phenomenal net game, Sedge never had the big shots of a Hoad, Kramer, Gonzales, or Segura, or the consistency in the backcourt of a Riggs or Rosewall. In the pros he ran into stars almost as good at the net (Kramer, for example), who had big shots—plus consistency. He was about equal to a much older Segura, had a slight edge on Trabert, but Hoad, Rosewall, Gonzales, and Kramer had the edge on him.

Nevertheless, Bobby Riggs considers Frank Sedgman, after Laver, the outstanding Australian in tennis history and the ninth best player who ever lived. Besides Laver, I give Hoad, Rosewall, and perhaps Jack Crawford a slight edge over Sedgman. (Budge calls Crawford the greatest of all the Australians.) Crawford served so deep and hit off both sides with such accuracy and depth that even Sedge would have had difficulty storming the net. Crawford was also capable of coming up with his "best shot" (as Riggs likes to call it) whenever his opponent attacked.

Riggs cites Sedgman's showing against Jack Kramer on their 1953–54 tour (56–41 for Jack) to support his high opinion of the blond wonder, and notes that Sedge had a far better record against Kramer than he did—or in fact than either Gonzales or Segura did.

A strong argument, but I never thought Sedgman encountered the Jack Kramer who trounced Gonzales, Riggs, and Segura. The 32-year-old Californian was having back trouble and had laid off competition for nearly a year waiting to sign up Sedgman as a professional. When Kramer and Sedgman finally squared off on their nightly junket, Jack's service was off, and it was his serve that was his ace in the hole against Riggs, Gonzales, and Segura. On the other hand, the stalwart from Mont Albert was right at his peak and gave a splendid account of himself against a great champion who was slightly past his.

There has never been a better volleyer than Sedgman; he had a good serve and his groundstrokes were solid. But when he had to face great serves and groundstrokes, these talents and being possibly the finest net player of all time wasn't enough. Many modern net rushers remind me of Sedgman, yet none has his anticipation or moves. It is why from one day to the next you can never tell who will win a tournament any more. If Sedgman were twenty years younger you probably could.

# 10

# Tony Trabert

LOS ANGELES, CALIFORNIA

BIOGRAPHY Born August 16, 1930, in Cincinnati. Height: 6' 1". Weight: 190 lb. Right-handed. Member Davis Cup team 1951, 1952, 1953, 1954, 1955. Preeminent American amateur of the 1950s.

DAVIS CUP RECORD Challenge Round 1951, 1952, 1953, 1954, 1955.

STYLE Classic orthodox stylist with Eastern grips and semiflat strokes. Lacks speed afoot as compared with the rest of the First Ten but quick for heavy build. Endurance compensated

114

for relative slowness. Best service return of any big man except Don Budge. Unsurpassed doubles player. Has strong, consistent depth on both wings, with a shade more severity off backhand. Almost unbeatable from backcourt. Big serve and overhead. Net game decisive, especially backhand. A self-disciplined, intelligent competitor not subject to bad days or bad losses. Only bulky physique precluded higher ranking.

The chapter on Frank Sedgman makes the point that the eight players ranked above him in the First Ten were undeniably better, in spite of the Aussie's unquestionable achievements. In contrast, Anthony Marion Trabert might well have been Number One in this book if he had been a step quicker.

Trabert resembled a football player more than a tennis star. With his muscular legs he was the slowest of the Top Ten, although he was fast enough to be an outstanding basketball guard at the University of Cincinnati. Kramer and Budge were the next slowest but had better moves. Tony's lack of agility shouldn't be exaggerated; he was as fast as either Stan Smith or John Newcombe, but because of his bulky build he couldn't shift direction as well. And he was a lot faster than 1951 Wimbledon champion Dick Savitt. It was fortunate for the other greats in the 1950s that Tony didn't have the speed or agility of a Hoad, for he had everything else.

After a year in the Navy, Trabert won Forest Hills and practically every other title in this country in 1953. The previous year he had been sent to Australia on leave to represent the United States on the Davis Cup team. As expected, the out-of-practice sailor lost to both Sedgman and Ken McGregor. But in 1953 Trabert was generally conceded to be the outstanding amateur in the world; however, a 19-year-old named Lew Hoad was expected to give him trouble in the Davis Cup. Trabert had beaten the other Aussie Whiz Kid, Ken Rosewall, in straight sets at Forest Hills. Vic Seixas had defeated Hoad in the other semifinals, but it was believed Hoad was playing below form. In the U.S. finals Trabert wiped out Seixas in straight sets.

In the opening Davis Cup match at Melbourne in 1953, Hoad defeated Wimbledon champion Seixas in three easy sets. Trabert did the same to Rosewall—an accurate barometer of the remarkable form that both the powerful blond Aussie and the husky American had attained.

In the doubles the next day the experienced team of Seixas and Trabert edged the newly formed tandem of Rex Hartwig and Lew Hoad (it was the last match this Aussie pair was to lose as amateurs). This gave America a 2–1 lead. Although the United States was now ahead, the pressure on Trabert was almost as intense as that on Hoad, because Rosewall was expected to beat Seixas (as he usually did). The stage was set for a memorable Davis Cup confrontation.

Trabert and Hoad exceeded expectations: Jack Crawford called it the best tennis on both sides of the net he had ever seen in the amateur ranks. The first set was a sixty-five-minute unbelievable exhibition, which Hoad finally won 13–11 as a thin drizzle of rain began to fall on the 17,000 who jammed Kooyong Stadium at Melbourne.

Trabert's request for spikes after the opening set was refused by the official referee, an advantage for the more light-footed Hoad. On instructions from coach Billy Talbert, Trabert began charging the net on everything to disturb Hoad's rhythm, but Lew kept slamming the ball past Trabert. At 4–1 in the second set, Trabert's request for spikes was granted, and his mobility improved even as the sprinkles continued. At 5–3 in his favor, Hoad found himself down 15–40 on his serve. Reaching deep, the powerful youngster hit four of the hardest deliveries in Davis Cup history, acing Trabert on two game points to win the second set 6–3.

Down two sets to love, Trabert broke Hoad's service for the first time at 2–1 and then broke it again to capture the third 6–2. In the fourth set, as the wet court slowed down Hoad's delivery, Trabert became even bolder on return of serve and took the set 6–3. It was now two sets apiece, and the entire nation of Australia stopped work to listen to the broadcast.

During the early games of the fifth set Trabert held serve with greater ease, but there still was no break at 4-all. In the ninth game Hoad cracked an overhead, but the undaunted Trabert took the blockbuster on the full stroke for a winning return. This proved to be the turning point in the match—but ironically to Hoad's advantage. Hoad looked down and found he had a broken string. The old strings had become sodden, and the new bat gave him more zing; this increased power bolstered his morale and confidence, and he won his serve to make it 5–4.

But in the tenth game Trabert hit two unbelievable shots to even the match at 5-all, after being down 15–30 on his own serve. Then Hoad held serve by acing Trabert on the last point and took a 6–5 lead. (Hoad hit 13 aces in the match, 9 with game points against him.) A tiring Trabert had his serve broken by an inexhaustible Hoad, and the historic match ended 7–5. Each player had won 31 games. Lew was overjoyed, and Tony was crying after the three-hour struggle. The Melbourne crowd went berserk.

The next day Australia stopped work again as Rosewall polished off Seixas 6–2, 2–6, 6–3, 6–4, and the Aussies retained the cup 3–2. It was Rosewall's seventh win over Seixas in the nine matches they had played up to that time.

During his career as an amateur Hoad was the only player who could give Tony consistent trouble, with the exception of the under-rated Aussie Rex Hartwig. For short periods Hartwig was one of the most sensational players who ever lived. During his "patches of brilliance," there was no one in the world, amateur or professional, who could cope with him, according to Hoad.

In the finals of the 1954 Queensland Hartwig ran off a streak of 12 games in which Hoad was almost helpless, even though Lew had won the first two sets. In the fifth set Hartwig became distracted by blistered feet and shoulder trouble and lost 6–1. The final score: 6–4, 6–4, 0–6, 0–6, 6–1.

Although only around 5' 9", Hartwig had a big serve, magnificent groundstrokes, and a superb net game. Gonzales calls his backhand volley the best. He was a bundle of nervous energy with superlative moves. He could overwhelm a player such as Rosewall by hitting a perfect shot every time for 40 minutes, then abruptly fold because one of his shots went out. Trabert was first surprised by the unpredictable dynamo when he lost to Hartwig in the Victorian championships at Kooyong just before the 1953 Davis Cup.

Trabert could handle Rosewall more easily than Hoad or Hartwig. An exception was in the 1954 Wimbledon semifinals. Trabert had captured the French championship at Stade Roland Garros, but lost at Wimbledon in five sets to Rosewall, who put on a performance that was hailed as the finest since World War II. Rosewall also upset Trabert in the semifinals of the 1955 Australian championship, but those were the only two times he beat Tony in major tournaments when they were amateurs.

Trabert was 6′ 1″, 190 pounds, and Rosewall was 5′ 7″, 143 pounds. Essentially their strokes were six of one and half a dozen of the other —splendid orthodox forehands and backhands; another case of a good little man against a good big man. Trabert didn't move nearly as well but he compensated for it by heavier shots, a longer reach, and a blasting serve. He was as cunning as Rosewall when they were amateurs, and his shots were more conclusive. He also played more net.

Trabert at his peak returned serve as well as Rosewall—and harder. In common with Rosewall and Budge, he had orthodox strokes, but as previously stated Eastern orthodox strokes have little disguise; that is, they telegraph direction. However Budge and Rosewall could respond faster to an opponent's volley.

As mentioned, the factor of speed was all that stood between Trabert and preeminence. It was only Sedgman's speed that gave him an edge over Tony. As amateurs their only important match was Forest Hills in 1951. Grass was always Sedgman's surface because of his speed and talent for rushing an opponent. But the number-three-ranked American pushed the Aussie to five sets; the only ones Sedgman lost in the tournament.

Another star of the era who could bother Trabert was Art Larsen, the 1950 national champion. Larsen managed to even off with the powerful Ohioan at 10 matches apiece, although Tony had a decided edge from 1953 to 1955.

Larsen had the groundstrokes and varied type of game that could spell trouble for the bulky Trabert. Gonzales has stated on television that Larsen was the toughest left-hander he ever faced. He was the first player to win all four American titles (grass, clay, indoor, and hard court). Trabert became the second.

The 5′ 10″ Larsen was one of the world's outstanding players. If he had quit smoking, kept regular hours, and single-mindedly pursued tennis he might have become one of the First Ten. He had the finest left-handed backhand in tennis history, and his forehand was as deep and sound but had less power.

Larsen was a left-handed Riggs with smooth Eastern strokes— marvelous to watch. Like Riggs, he was a superb counterhitter, who could turn a blaster's power against him—and he excelled in the use of the dropshot. A dropshot is treacherous unless a player has master-

ful control, and it must be coupled with splendid lobbing ability. Art had both. The mixture of shots allowed him at times to throw the powerfully built Trabert off balance and keep him guessing. His quick reactions and sound strokes also kept him from being overwhelmed by the big serve. Tony was chary of taking net-rushing liberties against Art. Although offensive-minded, Trabert only played the "big game" against run-of-the-mill returners. Against Rosewall or Larsen he would pick his spots before following in his serve.

To recreate Trabert's game, imagine the power and depth of a

Jimmy Connors off the ground with a better volley and a harder serve—keeping in mind that Jimmy is quicker. Once a player has totally controlled power and depth on every shot, he is practically invulnerable. He will not force until he is forced; and he can only be forced by exceptional shots, for example, by a serve of a Hoad, Gonzales, or Kramer.

The only possible strategy against a hitter of Trabert's soundness was the one Larsen (and later Gonzales) used—take advantage of his slowness and don't try to hit with him.

As the midcentury American champion Art Larsen is an important transitional figure. His predecessors as champions were Jack Kramer and Richard Gonzales, both identified with the "big game." His successor, Frank Sedgman, the 1951 and 1952 U.S. champion, was the epitome of the "big gamer" and a master at it. The fact that Larsen couldn't handle Sedgman, and was replaced by him as champion, augmented the popularity of the serve-and-net-rushing strategy.

What few of Sedgman's young admirers and emulators realized was that his amazing facility at the net is something that comes along once in a generation (in the same sense as Jack Kramer's second serve). Larsen's touch shots, dropshots, and lobs didn't bother Sedgman because of his speed, reactions, and anticipation. (Larsen also found these tactics didn't work with Hoad and Seixas, and for the same reasons.) The only way to beat Sedge was to put him on the defensive, not necessarily with the "big game" but certainly by forcing him at every opportunity. But Larsen was addicted to playing cat and mouse with opponents; he couldn't resist trying to toy with them. And trying to toy with Sedgman was mistaking a tiger for a pussycat.

Larsen's drawback was that he fell victim to his genius as a defensive artist. He relied too much on touch. Sound strokes, extreme quickness, and great reactions (such as Larsen's) were a necessity for anyone who wanted to keep up with Trabert.

Rex Hartwig had harder shots and a bigger serve than Larsen. Deep forcing groundstrokes off each wing plus his amazing speed and net game allowed Hartwig to upset Trabert at Forest Hills in 1954. It wasn't that Hartwig possessed stronger shots than Trabert; nobody did, but he had more energy and quickness, which made him invincible when he was "on." Indicative of Hartwig's unconscious form during this "patch of brilliance" in the 1954 U.S. championships was his easy straight-set victory over Rosewall the day after he beat Trabert. His inevitable lapse came against Seixas when he lost in a four-set finals. Hartwig, who turned professional in 1955 at the age of 25, never won a major world singles title, but in doubles he won practically everything because he felt less pressure.

Trabert made up for his losses to Rosewall at Wimbledon and to Hartwig at Forest Hills in 1954 by bringing the Davis Cup back to the United States that year. He defeated Hoad in four sets before 25,578 at White City Stadium (Sydney) in the opening match. This bolstered Vic Seixas to a supreme effort, and in a tenacious display of fighting tennis the 1954 U.S. singles champion defeated his nemesis Ken Rosewall. Under the guidance of coach Billy Talbert the doubles team of Seixas-Trabert also upset Hoad-Rosewall to regain the cup for America after a hiatus of six years.

The following year Trabert dominated the American circuit in a way no player had done before or has done since. He won 13 tournaments in a row, including U.S. Indoor and National Clay Courts, and also captured Wimbledon and Forest Hills without losing a set. In the semifinals of the U.S. Nationals he took Lew Hoad in straight sets and did the same thing to Rosewall in the finals. He also won the French title again, and if Rosewall hadn't upset him in the Australian championship, Trabert would have achieved the Grand Slam in 1955. As it was, he was the first player since Budge to capture the French, Australian, and Wimbledon titles in the same year. Trabert's biggest loss that year was in the Davis Cup to Lew Hoad.

By 1955 both Rosewall and Hoad were at their peak. Rosewall took the first Davis Cup match as he passed the net-rushing Seixas with needle-threading accuracy. Trabert, suffering from blisters on the fingers and palm of his racquet hand, lost to Hoad in four sets. In one of the most exciting and closest doubles matches since the war, Hoad and Rosewall edged Trabert and Seixas 12–14, 6–4, 6–3, 3–6, 7–5, to recapture the Davis Cup for Australia. Because of his hand Trabert didn't play in the remaining singles, and his place was taken by Ham Richardson (who lost to Rosewall). In 1955 the Davis Cup was played just before Forest Hills, and Tony skipped the finals match to make sure he would be ready for the U.S. nationals. His straight-set victories over both Hoad and Rosewall at Forest Hills proved he had fully recovered from his blisters.

The United States Lawn Tennis Association then declared Trabert a professional merely because he voiced his intention to accept an offer from Jack Kramer, even though he hadn't signed a contract or received a single dollar. Kramer came through with a large guarantee, and Tony had the dubious privilege of facing the surly giant from Los Angeles, Pancho Gonzales, who had just finished off Frank Sedgman on a tour. Gonzales was out for blood, as Trabert was slated to receive triple the money he was. Pancho was 27, at the height of his game, and leaner and meaner than ever.

Trabert went into a partial eclipse as a professional; his strokes were as good as ever but his body wasn't. The backgrounds in the arenas made him turn to glasses to correct a slight nearsightedness; his tendency to put on weight also proved troublesome. Gonzales was too wily and quick for the cumbersome Midwesterner and swamped him on the 1956 tour, 74 matches to 27. That Trabert won 27 matches was a testimony to the soundness of his game, as Big Pancho was awesome in the middle and late 1950s. The next year Gonzales beat Ken Rosewall (50–26), and the following year Hoad (51–37).

Trabert encountered Hoad again (for the first time since 1955) in a pro tournament at Forest Hills in 1957, right after the Aussie turned professional.

Lew had looked like a world-beater in his first two matches as a pro when he beat Sedgman and Segura in straight sets (although Segura was tired from playing three tough matches in four days). Against Rosewall in the next match, Hoad discovered he had a lot to learn as a professional and lost in four sets. Nevertheless he was still favored to defeat Trabert. His old rival from Davis Cup days proved as tough as ever; Trabert outlasted him 6–4, 10–12, 6–2, 3–6, 6–3. In the following tournament at the Los Angeles Tennis Club, Tony took his measure again, 9–7, 7–5. The Trabert victories cannot be discounted in view of Lew's sterling shot-making against Gonzales shortly afterward when he took an early lead on their tour.

Trabert didn't play much competitively after his tour with Gonzales. However, at 30 he made a comeback and got to the finals of the 1960 professional championships at Cleveland where he lost to a much younger Alex Olmedo 6–4, 7–5.

Even though Trabert wasn't as impressive as a pro, because of his eye and weight problems, in terms of the basic argument of this book he is a central figure because of his all-around soundness, with its corollary: return of serve. Indiscriminate net rushers were his meat.

Even Gonzales knew better than to go to the net on Tony before he had set him up.

Pancho was at his peak when he played Trabert; he had a string on the ball. It was his ability to jerk Tony around with a variety of spins and deep junk shots that allowed him to pick his openings for a net onslaught. This worked because Tony's relative slowness allowed Pancho to pull him out of position. Trabert found it difficult to switch direction once he had committed himself. In this caliber of tennis, a single step can spell the difference. (Gonzales also had the wisdom not to get into a slugfest.)

Trabert is tenth and Budge first in this book, although I would give the Trabert of 1955 a better chance against the Budge of 1938 than almost any of the others of the First Ten. For once in his life Budge would have found a big hitter who was as consistent as he—but, fortunately for him, a step slower.

# New Stars versus Old Myth

Only two present-day stars, Rod Laver and Ken Rosewall, make the First Ten and the "big game" gets the blame. All in all, the "big game" hasn't advanced tennis—no matter what it did for Jack Kramer. And the myth it promulgated—that always attacking the net in back of the serve is the formula for winning tennis—has been a positive detriment.

The link between the "big game" myth and the First Ten rests on one decisive factor: return of serve. Eight of the First Ten returned serve better than any of the modern net rushers, and the other two, Gonzales and Sedgman, could do at least as much with a return as the present "big game" stars.

The majority of the First Ten didn't rely on the "big game" because they didn't have to, any more than they would today. Here the analysis becomes paradoxical, for the First Ten would be likely to exploit the decline in quality of service returns by following in their serves more often. But the point is that they would have an alternate strategy if they encountered the service return of a Rosewall, Connors, Borg, or Vilas. The current proponents of the "big game" have no choice; their groundstrokes are such that their best chance is the serve and volley.

Obviously such "big game" exponents as John Newcombe, Dick Stockton, Arthur Ashe, John Alexander, Roscoe Tanner, and Stan Smith are fine players. On a given day they can be brilliant and might have upset any of our First Ten. But, as we have pointed out, they lack the one quality all the First Ten possessed: day-in and day-out consistency. The "big gamers" have not only lost frequently to those seeded below them, but almost as frequently to relative unknowns.

If their serve and net game is a little off, they're in trouble. This is in contrast to tennis in the days of Perry, Budge, Kramer, Riggs, Gonzales, et al.; when one of them was defeated it was really an upset, because it happened so seldom. Writers don't even use the word "upset" any more, because defeats of the Number One or Two seeds have become so commonplace. The massacre of Arthur Ashe, 6–1, 6–2, by Jan Kodes in the second round of the 1976 U.S. Open was barely noted. Or take the 1976 Pacific Southwest tournament in which upsets were so common they became a joke. Alex (Sandy) Mayer, the sixteenth seed, beat second-seeded Guillermo Vilas in straight sets. Unseeded Fred McNair whipped Harold Solomon, the seventh seed. Young Ferdi Taygan beat twelfth-seed Bob Lutz 6–4, 6–3 in the first round. The next day Taygan lost 6–1, 6–1 to unseeded Bill Scanlon. The young Britisher John Lloyd upset both Stan Smith and Roscoe Tanner. After Jimmy Connors had to default because of injury, Brian Gottfried upset Ilie Nastase 2–6, 6–4, 7–5 in the semifinals. Eight service breaks in the final set on a fast court indicate the importance of returning serve. Gottfried wisely abandoned his usual "big game" in the tournament and picked his spots for the net attack. In the finals he beat Ashe 6–2, 6–2 by returning serve far better. Ashe held serve only three times; Gottfried lost his only once.

In recent years, as tennis has attained its greatest popularity, it has become impossible to predict who will win a given tournament. A power server like Colin Dibley is liable to take Newcombe, Smith, and Ashe on successive days.

Today's players still concentrate on getting to the net "at all costs," and because of the poor service return of most of their opponents their success has generally perpetuated the "big game" myth. But if the younger stars are to dominate, they must learn to rely more on rocklike groundstrokes and return of service.

To return a hard serve, a sound groundstroker often has to deviate from his regular form. His backswing may shorten, and the stroke turn into an underslice, or almost a block. This is qualitatively different from intentionally chipping or blocking a return. In effect, he is intending to stroke the return of service but hasn't time. Here the concept of "deviation from form" becomes central. The forehand and backhand of a Riggs or Rosewall are like the talents of a playwright who knows all the rules of technique and can implement them in his drama. Therefore, he can deviate from form.

Is Rosewall doing something new that players of the past weren't aware of? If you cut off his head and transplanted it onto a Riggs or Elwood Cooke you couldn't tell the difference, especially returning serve.

The biggest test of a forehand or backhand is the ability to return serve. Rosewall's return of serve was crucial to the defeat of Newcombe at Wimbledon and Forest Hills in 1974—and Stan Smith at Wimbledon. There is a vast difference between groundstrokes that look good and the strokes of a Budge, von Cramm, Rosewall, Tilden, Connors, and Riggs, hit with such confidence that if they are missed it's an accident.

Budge talks about Gottfried von Cramm's return during the 1937 Davis Cup matches between the United States and Germany. Budge led 5–4 in the first set; all he had to do was hold his serve. "I did serve well the whole game. I held up the new balls and showed them to Cramm across the net. Right away I smashed a beauty at him. It clicked right in. I never touched his return. . . . As a matter of fact, the only thing I hit in the game were beautiful first serves." Von Cramm broke Budge at love by putting away four straight returns. Budge didn't even lay his racquet on the ball. Incredible, when one realizes what a heavy first delivery he possessed. More remarkably, von Cramm repeated his performance in the fourth set and broke Budge's serve again at love. In what he calls his greatest match, Budge managed to win the long contest in the fifth set, with a miraculous passing shot as he was falling to the ground. Budge claims he put in 175 first serves that day, and the Baron practically returned them all.

Von Cramm's and Budge's serve and volley were on a par with that of today's stars. But they knew how disastrous it could be rashly to charge the net. Today many players rush the net because they feel safer there than in the backcourt. The irony is that they often get away with it because their opponents are equally inconsistent. The truth is that "big gamers" don't generally have outstanding groundstrokes because they don't use them that much. And they don't use them because they haven't perfected them; it's easier to rush the net, which covers up their inadequacy off the ground.

Jack Kramer has generally been credited with revolutionizing tennis. Actually, there was nothing new in the "big game" of Jack Kramer. Maurice E. McLoughlin won the U.S. nationals in 1912 and 1913 with his constant serve and net attack, but the California Comet's tactics were neutralized by exponents of the all-court game. He lost to Anthony Wilding in the 1913 Wimbledon finals because of the Englishman's ability to return serve. In 1914 the remarkable R. Norris Williams took the title from McLoughlin by utilizing the same net-rushing tactics. As I mentioned, Williams probably had the finest coordination and ability to take the ball on the rise of any player who ever lived. But in 1915 neither Williams or McLoughlin could handle William M. (Little Bill) Johnston. Johnston was a fine volleyer, but he relied on all-court expertise to neutralize the net-rushing Williams and McLoughlin. Strange as it may sound, McLoughlin's net-rushing strategy was old even then. In a very old book, the famed Doherty brothers wrote,

[About Malcolm Whitman, U.S. champion from 1898 through 1900] He gets up to the net on every possible occasion and when at the net is very hard to pass.
[About William A. Larned, seven times U.S. champion from 1901 to 1911] Among his strongest points are his forehand volley and his service . . . which as a rule he follows to the net.
[About Beals Wright, champion, 1905] He has a good service which he follows to the net.
[About William Clothier, champion, 1906] Service much the same as Whitman's and he always follows it up to the net.

The British star Hugh Doherty was able to defeat all of them. He won five straight Wimbledon titles from 1902 to 1906 because he was an all-around player. Billy Johnston and Tilden did the same to the "big game" of Gerald L. Patterson, the outstanding Australian champion.

It sounds like history repeating itself, as "big game" exponents are neutralized by all-court artists Connors, Panatta, Borg, Orantes, Nastase, and Vilas. And of course Ken Rosewall has been winning with an all-court game for years.

Actually, Kramer never claimed his "big game" was revolutionary. He admits it was the media who originated and popularized the term. Since it helped to build him as a gate attraction, he never bothered to clarify the issue.

The myth really stems from what might fairly be called an accident of tennis history. Kramer's predecessor as national champion, Frank Parker, and the other major star in 1944 and 1945, Billy Talbert, were relatively small men who lacked big shots. Neither of them had a powerful serve (although they were noted for getting their first delivery in). They were essentially well-grounded, consistent players and superb tacticians. Although they were both good volleyers, they were known primarily for baseline steadiness. When Kramer returned from the war he looked like something new because his power serve and net-rushing tactics were such a contrast to Parker and Talbert's game styles. The fact that Kramer's other main rival in this period, Tom Brown, was another backcourt stylist accentuated the contrast and helped promote the "big game" myth.

Budge had a severe enough delivery to have constantly attacked the net on his serve; it was roughly as good as Stan Smith's and he was faster afoot. A return by Budge would send a 115 mph serve back at 150 mph—just as Connors' returns shatter modern-day net rushers. Remember: a service return of a Budge, Trabert, Laver, and Connors comes back faster than it went over.

With us old-time stars it was an axiom that return of serve was as important as serving itself; both meant only a point. And if you could break serve you had a definite psychological advantage. The irrefutable logic of this seems lost on performers addicted to net rushing.

Connors used to rush the net on serve more than he does now—until Pancho Segura told him it was better to be less predictable. He noticed that an aging Gonzales had Jimmy lunging all over the place in the finals of the 1971 Pacific Southwest at the Los Angeles Tennis Club. The 43-year-old Gonzales was giving the 19-year-old a lesson in the futility of employing "big game" tactics against him (unless you could serve like a Kramer). After Segura pointed this out, Connors concentrated on groundstrokes to force the net. Because of Connors' absolute sureness off the ground, he knows he can control the play and stay on the offensive without going in on serve.

The "big game" exponents of the First Ten—Kramer, Hoad, and Sedgman—had special qualifications and reasons for taking the net in back of serve. Kramer did it because both deliveries were superlative. Jack used to say, "In this racket you're as good as your second serve." He was also adept at "cheating" on his backhand; that is, he would favor the left side of the court so he could get in position to use his superb forehand. "I even did it awaiting serve," Jack admits. John Newcombe does the same thing. Both these classic net rushers "covered" for their backhand, but they had so many other guns going for them (serve, forehand, net game) that to put baseline pressure on their backhand was a decided achievement. (Budge was able to do it to Jack in their historic 1948 pro match at Forest Hills, and Rosewall beat Newcombe at Wimbledon and Forest Hills in 1974 by doing the same thing.) Yet neither the Kramer nor Newcombe backhand was really weak—only weaker than the forehand.

Hoad accelerated so fast, and volleyed so well, it was just natural for him to go in on everything. Unlike Newcombe and Kramer, he wasn't covering for a relative weakness off the backhand when he stormed the net. But I maintain Hoad would have been as great a player if he'd "picked his spots" for the net onslaught, as Connors does. But Hoad was impatient; his lightning takeoff, endurance, and reflexes made the trip to the net seem very short. As with Kramer, the "big game" fit Hoad's temperament and his physical attributes. But that doesn't mean others should model themselves after either of these unique men's experiences.

Sedgman is a different case; he *had* to get to the net to win. In his day, several players were as good off the ground and served as well, but none equaled him on the volley. More than any other champion Sedgman illustrated the tactic of using a chop, slice, or chip on return of serve to get some semblance of position at the net. His maneuverability and unique ability to volley from the service line allowed him to get away with it. By developing this strategy he was taking advantage of his unusual anticipation, agility, and volley talent.

Whether Pancho Gonzales should be categorized as a "big game" player is open to question. In *Court Hustler* Riggs calls Pancho a "defensive" player. Even though defensive is an inappropriate word to describe his game style, there is no doubt that Gonzales played better defensive tennis than any other big man in the game's history. (What is defensive tennis? Blunting your adversary's offensive without going on the offensive yourself is a good rule-of-thumb definition.) Gonzales was above all a heady player. He wasn't locked in to a "big game" strategy. Sometimes he followed in his serve, sometimes not—it depended on his opponent.

A subsidiary myth of the "big game" should be exploded here. On their long 1949–50 tour in which Jack Kramer overwhelmed the relatively inexperienced Gonzales, neither worried about the net when they were attempting to ace the other. It's the same with every big server who ever lived. The all-out effort of an ace attempt precludes cutting off the return at the net. Another result is that "big ones" from these powerhouses are flat, that is, have less spin than usual. If they are able to get the serve in, it's an ace (opponent misses it completely), a forced error, or it is returned. If returned, it is coming back terrifically fast (à la Budge), or just barely. The server is instinctively ready for either eventuality; if the return is utilizing the server's severe pace he's lucky to have time to get set; if short, he is prepared to move in.

An ace serve demands a total output of resources. The more it's used, the less the power. With the introduction of the "sudden death" point system in 1968, ace attempts are more in evidence because the endurance needed for extra long sets is now a thing of the past. Before the advent of the "sudden death" and "lingering death" tie-breaker, a player could not lose if he held serve. Now he can. Yet the tie-breaker hasn't kept Rosewall, Borg, Vilas, or Connors out of the winner's circle—and none of these men are noted for aces. A confusion surrounding "the ace" is caused by the momentum that pushes the server forward, leading spectators to believe he is net bound—which he may or may not be. Thus the ace has become identified in the public mind with the "big game."

Because Gonzales and Laver were noted for their power and net play, young players emulated the myth instead of the reality. Gonzales—more often than not—was a larger version of Bobby Riggs. When he became the accomplished artist who dominated the pros in the fifties he concentrated on "jerking his opponents around." Sometimes he'd ace them, chip a shot at their feet, lob, or send over a collection of deep junk shots. But one thing was certain, he always had the "big guns" in reserve: the big serve, the net game with his enormous reach, or the clincher forehand available after working the opponent out of position.

Laver is another borderline "big game" player, although his style is different from that of Gonzales. Gonzales says of Rod, "Laver hits all shots—topspin, flat, slice"; whereas Gonzales tended to rely on a semiflat groundstroke. Except for his serve, Laver generally hit harder and volleyed more decisively than Pancho. None of his shots —especially return of serve—could be called defensive. He was always moving, always attacking. Because of this, Laver is often assumed to be a "big game" advocate when in actuality his net attacks were often forehands or backhands. With both Gonzales and Laver it depended on what match you were watching. Against poor returners they'd go in; but neither was committed to a "big game" strategy in the sense that so many of today's youngsters are.

Another player who helped foster the myth was Vic Seixas, who succeeded Sedgman as Wimbledon champion in 1953 and also took the U.S. nationals in 1954. Seixas was a superbly conditioned athlete who won his matches by rushing his opponent. He was as fast as Hoad, taller, and had a fine spin serve to attack the net. At 6' 1", 180 pounds, Vic was so quick and strong that his unsound looping (semi-Western) forehand and sliced backhand, instead of being a disadvantage, oddly fitted in with his fine conditioning. As Will Grimsley notes, "he blunted superior games with his unorthodox style and tenacity." He adopted the Sedgman tactic of charging the net on everything . . . which he did with lightning acceleration. Once up there, he could crowd the net and utilize sharply angled volleys. Lobbing was ineffective against him, for he had an uncanny ability to move backward and dispatch a lob while off the ground. Seixas was a classic example of a player who overcame groundstroke weaknesses by assailing the net.

He had hung around the First Ten for years before this game-style revelation hit him. His career took off at 29 when he upset Sedgman 6–4, 6–4, 6–4, in the 1952 Pacific Southwest. The odds were 20 to 1 against the erratic Seixas. Vic pulled it off by beating Sedgman to the net. And though it didn't work against service returners like Trabert and Rosewall, it was the strategy that best fit his limitations. Seixas is a perfect model for examining the strengths and weaknesses of the "big game." His groundstrokes were so peculiar that he had nothing to lose by moving to the net in back of a service return—and because his strokes were unorthodox he often hit a deceptive passing shot by accident on his way in. Vic had a hard spin serve but it wasn't a flat ace serve so he always sallied forth. Of course, if his opponent could serve—and return serve—he didn't have any defense to speak of. In this regard he resembled the net rushers of today, except that he had more physical qualifications for the "big game" than most of them do.

Why Kramer, Sedgman, Seixas, and Hoad have so many disciples is understandable. A big serve and net game has the advantage of rushing an opponent off his feet before he can get into the match. The run-of-the-mill tournament player would find himself being overwhelmed; and as he becomes more flustered his service return would worsen and his groundstrokes become shakier. The distinct psychological advantage of this blitzkrieg strategy is obvious.

What is less obvious is that the "big game" *is just one tactic.* If a player has a penetrating second serve, such as Kramer and Newcombe, backed up by conditioning and a net game, it can be a decisive tactic—especially against service returns on fast surfaces. But there hasn't been another second serve like Kramer's, and hardly any have equaled Newcombe's.

The problem is that many of today's hard servers imagine they can duplicate them. (Even Newcombe who has all the equipment for the "big game" has been frequently upset.) This is a damaging side effect of the "big game" mythology. For players are constantly wearing themselves out against sound performers like Solomon, Nastase, Rosewall, Kodes, Borg, Orantes, Vilas, Richey, and Connors, who don't play the "big game." Like Budge, all the above take the net when expedient but rely primarily on control of the "third shot."

I'm not contending that groundstrokes are solely what determine a great player; it is simply that without them there is no consistency, and it was consistency, plus power, that made Budge the greatest player in the past thirty-five years. This leads to the question of whether the Budge of 1937–42 will ever be surpassed. To my mind the most likely prospect is Jimmy Connors. Despite some ups and downs in 1976 and 1977—losses to Orantes and Vilas at Forest Hills, to Borg at Wimbledon—Jimmy seems more mature, his game grows steadier, and his competitive spirit remains as fierce as ever.

The consensus of leading players is that Connors' return of serve and ability to apply pressure are what make him so tough. Here is what three have said:

> It's something when you hit what you think is a great serve and it comes back twice as hard, to a corner. You're always stretching. It's not as intimidating physically as it is demoralizing [Brian Gottfried].
> The big thing is that it rarely matters how well you serve. He puts so much pressure on you from the return on, that he's always in control [Marty Riessen].
> Yeah, it's that service return [Arthur Ashe].

What isn't mentioned enough is Conners' ability to lob. He can pull off a surprising topspin lob that brilliantly complements his great passing shots.

It is worthwhile recalling that Arthur Ashe, a long-time "big game" exponent, didn't employ his usual net-rushing tactics when he upset Connors at Wimbledon in 1975. An in-and-outer for several years, Ashe had finally smartened up as his comment to Edwin Newman over national TV indicates: "Whatever it takes to win under a given set of conditions, that should be the 'big game.'"

Discounting Connors' slight leg injury at Wimbledon, Ashe did play "out of his mind," as Jimmy remarked afterward. He got in 70 percent of his potent first deliveries and also played it "smart," a quality sometimes lacking in his game style in the past. He gave

Connors nothing to hit, and only employed his big shots when he had him off balance.

After watching Connors carve up net-rushing Roscoe Tanner in the Wimbledon semis, Ashe realized the futility of indiscriminate power tactics against Connors. An overconfident Connors, who had nearly always taken the measure of his fellow UCLA alumnus in the past, suddenly became confused when he found himself confronted with such an odd mixture of shots from this hard hitter who normally was a "big gamer" par excellence. It threw him off enough so that Ashe got the jump on him, and by the time Jimmy settled down it was too late. Ashe had learned what most players on the circuit are finding out: against Connors the "big game" is futile.

Because of Connors' losses at Wimbledon, Forest Hills, and in the Davis Cup in 1975 there were those in the tennis world who said he had been overrated. After his invincibility in 1974 this is somewhat understandable. What is forgotten is that Ashe at Wimbledon, Manolo Orantes at Forest Hills, and Raul Ramirez at Mexico City all played the matches of their lives . . . and all three on a given day on the right surface are capable of defeating anybody.

The Mexican team captain acknowledged that Ramirez was serving better than usual in the Davis Cup contest against Connors. Ramirez had annihilated the other half of the American team, Brian Gottfried, on the previous day; the straight-set victory over a sound player who ordinarily gives every opponent a tough match indicates that Raul was at the height of his confidence and form.

Ramirez' game style is particularly suited to give Connors a battle. He returns serve beautifully, serves well himself, and his very short backswing allows for deceptive passing shots. But above all Ramirez, at 5' 11", is quick as a cat.

The last point is central. An opponent has to have outstanding reflexes and speed—besides sound strokes—to handle Connors' power. He also has to have a change of pace. Connors can only be defeated by "being jerked around." Ashe hadn't been noted for the ability to do this in the past, but at Wimbledon he was a veritable Riggs. Orantes at Forest Hills did even a better job of it, and apparently Ramirez learned from the other two. Then Vilas, in the 1977 U.S. Open, after succumbing in the first set to Connors' power, thereafter managed to upset his rhythm and won the next three sets—the last at love.

What does "jerking around" mean in Connors' case? It means,

first of all, neutralizing Jimmy's power. To do this, solid ground-strokes are axiomatic in order to withstand the onslaught of his two-hand backhand and left-hand forehand. To counterhit Connors requires the amazing reactions that Ramirez has. Raul also used an adroit change of pace, and he didn't make the fatal error of trying to outhit Connors.

Few players in the history of tennis could have beaten Connors by outhitting him. Gonzales demonstrated the best way to stop Jimmy in the finals of the 1971 Pacific Southwest: get him lunging. By employing soft deep shots, tantalizing short ones at the appropriate moments, plus his heavyweight forehand when he had an opening, Gonzales achieved the difficult objective of "breaking up" Jimmy's game.

To get Connors lunging requires an all-court mixture of shots to throw him off balance so he has trouble getting set for groundstrokes —which is easier said than done, because Jimmy is fast and his reflexes superb.

In the finals of the U.S. Indoor in February of 1976 Ilie Nastase upset Connors, who had won it the three previous years. He also defeated Connors in the finals at La Costa the following month. The Rumanian has to be given great credit for defeating Jimmy on fast surfaces. For once Nastase kept himself in check, put all his undeniable talents to work, and above all didn't give Connors anything to hit. Ashe, Orantes, Ramirez, Nastase, and Vilas all played Jimmy the same way: they steered clear of the "big game" and didn't give him "anything to hit."

This strategy may be the only one that works, but it is far from a guarantee of victory; everything else has to be working very well too, as Connors' destruction of Orantes in the $250,000 Las Vegas challenge match showed. Orantes was obliterated 6–1, 6–2, 6–0 in the nationally televised contest. This laid to rest any idea that Orantes was better, even though he had beaten Jimmy 6–4, 6–3, 6–3 in the 1975 U.S. nationals.

The first thing to be said in comparing the two matches is that Connors played a lot better in Las Vegas on February 28, 1976, and Orantes didn't perform nearly as well as he had at Forest Hills, even though Manolo tried to use the same neutralizing strategy. Secondly, the Caesars Palace surface is faster than the Har-Tru used at Forest Hills, and this was decidedly in Connors' favor. The surface assuredly made a difference, but I believe an error in strategy by Connors at

Forest Hills was more fundamental. Whenever he attacked the net with his famed down-the-line (lefty) backhand he kept running into the Spaniard's left-hand forehand.

Orantes can do as much with a left-hand forehand as any player who ever lived. He can hit it hard or soft, deep or short, dropshot or lob with it. His usual forehand is semiflat—similar to Connors'—with an inherent disguise for passing shots because he's a lefty. It is flatter than the topspin shot of left-handed Guillermo Vilas, and as a result Manolo gets more consistent depth; he is also more capable of changing pace with the forehand than either Vilas or Connors.

If Connors has a weakness it is handling low, skidding balls in midcourt with his backhand (he will murder topspin in this area off both sides). Both Ashe at Wimbledon and Orantes at Forest Hills exploited this relative shortcoming. (Two-hand strokes are uncertain on low, midcourt shots; even Segura used to switch from his two-hand forehand to one arm when he was in "no-man's land" and had to handle a low ball.) At Las Vegas Jimmy directed his attacking shots at Orantes' less flexible backhand. He played smart, made no mistakes, and kept the pressure on from the start. He never let Orantes into the match.

Actually, Connors had no bad losses in 1975. He gained the finals of Forest Hills, Australia, and Wimbledon, and in the big money challenge matches at Las Vegas he defeated Laver and Newcombe. The previous year Jimmy was high on a burst of confidence which made him temporarily invincible.

In Jerry Cohen's column in *The Los Angeles Times* on March 24, 1976, Rod Laver commented: "What happened is that Ashe figured out how to beat him last summer at Wimbledon. Then the other players began to talk among themselves about how to beat Connors —and others did beat him."

One thing the others (Orantes, Ramirez, Nastase, and Vilas) didn't do was employ the "big game." Even Roscoe Tanner, who defeated Arthur Ashe in the semifinals of the American Airlines games on March 27, 1976, with the "big game," didn't use it against Jimmy in the finals . . . although the fast courts at Palm Springs were conducive to it. (He gave Jimmy a tussle but lost the $35,000 first prize.) And in the 1976 Wimbledon, Tanner did manage to beat Connors by steering clear of his usual "big game" strategy and achieving an extraordinary percentage on his first serve—the hardest serve in tennis.

Despite his many achievements, Connors still has something to learn before he realizes the full potential of his game. He doesn't have the serve of a Budge, Kramer, or Hoad to get himself out of trouble. They didn't have to worry about a change of tactics; Connors is now finding out that he does. But in one aspect of his game, Jimbo is already perfect: he knows when to follow in a serve.

On serve, when it comes to playing net, Connors follows the Budge policy; he picks his spots, depending on the game style of his opponent. In the Forest Hills finals of 1974 he followed in his serve more than usual, taking advantage of trampled-down grass. A tired Rosewall was serving poorly, so Connors went in on his return of serve. He reasoned correctly that once he had the jump on Kenny it was an excellent idea to rush him off his feet, before he could get his groundstrokes grooved. His own serve was zinging, and the poor condition of the court made his strategy pay off.

Connors is extremely well coordinated. John Faunce says, "He reminds me of a coiled spring . . . like Segura. And like Segura he really unleashes." Adds Faunce: "You have to get your first serve in on Jimmy or he'll move in and kill you on the second." One of Connors' strengths is the way he can splash a shot at the net with his two-hand backhand volley. This shot is definitely unorthodox. However, according to Glenn Bassett, who coached him at UCLA, "Jimmy's regular two-handed backhand is essentially hit on very orthodox principles. The same goes for his left-hand forehand."

A Connors match against a net rusher usually follows a pattern. Obeying the habit of following all serves to the net, a "big game" exponent finds himself in constant trouble. He is either passed outright, or at best lunges and makes an ineffectual shot—either way he loses the point. If he is lucky enough to make a fairly good volley, the speedy Connors will either pull him off the net with his topspin lob or rifle a bullet off his deceptive backhand or his almost equally brilliant forehand (because he's a lefty it is more difficult to sense the direction of the shot than from a right-hander). If the volley is short, Jimmy jumps on it like a tiger.

In order to take the net on Connors, an opponent has to have the hard penetrating first serve of a John Newcombe. (Jimmy's two-hand backhand allows him to dispatch kick second serves in a unique manner. Bjorn Borg is another who can do this.) Connors' hand-eye coordination is so remarkable that even deep, hard first serves don't bother him.

The best policy against Connors is not to attack the net in back of the serve, as Manuel Orantes demonstrated at Forest Hills. However the "big game" stylists usually have no choice but to try to storm the net against Connors, as they aren't sound enough off the ground to trade strokes with him. They're on the horns of a dilemma: if they rush the net on serve they lose; if they stay back they lose.

Vilas, the winner on Grand Prix points in 1974 and 1975, simmered down in 1976, but in 1977 came back to beat Connors at Forest Hills, and later at Madison Square Garden early in 1978. Like Connors, the mainstay of Vilas' game is groundstrokes. Out of his repertoire the sturdy Argentinean has developed a very deceptive, sharply angled topspin backhand. He also uses heavy top on his left-hand forehand. He has as good passing shots as the game has ever seen. He hits very hard, and much of his game is reminiscent of Laver's, although he doesn't volley as well. The inevitable imitators will be fascinated by his unique backhand, just as they were by Laver's wristy shots . . . and they'll be just as unsuccessful in duplicating them. Like Laver, Vilas has the wrist of a Sonny Liston.

A dazzling, unorthodox shot is usually a natural gift growing out of the individuality of a given player. Through experimentation he has devised something that works for him. This "something" is usually inimitable. These inimitable shots cannot be learned . . . only admired. By contrast, orthodox strokes can be taught. Besides being more consistent, they are the result of a solid body of technique which provides a blueprint to follow.

How about experimentation? Experimentation is essential . . . this sounds like a contradiction in light of the last paragraph. But there has never been a top tennis player who didn't experiment. To improve, a player reads, observes, thinks, talks to other players—then analyzes, and through a process of trial and error finds out what works for him. Finally he arrives at a point where it "all hangs together."

The ultimate test of any shot in tennis is its reliability under pressure—be it orthodox or unorthodox. The advantage of orthodox form is that it provides a shortcut to excellence because it is the result of a historical process. As with other disciplines, the student can avail himself of the refinements of past experience and knowledge concerning technique. Sometimes he finds he has a special talent that doesn't quite fit into the accepted form, and through experimentation perfects it. Vilas is a case in point, as are Laver and Bjorn Borg.

All three are noted for their use of topspin, and herein lurks a danger similar to that inherent in the "big game" myth.

Hearing the constant refrain that "topspin is king" makes me fearful that another myth is about to be spawned. Youngsters and newcomers to the sport will be gulled into thinking that "topspin" is a magic formula and something new. As a technique, topspin has been around even longer than the "big game" has been a strategy—Billy Johnston's topspin Western forehand was the most famous stroke in the world in 1915. The major breakthrough with topspin today has been on the lob, not on regular strokes.

It is not difficult to understand why heavy top came into vogue. With the serve-and-net-rushing tactics dominant on the circuit until recently, extremely topped shots had an inherent disguise and dip, which made them difficult to volley. Nobody denies topspin shots are effective when used by Laver, Vilas, Okker, or Borg. But it is a hard shot to control consistently. When Tom Okker is "on," his flashy Ping-Pong forehand is terrific; but when he is off, he can lose to an inferior player, as he did in the first round of the 1975 U.S. Open. A wristy topspin forehand like Okker uses simply can't be grooved in the way a semiflat topspin can. In Bjorn Borg's case, the excessive topspin on his forehand comes as much from his Western-style grip as from the wrist. Vilas has the looping topped forehand which is natural with many left-handers, although he cuts his depth by dropping the head of the racquet.

Now that the "big game" is (hopefully) on the wane, extra topspin should also be on the decline . . . but it isn't. With the slower courts many players are being forced to stay back more, so there is less need for topped "dip" shots to thwart net rushers. The serve is giving way to groundstrokes as the method for paving the way to the net. But an excessively topped stroke is inferior to a flatter one as a net-attacking weapon, because the high follow-through restricts forward momentum. Watch Connors, Orantes, Kodes, and Rosewall ride with the shot as they move to the net; their semiflat stroke allows them to retain the ball on the strings, whereas Borg's high roundhouse finish doesn't.

Nevertheless, Borg's forehand meshes perfectly with the rest of his game. Besides being deceptive for passing shots, his semi-Western grip has great consistency, and the jumping bounce makes it hard to handle for the average groundstroker. But with all Borg's artistry, his topspin shots are not consistently deep. No heavily topped stroke can be, because the amount of drop cannot be controlled and the shot is likely to go out if you try for *too* much depth. The same goes for his two-hand backhand, which has far more wrist and top than Connors' two-hand shot. Deeper shots, and maximizing the forward body motion, are what allow a player to get to the net off the ground.

Two other disadvantages are inherent in extreme topspin: the ball simply doesn't go through the air as fast because of the excessive overspin, and the high follow-through requires an inordinate expenditure of energy as compared to an orthodox forehand.

It is axiomatic in tennis that the more spin, the less speed. For this reason Borg's forehand is not as forceful as Tilden's, Budge's, Perry's, Segura's, Kramer's, von Cramm's, Hoad's, Trabert's, or Connors'. All this said, my reservations about extreme topspin should not be construed as a criticism of the way Borg plays tennis. His game "hangs together" beautifully; topspin is part of it, and along with Laver, Vilas, and Connors, he possesses the best passing shots in the history of the game. What I am saying, though, is that excessive use of topspin—unless your name is Borg or Vilas—can be as dangerous as it is tempting.

The Connors-Laver challenge match at Caesars Palace in February 1975 was another illustration of the shortcomings of excessive topspin. Rod played very well while losing the four-set contest, but again and again Jimmy's lefty forehand proved deeper and sounder than Rod's dip shots. Jimmy hits straight through the ball with a high follow-through which imparts the topspin. He does the same with his two-hand backhand. This sends the ball zooming an inch or two above the net, invariably deep, always in.

Connors' passing shots proved more effective than Laver's dip variety, thus debunking a widely held theory that dip shots are inherently superior in thwarting a net rusher. An excessively topped shot clears the net higher and stands up before it dips. (Newcombe used to be able to cut it off before the drop, as did Adriano Panatta consistently against Harold Solomon in the French finals in 1976.) (Besides lacking the speed of a flatter drive, a heavily topped shot is subject to mishits, even by consummate masters of the stroke such as Borg and Laver.) There is no denying that the disguise on a dip shot and the drop make it difficult to volley; it is a splendid weapon for a player to have in his arsenal—but not essential. If Bill Tilden were playing today he would use it as a variation, not as his fundamental forehand. Ken Rosewall doesn't use heavy topspin. Connors' long, high follow-through gives him topspin, but his strokes are primarily semiflat. This allows his passing shots to skim the net, and because there is less spin they go over faster. Guillermo Vilas hits his highly topped forehand with tremendous force but the extreme spin cuts the speed. In his 1977 U.S. Open finals against Connors, Vilas mixed topspin and semiflat strokes to devastating effect.

The two-hand backhand is coming into vogue. It's the shot that usually spells the difference in a Connors match. Although more difficult to learn than a standard backhand, it does embody orthodox principles (although Borg's open stance and wristy dip stroke are definitely unorthodox). It can be taught to beginners with a certain natural aptitude. Unlike the "big game," it could be an advance in tennis because it grew out of a need: how to handle the kick service of a net rusher.

The main advantage of a two-handed backhand is on return of serve. No matter how flawless a one-hand backhand is, it's nearly impossible "to kill" a ball that bounces above the shoulder. Laver and Vilas are exceptions because of their extraordinary wrists. And Don Budge at 6' 2" was able to jump a kick serve before it rose above shoulder level. But as I noted earlier, Budge's stroke was orthodox and the direction could "be read," whereas the two-hand backhand has a natural disguise. Those who use the shot also say it can be made more quickly, that the weight moves in more naturally, and that there is more racquet-head control, which allows the direction of the shot to be changed later.

Sounds great. But there are disadvantages. You have less reach on wide shots, and unless you are naturally ambidextrous, it's tough to learn—and much tougher to learn if you're already using the one-hand variety. Nevertheless, Connors, Harold Solomon, Eddie Dibbs, and Bjorn Borg are being copied all over the world by youngsters just starting out. Solomon has the most consistent backhand in tennis today, and it's a two-hander.

Just as innovative and far more prevalent on the pro circuit is the topspin lob. Like the two-hand backhand it is difficult to learn, but worth the trouble because it's almost a sure point getter. Vic Seixas was the first champion to use it extensively, and Roy Emerson and Rod Laver further popularized the shot. Today's leading exponents are Nastase, Borg, Vilas, Solomon, Ramirez, and Connors. It is a more offensive weapon than the conventional lob and grew out of the need to thwart net rushers (just as "dip" shots and the two-hand backhand did). The present tennis balls are such that controlling this type of shot is far easier than in my day. It's the one form of heavy topspin I'm in favor of . . . provided you can keep it under control!

There is an oft-heard argument that because people have gotten bigger and faster, and because training methods have improved, all sports are better today than they were twenty years ago. It is incontestable that track, pro football, and basketball have made vast strides; but it is my considered opinion that tennis has not. Track, football, and basketball are more physical than mental. Tennis is the reverse—it is a game of technique like golf. A man of 50 in reasonable shape if he has better shots can defeat a 20-year-old physical marvel.

If, as I believe, tennis is primarily technique and only secondarily physical, then a wrong approach about how it should be played can adversely affect its evolution. Golf has improved because it steered the right course by building on previous development. But around midcentury tennis took the wrong road, and the "big game" must bear the brunt of the responsibility. The younger players today are aware of this . . . and as a result I look to an upswing in the quality of tennis in the years to come.

# PART II

# METHOD

Technique, Strategy, and Tactics

# Grips

How important is the grip?—not as important as stroke production but important nonetheless, because to a large extent the effectiveness of a stroke depends on the grip you use. The grip influences the angle of the racquet face, how long the ball stays on the strings, and above all your power.

Most instruction books say there are three basic grips: Continental, Western, and Eastern. Obsolete. The grip now most used among circuit professionals is none of these but a variation on the Continental, variously called the composite, the in-between grip, or the Australian. (Because Rod Laver uses a "Continental," that term is still the most common one in tennis books.) Laver began with an Eastern, but because of the wrist action he favors he moved to the Continental. There are very few Continental forehands in big-league tennis, but it is so close to the Australian it's easy to confuse the two. (American pros call it the "in-between" but I'll stick to the formal name of Australian.) Of the First Ten, Laver is the only one to use the Continental. Of the remaining nine, three used the Australian and six the Eastern. Kramer, Riggs, Budge, Segura, Gonzales, and Trabert all used a form of Eastern. Hoad, Sedgman, and Rosewall—all Aussies— used the Australian. The Eastern is still a popular grip among the rank and file of tennis players and runs second to the Australian among world-class professionals.

The question of grips can get complicated because we are dealing with fractions of an inch—perhaps an eighth of an inch or so—of adjustment. And though there is only one Continental grip and one Australian, there are two Westerns and three Easterns. This makes seven grips in all, although three could be construed as variations.

In the following discussion consider the racquet face to be held perpendicular to the ground, with the handle pointing toward the body. This means you will be looking down on the top of the handle.

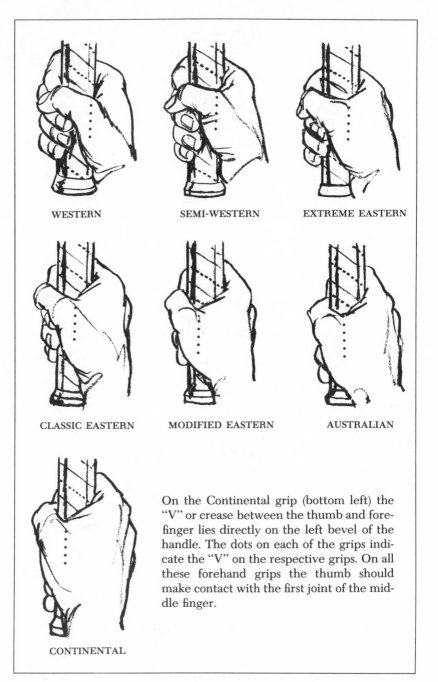

WESTERN

SEMI-WESTERN

EXTREME EASTERN

CLASSIC EASTERN

MODIFIED EASTERN

AUSTRALIAN

On the Continental grip (bottom left) the "V" or crease between the thumb and forefinger lies directly on the left bevel of the handle. The dots on each of the grips indicate the "V" on the respective grips. On all these forehand grips the thumb should make contact with the first joint of the middle finger.

CONTINENTAL

FOREHAND GRIPS

The central reference point is the "V" of the hand, that is, the crease between the thumb and index finger. The hand, and the "V" it forms, can rotate over the racquet handle, and it is this rotation that determines which grip is formed. The most commonly taught hand position on the forehand is the classic Eastern—the so-called "shaking hands" grip. When shaking hands with the racquet (while it is on edge) the "V" lies in the middle of the top surface of the handle. The fingers are curved around the handle naturally with the thumb making contact with the first joint of the middle finger; the forefinger is slightly extended. (I don't favor a big extension of the forefinger on the forehand no matter what the grip, although some players get better control that way.) You can move to a modified Eastern by rotating the hand a fraction to the left of the middle (the classic Eastern). By moving a fraction to the left of the modified Eastern you form the Australian; and a fraction to the left of the Australian gives you a Continental. When you rotate a fraction to the right of the classic Eastern you're holding the extreme Eastern (in this position the "V" is just to the right of the middle of the top surface of the handle). A fraction to the right of the extreme Eastern is a semi-Western (by a fraction I still mean roughly one eighth of an inch).

### THE WESTERN AND SEMI-WESTERN

For the Western grip, think of the way you grab a frying pan (the "frying pan" nickname has stuck with the grip through the years). Its greatest proponent was Billy Johnston. The legendary Johnston was short, about 5' 8", and brought up on the high-bouncing courts of the San Francisco Bay area. He was able to hit his backhand (called the Western backhand) with the same side of the racquet as the forehand. Helen Wills, who came from the same area, used a form of semi-Western and switched grips for the backhand. Bjorn Borg and Harold Solomon's forehand grips are close to Helen Wills's.

The Western forehand is fine on high balls; awkward on low ones. For waist-high shots it has no advantage over any of the Easterns, and you can't reach as far with it. Its biggest drawback is difficulty encountered when shifting to the backhand. A Western backhand (hit with the same side of the racquet as the forehand) is so awkward it hasn't been used by a top player in thirty-five years. And for most people, switching from a Western forehand to an Eastern backhand is also awkward; it requires half a turn of the handle and takes too much time. All in all, the Western is not as sound a grip as any of the others.

The semi-Western is coming into vogue again because of the prodigious accomplishments of Bjorn Borg. Borg gets around the awkwardness of the backhand shift by using a two-hand backhand. Borg is not only consistent but pulverizes the ball with his semi-Western forehand. He makes an excellent passing shot because of the disguise and dip he achieves in the way he produces it. But Borg is one of those unorthodox one-of-a-kind phenomena whose strokes are best not copied. Vic Seixas used a semi-Western forehand, and although it fitted his game style, it was ultimately an unsure shot.

### EASTERN GRIPS

The three Eastern grips are best discussed together. They are all "shaking hands" grips, with the palm and wrist solidly behind the handle for power. As mentioned, a slight hand rotation either way from the middle position of the classic Eastern gives you the other two grips: for extreme Eastern, a fraction to the right; for modified Eastern, a fraction to the left.

The players who used the Eastern are legion: in the First Ten Budge, Kramer, Gonzales, Segura (two hands), Riggs, and Trabert; others include Bill Tilden himself, Joe Hunt, Don McNeil, Art Larsen, von Cramm, Cochet, Budge Patty, and a fellow named Vines. Just which champion used which Eastern is academic. Each of them was flexible. If it didn't feel quite right they shifted the "V" slightly and chose the Eastern that felt the most comfortable. But they all had a problem in common: how easily could they shift to the Eastern backhand? Using an extreme Eastern requires over a quarter turn to the left for the backhand. The classic Eastern forehand presents less of a problem on the switch. With the "V" in the middle of the top surface of the handle, the shift to the Eastern backhand is less, but still entails a quarter turn to the left. I prefer the modified Eastern (the "V" a fraction to the left of the middle) because it only requires an eighth of a turn to achieve an Eastern backhand. Which Eastern grip you should use is largely a matter of "feel" and how smoothly you can shift. Above all, feel comfortable.

### BACKHAND

The Eastern backhand is roughly the same as the Continental forehand except the thumb is advanced diagonally across the back of the handle for support. The thumb across the handle gives greater power and control than the original thumb-along-the-handle method. The latter is a valid Eastern backhand, but awkward on low balls. On the Continental backhand, the thumb is wrapped around the handle and makes contact with the first joint of the middle finger. This is the identical grip to the Continental forehand in most cases. The "V" formed by the thumb and forefinger is roughly in the same place on both the Eastern and Continental backhands; that is, the "V" lies on the left bevel of the handle and the palm is on the top of the handle. Some players, such as Art Larsen, moved the "V" farther left toward the back of the handle . . . an individual matter and the natural backhand grip for certain players.

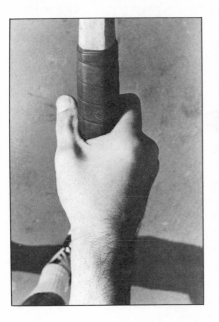 

**BACKHAND GRIPS**

### THE AUSTRALIAN

The Australian is a grip "in between" the modified Eastern and the Continental. The grip is more of a Continental than Eastern because the wrist is no longer completely behind the handle as on all Easterns. With the Eastern grips you have a feeling of being more behind the ball, whereas with the Australian you feel more beside it (just as you do with the Continental).

It is also similar to the Continental because the wrist is more in line with the handle instead of in back of it (as with the Easterns and Westerns). But the most obvious similarity is that there is no grip change required on either the Australian or Continental. Possibly the reason the Continental gets talked about more than the Australian is that the Australian is a hybrid grip, a variation of the much older Continental, and definitely belongs to the Continental school.

The Australian grip didn't come into prominent use until after World War II. Who invented it remains a mystery, but Harry Hopman popularized it Down Under. It is a grip with no intrinsic weakness, especially good for return of serve and for volleying, although it doesn't have quite the punch of the Eastern forehand at net. It was made to order for Lew Hoad.

Because he was spared the necessity of changing grips, Hoad was able to utilize his lightning moves and power to stay on top of the opponent. His wrist and strength were such that he didn't need any of the additional power that the Eastern forehand and backhand supply. Like the Continental, the Australian grip has a faster wrist action than any Eastern. A strong wrist is not a major requirement with Eastern strokes. The Eastern wrist action is more gradual and the follow-through longer. It also produces more hitting surface, allowing the ball to stay on the strings longer, which gives maximum power. But Hoad had that extra degree of wrist strength which made his Australian forehand and backhand as hard as anybody's . . . no matter what their grip.

Besides eliminating the time lost in changing grips, the backswing on the Australian is slightly shorter (as with the Continental this has nothing to do with form; the grip itself determines the shorter backswing); thus the receiver is less likely to be late in meeting the ball on the service return. The same reasoning applies when the opponent is at the net; that is, the Australian or Continental gives you more time and deception on passing shots because the swing is shorter and you don't have to change grips.

The Australian is used by a majority of world-class professionals now that heavy topspin is the rage. The shorter swing and constant grip allows the pros to utilize more wrist and achieve a higher finish on both forehand and backhand. But it seems to me this extreme topspin trend causes losses in accuracy and consistency that offset gains in deception. The Australian is almost as deceptive on "flatter" shots—and is more reliable.

On high forehand drives and volleys, the Australian is less restrictive than the Continental. However on the backhand side it is easier to impart "normal" topspin with a Continental because the "V" is farther to the left. (Frank Kovacs could hit a marvelous topspin shot with his Continental backhand, whereas Ken Rosewall is rarely able to put top on with his Australian backhand.)

### THE CONTINENTAL

The Continental is the grip that Fred Perry made famous. The "V" lies on the left bevel of the handle. The Continental forehand (and backhand) has roughly the same "V" position as the Eastern backhand, but the thumb, instead of being extended diagonally in back of the handle, is wrapped around it and makes contact with the middle finger.

The Continental forehand's drawback is that maximum power is restricted as compared to the Eastern, particularly on high balls. Perry got around this by taking the ball very early (on the rise). Kovacs did this too. It is a fine stroke on low balls; and Kovacs was 6′ 4″, but he kept his wrist locked, whereas Perry usually snapped his wrist on the forehand. Kovacs was so strong that the relative power restriction the Continental grip imposes only showed up when he was trading strokes with Budge.

Continental groundstrokes have a disguise lacking in the Eastern. At the net, the Continental gives you the advantage of not having to change grips, and it is also good for handling low volleys, in fact, anything a net player has to stretch for. Its disadvantage is that, because of the position of the wrist, dealing decisively with high forehand volleys is difficult. It is also awkward on the forehand to deal with straight-on volley directed at your midriff. On the serve, the Continental is still the most common grip because the spin it imparts allows for more control.

The use of the Continental grip is on the wane among today's major players. Nonetheless, it is a constantly mentioned grip—perhaps because tennis books often lump it together with the increasingly popular Australian. There are understandable reasons for doing so. Both have some wrist and palm the top surface of the handle (with the Continental the center of the palm actually is on top of the handle and the wrist directly in line with it); both demand a strong wrist; both have an inherent camouflage as compared to Eastern grips; and neither requires a grip change. Yet the Continental and Australian are far from being identical.

The critical point is that with the Australian some wrist is in back of the handle, whereas with the Continental the wrist is in line with it. Frank Kovacs, as I have mentioned, was the Continental stylist par excellence. His impeccable strokes and mighty physique allowed him to initiate great pace. Yet in the 1941 U.S. nationals against Riggs, Bobby took this power in stride and counterhit with Eastern strokes. When Kovacs traded backhands with Budge, the intrinsic drawback of the Continental became more apparent; although Kovacs had the finest Continental backhand of all time, even his strong wrist couldn't stand up against Don's bludgeons. Without the diagonal thumb for support, the wrist just wasn't firm enough to counterhit the way Riggs could. The importance of Eastern strokes rests as much in countering power as in initiating it.

The firm wrist of the Eastern forehand and the diagonal thumb of the Eastern backhand lend a support for handling a heavy-hitting opponent that no other grip equals. Support is the operative word here. Don Budge could handle my speed because his wrist didn't waver when parrying the force of my flat strokes. Riggs in a sense did the same to Budge—he could use Budge's power against him and counterhit with Eastern strokes.

The disadvantage of Eastern in ground duels is that the grip change must be effortless . . . automatic.

How is the Australian grip for counterhitting as compared to the Continental? About the same on the backhand, but the Australian is better on the forehand because some wrist is in back of the handle. Therefore if you want a firmer forehand, the Australian is better than the Continental. The Australian is also a better grip on the forehand volley for the same reason—the wrist.

But the truth is that grips are part of the individuality of a given player. Gene Mako, an outstandingly astute athlete, used the Continental . . . and as Budge's doubles partner he knew everything about the Eastern. The Continental fit his game style. The same held true for Perry, and holds true for Rod Laver.

I advocate Eastern strokes, but the Continental, semi-Western, Australian, and even the Western are correct grips (although the last has no advantages over the semi-Western, and more than its share of disadvantages). If you are having good results with a grip other than the Eastern, it is far from mandatory to change. In tennis, if something is working well, it is usually best to stick with it . . . and this includes grips, provided the grip is a legitimate one. Grips by themselves never made a tennis player and never will. A player with an inferior grip and good form will always defeat an adversary with the right grip and poor form. But the right grip becomes important when it comes to attaining the heights.

I am certain Budge would never have reached the level of controlled power he did if he had used the Continental instead of the Eastern. In this regard, the grip is pertinent to the present-day standard of forehands, most of which are Australian. The situation may lead one to ask, where are the big forehands (all Eastern) of a Tilden, Budge, or Kramer? It is only in talking about the ultimates in tennis power that the question of the grip becomes central.

# Shortcuts to Technique

The following pointers, which are the bedrock of tennis technique, will enable you to keep your game together under pressure. After all, the ball comes over fast, and you have only a split second in which to respond (I'm assuming that the reader has some experience and familiarity with the sport). There is a rapid-fire sequence in technique which lets you respond properly . . . if you can combine several operations into one. The basic problem with most tennis instruction is that it's too complex; thinking about eight things at once is impossible: If you've been worrying too much about where your shoulder or head is, whether your feet are in proper position, and so forth, don't! If you can absorb a few basic ideas, all the rest follows. "Combining several operations into one" is the key to tennis, and the purpose of this chapter is to unlock the door.

The best place to wait for groundstrokes is behind the baseline at the center line. Always return to the center line, for it's the place from which you can move most easily to either side. The basic "return to" grip is the forehand.

The proper stance is the natural one—knees flexed, leaning forward slightly, with weight on the toes, as the fingers of the left hand cradle the throat of the racquet.

These tips on technique fit the widest range of players and are the simplest to learn; they are roughly the orthodox form of Budge, Riggs, Tilden, and Rosewall. The only promise I make is that if you can incorporate them into your game you will become a sound player, and that generally spells victory over unorthodox opponents. It means you'll have achieved the one crucial objective of tennis: getting the ball back one more time than your opponent. Generally speaking, if you get the ball safely over the net you have a 75 percent chance of taking the point.

Before going into groundstroke technique, there is an axiom of

154

tennis so elementary I hesitate to mention it: try to hit the ball in the center of the racquet. Enough said.

### THE FOREHAND

The forehand is the essential shot in tennis. It is the staple of a player's game; it is used more than any other shot, and in theory a forehand can be "killed" whether taken low, at waist level (recommended), shoulder level, or above.

The forehand grip I recommend is the modified Eastern. As already described, it is achieved by shaking hands with the racquet, with the thumb and forefinger forming a "V" just to the left of the middle of the top surface of the handle. I favor the thumb making contact with the first joint of the middle finger, because it makes for a firmer hit.

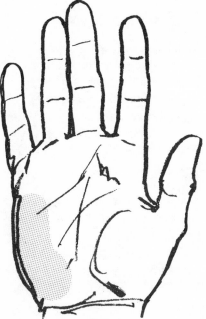

PRESSURE POINT

On the forehand it is important to keep a pressure point at the heel of the hand. Use of the correct "pressure point" means the ball will be hit solidly; the racquet on contact with the ball won't falter or twist in the hand.

As soon as the ball leaves the opponent's racquet your mind will

signal whether a forehand or backhand is coming. The first requirement on the forehand is to "line up" the ball properly. This is done
by starting the head of the racquet "above" the oncoming ball which
gives you the vital loop required in the backswing or, to be more
precise, a short arc which flows into a straight line on the forward
swing. Many instruction books advocate bringing the racquet
straight back. I disagree. There has never been a top player who
employed this method, because with it a "hitch" or break in rhythm
is inevitable. Another piece of horrendous advice is: Get your racquet back right away, the implication being that you "hold it back
there" and then swing. A proper stroke has to be timed to the speed
of the oncoming ball . . . and has to be continuous. If the racquet
"stops" at the end of the backswing, there is an even worse break in
the essential rhythm of the stroke than there is in the straight-back
forehand. *A stroke in tennis is a smooth continuous motion*—not a
jerky one or a "swipe" at the ball.

Tennis assumes a certain "ball sense," or timing, on the part of the
participant, and most people do have the modicum of ball sense
required. Keeping this qualification in mind, a given player usually
has enough hand-eye coordination to be able to line up the ball by
starting the "head of the racquet above it." Besides providing an
automatic arc (or loop) in the backswing, it pivots the body around
to the right for the correct hitting stance. This "lining up" technique
also allows the player to strike the ball at a comfortable distance from
the body.

Where should ball contact be made? I advocate in a direct line with
the left shoulder (roughly, a line which would run parallel to the net).
Many players try to hit the forehand opposite their left foot (or knee).
The problem with this is that a player's left foot is liable to be any
place when he is caught out of position. I like the "shoulder" theory
because it gives you a point to "move on" as you step into the ball.
This also causes you to watch the ball so you'll contact it opposite the
shoulder point.

A word about the bugaboo of "watching the ball." It may sound
strange, but I've known few big-name players who really worry
about it. Unlike golf, the ball in tennis is not a stationary object; the
tendency is to watch it simply because it is liable to hit you. Overemphasis on "looking at the ball" can cause you to overreact and stress
watching to the exclusion of shot production itself. By trying to hit

the ball opposite your left shoulder you will automatically watch it; it will make you keep your head down and will also help your footwork by giving you a point to move on. I'm not saying "don't watch the ball"; I'm only cautioning against becoming overly preoccupied with it.

When you line up the ball by starting the racquet head above it, there is a wrist break in the backswing. This wrist break is such a natural consequence of the stroke it is automatic with most players. (Budge likens it to the opening and closing of a gate.) At what point should the wrist break and how much? This is no trivial matter, for the entire forward motion of the stroke hangs on the hinge of the gate as it were. Yet the player is so busy lining up the oncoming ball he is unable to see the wrist break. The question arises: how can he break the wrist (for the closing of the gate) at roughly the same spot and in the same way every time?

The answer is: swing through on the level of the ball. This means that if the forward swing is made in a direct (straight) line with the oncoming ball, the wrist breaks automatically at the right place and in the right amount. Why the wrist break and the forward swing correlate so perfectly is a mystery. All I know is—it works. (On the ordinary forehand, the racquet is pointing straight back at the fence at the farthest point of the wrist break.)

On contact with the ball, the wrist should be straight, or "locked," and remain that way until the follow-through is completed. Additional wrist for power (à la Laver) is unnecessary. If the basics of the stroke have been executed properly, the head of the racquet will be accelerating so fast that a hard deep forehand inevitably results.

The greatest bonus of the "level of the ball" concept is that the follow-through automatically finishes higher, imparting just enough topspin for this relatively flat shot to stay in the court. Another bonus is that you can hit it even harder on the run . . . especially if the bounce is low. Bill Tilden was the supreme master of the "level of the ball" concept, and it was death in the afternoon to let him hit a low running forehand. A secondary bonus is that "level of the ball" implies getting down to the ball when you hit it. There is also the psychological bonus of a marvelous confidence that comes from knowing that once you're in position you can "hit out" and be sure the ball will go in.

Besides these basic precepts, a couple of secondary pointers are worth remembering about the forehand. For added impetus, I gripped my forehand with the heel of the hand at the extreme bottom (mound) of the handle, which added extra zing. It was harder to control, but the additional power made it worth it. (However, in returning serve on the forehand it helps to choke up a little on the racquet; not much, but enough so the wrist won't waver on impact.) Also, when I switched to the backhand I moved slightly up on the handle for a firmer stroke, for on the backhand you don't have the wrist for support the way you do on the forehand. The second pointer (although natural to most players) is: stick the nonracquet arm out as a balancer. It gives you "space" to step into and facilitates smooth footwork. There are good forehands which don't involve putting out the other arm—such as Andrés Gimeno's—but they are a distinct minority. *However there are no good forehands that are hit late.*

Hitting the ball late will spoil the best preparation . . . for a player's back and forward swing, plus the weight shift, are all coordinated to the objective of the contact point, as determined by the "left shoulder." For if the ball gets past the shoulder, the other two cardinal principles (racquet head above ball, then swing through on level of ball) are to no avail.

To recapitulate: (1) Start the head of the racquet above the ball. (2) Swing through on the level of the ball. (The wrist has broken sufficiently when the racquet head is pointing directly at the rear fence.) (3) Hit the ball opposite the left shoulder.

It goes without saying that all three operations must blend into each other in a rhythmic continuity of motion. If you can keep these three cardinal tenets in mind, I think you'll soon find the unconscious will supply the unity.


### THE BACKHAND

Most tennis coaches agree that the backhand is a more natural stroke than the forehand, but it affords you less power, reach, and ability to shift your grip. As your opponent strokes the ball your brain signals a backhand is coming up, and by moving your hand counterclockwise (left) an eighth of a turn you have switched from the modified Eastern forehand to the Eastern backhand. Then the first decisive step is to give yourself plenty of space to make the stroke. This is tricky as the tendency is to get closer to the ball than you have to—in the belief you are farther away from it than you are. You have to get so far from the ball that you say to yourself, "I'm almost going to miss it." Crowding the shot is a major flaw in backhands (of left-handers in particular). Budge was famous for the wide sweep of his stroke. This "plenty of room" concept leads directly into my second cardinal principle: *start the elbow away from your body.* In other words, your arm is fully extended when reaching for the ball. Lloyd Budge—who taught his brother—stressed the elbow-away-from-the-body technique. It is the best way of incorporating several technical points through one essential move. For right-handers hitting backhands, moving the elbow around to the left automatically pivots the body to the left . . . which places it in the correct stroking position. The body is now sideways (more so than on the forehand), and the right foot is in front and to the left of the back foot. (Obviously, the body and racquet should move to the left in unison.)

With the backhand, the wrist break and forward swing are no problem. The elbow-away technique automatically supplies the proper arc and wrist break for the follow-through . . . and the accelerating head comes through at the proper level without your having to think about it. So far we have covered two points; as with the forehand, the second flows from the first. By staying far away from the ball, you have to stretch to meet it; this forces you to extend your arm (and elbow) and swing your body around to the left. The proper stance, wrist break, and swing are all natural if you follow these precepts.

The third vital point is: "swing easy." Next to crowding the ball, the worst fault on the backhand is trying to swing hard. When you do, your swing ends up a swipe instead of a stroke. By swinging easy, you rhythmically shift your weight as your body flows into the ball. As with the forehand, power comes from the accelerating head on the forward swing as the weight is moving into the shot. The racquet head is doing all the work (in the same way as the club head does in golf). The easy swing is the key to smoothness of stroke, footwork, and —believe it or not—power.

On the backhand, you hit the ball opposite (in a direct line with) the right shoulder instead of the left. But all the reasons why the shoulder is your focal point are the same as for the forehand. However, as contact with the ball is made, the wrist plays a different role in the two strokes. On the forehand it is preferable to have the wrist straight on contact and kept locked until the follow-through is completed. On the semiflat backhand the wrist is also locked on contact, but the wrist gradually breaks after contact. The racquet head should move to the right across the body. This is largely automatic. On the undersliced backhand (the racquet face angled, with the strings brought across the ball) the wrist stays relatively locked on the follow-through.

The rising follow-through on the semiflat backhand provides a natural topspin without your having to worry about it. You'll note that on both the forehand and backhand I don't make a big point of the follow-through, because the follow-through is a natural outcome of all the previous steps.

The fifth principle of the semiflat backhand is the gradual unfolding of the wrist.

To recapitulate the five steps. (1) Be far away. (2) Start with the elbow away from the body. (3) Swing easy. (4) Hit the ball opposite the right shoulder. (5) Unfold the wrist. An additional point—but not essential—is to rotate the hips for extra power. The more pronounced sideway stance on the backhand side leaves room for this additional power.

There is one backhand shot in tennis (oddly seldom mentioned by instruction manuals) that calls for special footwork—a very high-bounce backhand. Even good backhands have trouble with it.

Pancho Gonzales is one of the few players to single out "the high backhand" for special mention, and it's possible to attribute much of his success to his realization of the danger inherent in treating the high-bounders on his left side as calling for just another backhand. Pancho says, "I move one step back so that I can move into the ball. I never want to hit a ball when moving backward." Gonzales steps back to get into position so he can move forward. It also helps to keep the shoulders level when hitting a high backhand, especially if you haven't got time to get properly set.

### FOOTWORK

The principles of footwork apply to both forehand and backhand. The weight should be on the balls of the feet with the knees flexed (never stand stiff-legged). On both the forehand and backhand the weight starts on the back foot and ends on the front. With any good tennis player the weight has shifted *before* ball contact is made. As with other aspects of footwork, this is automatic *if* the following cardinal rule is observed: *hit the ball as if you were going into the net to volley.* You may, in fact, take the net (or may not, as the case may be), but always move on the ball as if you were going to the net. This footwork is inherently connected with the "shoulder" contact point, with putting the nonhitting arm out in front on the forehand as a balancer (and to gain "space" to step into), and to Pancho Segura's dictim, "Never let the ball come to you."

It is even possible to hit an adequate drive off the wrong foot as long as your weight is shifting forward. It is more awkward, certainly not recommended . . . but sometimes necessary when you are caught out of position in a fast interchange. Once you've incorporated the invaluable "going to the net" rule into your game, your footwork should soon become largely automatic—you won't have to think about it.

Tennis experts agree that for left-handers the forehand is the more natural shot. Don't ask why. It's like trying to explain why they throw a natural curve in baseball. The natural forehand is the result of the loop in the backswing which is not something lefties have to learn. For southpaws the backhand is the difficult shot because they tend to crowd it. Nevertheless, all stroke technique advice in this chapter also applies to lefties.

### THE NET GAME

The nature of net play is so split second that unless a change of grip from Eastern forehand to Eastern backhand can be made without thinking, holding the in-between grip, the Australian, is recommended. Players who began changing grips very young—so it is second nature—are the most successful employing the Eastern forehand and backhand at the net. Today they are in a distinct minority. Most professionals teach the Australian for the volley, and the majority of the world-class players use it. Nowadays the majority of big-time stars volley superbly (although no better than Perry, Schroeder, Kramer, Mako, Sedgman, Riggs, Trabert, and several other greats of the past). This isn't remarkable; with the "big game" they have to be fine net players or they'd be dead.

I've also mentioned their proficiency in the half volley, a tricky and often difficult shot but one which any complete player must have in his repertory of strokes. (Pancho Gonzales has reservations about the half volley. He says: "Avoid the half-volley as much as possible, since it is a defensive stroke.") On the half volley the ball is hit immediately after it bounces. However it differs from a regular forehand in that the swing is shorter—straight back with the racquet head at least level with the wrist. The last two points are the antithesis of the ordinary forehand drive in which there *must* be an arc in the back-swing and the racquet head should *never* drop below the wrist. The follow-through on the forehand half volley should be short, level, and with a locked wrist.

On the backhand half volley the swing is also much shorter than on the regular backhand and so is the follow-through. Unlike the regular backhand, the wrist should be kept locked on the follow-through. Like the forehand half volley, the follow-through should be straight and short. And it is very important on both the forehand and backhand half volleys *to get down to the ball.*

### THE FOREHAND VOLLEY

The ready position at net is almost the same as in the backcourt. The throat of the racquet is in the left hand with the head pointed upward to the left, and the "pressure point" is at the heel of the right hand. Weight is on the toes, the knees flexed. This ready stance is the basic position in tennis, but at the net the racquet is slightly closer to the body with the racquet head slightly higher. The volleying stroke is actually one of the simpler things in tennis, far less compli-cated than groundstrokes or the serve. Nonetheless it has been one of the most poorly taught aspects of the game. (For one thing, the pressure point is usually overlooked, and it is absolutely essential to locate it correctly.)

For many years, particularly in the 1950s, it seemed the Austra-lians were the only players who thoroughly understood the forehand volley. Their volleys simply had more punch, especially off the fore-hand. Superficially the American players seemed to use the same form, but what may appear a minor point was a major difference: the Australians rarely bent forward to hit a volley off either side; whether the volley was high or low, they kept their backs straight, even when catching the ball off their shoelaces. They crouched, but didn't lean forward. The straight spine allowed them to step into the ball like a solid wall and punch from the small of their back; their whole body went into the shot (this was particularly true off the forehand side). Watch Rosewall, and you'll notice he rarely bends forward when he hits a volley (bearing in mind a wide variety of body positions can result from the rapid fire of net play).

Gonzales often leaned; and for this reason his volleys generally lacked the punch of Ken's. He made up for this by his remarkable agility and the fact he could use his gargantuan reach to blanket the net. Because of these he could get away with volleys that a smaller, less agile player would have found disastrous. You can't always put away a volley, but it has to be offensive or you are a setup for a passing shot. An offensive volley means you've forced your opponent; he's still liable to pass you, but he hasn't got all day to do it.

The best way to tell where your opponent is hitting the ball is to watch his racquet. This is true on groundstrokes, but at the net the information is absolutely essential; otherwise you won't have a clue to the direction of his shot.

The forehand and backhand volley action is far shorter than backcourt strokes. The ideal volley off either side is a one-foot punch. There is very little backswing, almost no follow-through, and the wrist stays locked (although some players may snap their wrists on high forehand volleys and make putaways).

The first thing to do when the mind gets the signal for a forehand volley is to "open the wrist," which automatically pivots the body to the right for the correct hitting stance. When the wrist is in line with the rest of your arm you've moved the racquet back far enough (the same position as in catching a baseball). Then step in and catch the ball parallel to the left shoulder (the same as on the forehand drive). Many pros advocate hitting the ball as far in front of the body as possible; others suggest just blocking the shot. I find the left shoulder is the ideal point "to move on." This gets your whole body into the shot and still keeps it in the court whether it is a low, high, or medium-height volley. It helps to put out the nonhitting arm as a balancer just as on the regular forehand.

On making contact with the ball, stop the stroke instantly! There will be a slight follow-through from the momentum of the swing, but it should not be a conscious effort. The whole body is moving as a solid wall in unison with the open (straight) wrist and stiff spine providing the punch.

Because the racquet head moves to the right side as you lay open the wrist, there is a tendency to take your eye off the ball. The forehand volley and overhead are the two shots in which watching the ball is imperative. On the backhand volley it is less vital because the nature of the shot puts the ball almost directly into the line of vision.

To recapitulate: on the forehand volley watch the ball, open the wrist, keep the spine straight as you move in on the left shoulder, and stop the swing on contact with the ball (and don't drop the racquet head below the wrist). If you follow these guidelines you won't have to worry about footwork (you're moving in on the shoulder), bevel of the racquet, follow-through . . . or consistency. Naturally, you should get your body down as far as possible on low volleys (crouch but keep your spine straight).

### THE BACKHAND VOLLEY

The key to this shot is *punching from the elbow*. This means you move the right elbow out in front of you as you go into the swing. This tip serves the same function as the "open wrist" on the forehand volley; that is, it pivots the body to the left and automatically provides the proper length backswing and wrist angle. The "punch" volley action is similar to the forehand and has the same locked wrist; you also get down to the ball, keep a straight spine, and stop on contact. The main difference is that on the backhand volley you move on the right shoulder as the contact point. But always remember the straight-spine principle—it's absolutely essential on the backhand side, for this automatically puts the elbow out.

On very high backhand volleys, if your opponent catches you by surprise at the net and lobs to your extreme left, you snap the wrist in a badmintonlike action just as the ball is about to get past you. It is not as tough as it sounds. You can't get into position for an overhead, anyway, and as your back is almost to the net it's about the only way you can hit it. And if you can pull off one of these rarely needed "backhand flips," it looks sensational.

### THE SERVE

Before going into the mechanics of the serve it is crucial to say a word about the nemesis of countless servers: the toss. The windup of the serve should be slow, as if you were just going through the motions to illustrate the stroke. Always keep in mind an overall idea of striking the ball easily. The value of this approach is that it will avoid a jerky toss. The hurried windup, with lots of effort, consumes energy and throws off the toss. And if the toss goes wrong nothing else goes right. Once you achieve an unhurried preparation, expediting a smooth toss, the racquet head automatically accelerates on the forward swing, maximizing power on impact. (Height helps. A longer arm, and more trajectory, usually spells a harder delivery.)

Correcting a serve once your windup, toss, and other bad habits have been formed is more difficult than correcting any other shot. It is a truism of tennis that great servers start out that way; they have a natural facility, plus good instruction at the start. It is damned hard to develop a fine serve once you've been in the game for a number of years. Ken Rosewall was never able to develop a strong delivery, yet I'm sure he knows everything about it. Only his serve kept the talented Dennis Ralston from being world champion as an amateur. (At that he was ranked Number One in the United States three years in a row.) Bob Hewitt—the Australian transplanted to South Africa —is another marvelous player whose serve lets him down at critical points in singles.

It is also a truism that a reliable big serve will get you out of more trouble than any other shot in tennis. As mentioned earlier, before the introduction of the tie-breaker in pro tennis, you couldn't be beaten if you held serve.

The serve is a unique shot in one respect: you entirely initiate the action; you are not reacting to an opponent's shot. There is a parallel with golf; in both cases you have plenty of time. But this time presents a psychological pitfall: you are liable to end up fighting yourself. So the first bit of advice is: go right into the windup. Too much dilly-dallying and thinking break the rhythm. In this regard, bouncing the ball before going into the serve sometimes helps the rhythm.

The usual grip for the serve is the Continental (although some prefer Eastern or Australian), with the forefinger separated from the other fingers. The racquet should be held loosely, which facilitates an easy motion (the grip automatically tightens on ball contact). The body should bisect the angle of the opponent's court, with the left foot somewhat diagonal to the net and pointing slightly to the right. As with other shots, you should not stand flat-footed but have the weight on the balls of the feet.

As you go into the motion, the weight should start on the left foot, with the body leaning forward slightly; then as the swing begins the weight shifts back to the right foot, and gradually, just before the ball is hit, the weight swings back to the left foot, thus putting the full power of the swing and weight behind the serve.

The service swing should be full and continuous from start to finish (somewhat like the windup and follow-through of a pitcher throwing a baseball). Swing and toss of the ball should be simultaneous. Throw the ball slightly to the right and hit it at the highest possible point that you can reasonably reach. This gives a better trajectory into the service court.

Spin is imparted by either coming around the outside of the ball, putting a right to left curve on it, or by coming over the top of the ball with the racquet motion from left to right with the follow-through finishing low on the right. This puts overspin on it, which makes it kick high upon hitting the court and spin away from the receiver. The outside-of-the-ball method is the slice serve, and the latter is a type of American twist, sometimes called topspin.

On the "flat" serve you come right down on the very top of the ball. Certain players use an Eastern forehand grip for this cannonball style delivery and also on the slice; it's an individual matter.

However, on the modified American twist (topspin) serve, it is definitely better to use a Continental grip, preferably with the thumb touching the forefinger, which automatically forces the racquet face across the ball and maximizes the desired spin. (On the regular Continental grip the thumb contact is the middle finger.)

Service variations from slice serve to spin serve to flat serve can be obtained by tossing the ball to the right for the slice, more behind for the topspin, and more in front for the flat serve. There are different wrist motions at the time of impact. The slice at impact has the wrist facing left; on the topspin serve the wrist is facing downward; and on the flat serve the wrist is facing forward.

Don Budge advocates copying the motion of a baseball pitcher and advises keeping the arms away from the body as you go into the windup. It is also usually a good idea not to lower the ball below the waist in the windup.

One tip I wish to stress I haven't noticed in tennis books. It is called the "open wrist." This means when you break the wrist in the backswing while the racquet is behind you, your wrist should "open." This shortcut automatically causes the racquet head to drop and "scratch" the back (something common to strong servers) and bolsters power.

I've often been asked whether there was any secret to the wrist snap which augmented the severity of my serve. Outside of the usual recommendations such as imitate cracking a whip, simulate throwing the racquet at the ball, or act like you're driving in a nail with a hammer, I can't offer any new suggestions. The ideal wrist snap is a gift which can only be developed up to a point. Just why such servers as Kramer, Les Stofen, and Bob Falkenburg were able to do it so well is as difficult to ascertain as why certain pitchers have a snap which gives them that extra something on a fast ball.

Besides using the wrist, some players (Riggs for one) find that "anchoring" their front foot on the hit and follow-through enhances power. A last bit of advice on power: don't bend the back knee too much when the weight is on the rear foot; this throws off your balance and cuts your power.

I realize that for serving instruction this has been brief, but more good writing has appeared on the serve than on any other aspect of tennis . . . and it hasn't helped much. This is understandable because the service is the most complicated stroke in tennis. There are tips —such as I've imparted—but few shortcuts. The best advice is to start out with a good instructor.

### THE OVERHEAD

The overhead smash isn't as difficult a shot as often assumed. It is actually easier than the serve itself and the best grip for it is the usual service grip (Australian or Continental). When you see it is going to be an overhead, move right under the ball and get into the ordinary service position . . . and then *anchor* your weight on the rear foot. Anchoring of the back foot is vital; it is the one critical difference between the overhead and your regular serve. Hitting with an "open wrist" is also important for a good smash. On the overhead, as I mentioned earlier, you really have to watch the ball in order to contact it while your racquet arm is fully extended; then hit down on the very top of the ball. This "hitting down" is what assures it stays in court. Let it bounce first if it can't be handled comfortably; otherwise catch it in the air.

### THE LOB

On the forehand lob the swing is greatly shortened, the face of the racquet opens, and the wrist locks on contact. The trajectory of the racquet is high, with the wrist kept locked during the long upward follow-through. It is vital to "get down" to the ball on all lobs.

Lobbing can also be an offensive weapon when the opponent at the net is expecting a passing shot; many of the top pros use the topspin lob to catch their opponent off guard. It is a tricky shot to make but highly effective. The deceptive short swing is the same as on the regular lob, but there is a highly accentuated wrist action in the follow-through which causes the ball to dip sharply on its downward flight. The topspin lob off the forehand is the only genuine innovation of modern tennis and is definitely worth learning. However, a topspin lob off the backhand side is much too difficult and uncertain for most players . . . and best left alone.

The ordinary backhand lob is hit with underspin. There is the same short backswing as on the forehand lob, plus the long upward follow-through. The major difference between an ordinary backhand and the backhand lob is in the function of the wrist. On the backhand lob the wrist stays "locked" during the follow-through instead of gradually breaking as it does on a regular backhand. As with the forehand lob, it is essential to get your whole body down to the ball.

### THE DROPSHOT

The dropshot can be used when you are inside the service line and your opponent is on or behind the baseline. The dropshot is hit with a volley action and almost always off the forehand side. The idea is to make the ball drop just over the net and then die. Dropshots work best on clay or grass. If the opponent is able to get to the dropshot, your parry should be the lob . . . he has been running forward and now has to reverse himself to run back.

Surprisingly few of the big-time pros have an outstanding dropshot; Chris Evert has a better one than any of the men. None of the present stars has the dropshot of Riggs or Segura. Now that clay is coming more and more into prominence, it can cause a very effective change of pace. The problem with the dropshot is that it is less a matter of technique than touch. With the dropshot the element of surprise is everything; if your opponent can get to it you are often put on the defensive. It is not a shot that should be used too much, because the opponent will start to anticipate it even if you're one of the lucky ones who have "the touch."

# Return of Serve

It is no accident that the best service returns in tennis today belong to the best groundstrokers—Connors, Orantes, Rosewall, Nastase, Solomon, Borg, and Vilas.

Returning serve is the shot every player has to make on half of the points he plays and offers the best chance to put the server on the defensive. The moment the ball is coming back on return of serve, the scales are almost evenly balanced. If you're unable to return serve well, you'll lose the games your opponent serves; he will win points without a struggle—and probably serve better due to the confidence you've given him. But if you start returning serve well, he'll immediately know he's in a match. A poor service return puts a self-imposed pressure on you to hold your own serve at any cost.

When you handle your adversary's best serves you deal him a psychological blow, especially if he relies on his serve for victory. He will become discouraged and probably try to compensate by hitting even harder, which will require a greater expenditure of energy. Very likely he'll start missing his first serve and tightening up on the second, which can lead to double-faults. If he cuts down on his power and becomes content to put the ball into play, you will have blunted one of his best weapons.

The first prerequisite of returning serve is to get the ball back— hopefully offensively. I favor the same ready position as on regular groundstrokes, that is, weight on the balls of the feet, knees slightly bent, with the throat of the racquet cradled in the fingers of the left hand (some players bend farther forward and bounce on the balls of their feet). The racquet is roughly 45 degrees to the left with the head higher than the handle. Studies have shown that the more upright position is better.

The grip for returning serve depends on the individual. I changed grips on return of serve; so did Tilden, Budge, von Cramm, Riggs,

Parker, Schroeder, Kramer, and Trabert; in fact, until the advent of the Australian (which requires no grip switch), the vast majority of players shifted grips unless they were Continental strokers, in which case it was unnecessary. The criterion for changing grips was and still is: how effortlessly can it be done? In other words, it has to be second nature.

I had little trouble switching to my backhand on the service return because my forehand was a modified Eastern and my backhand an Eastern one, that is, my thumb made a diagonal across the back of the handle as on the standard Eastern backhand. Holding a modified Eastern required a very short hand-position move to the left. I shifted to this grip on all backhands, and as I started out this way I never had to think about it.

Placing the thumb at a diagonal across the handle makes for a firmer hit and more support.

In my day, several of the players—Borotra for one—used the old style of putting the thumb straight back along the handle for support. This grip has a built-in adaptability for handling high serves, but the straight-thumb method also has a built-in restriction of power. (Most Eastern strokers employ the forehand grip awaiting serve, but a few, such as Art Larsen, prefer to hold the backhand grip and then switch if necessary.)

George Toley, an outstanding instructor and coach, advocates Eastern strokes and changing grips on the service return, and he has strong historical support. Tilden, Budge, and Trabert—three of the greatest service returners—all switched. Of our First Ten, Gonzales held a form of modified Eastern but didn't switch on the service return. Kramer and Riggs shifted for the backhand. Rosewall, Hoad, Laver, and Sedgman used the Australian, which, you'll recall, doesn't require a grip change.

Despite this impressive evidence for the Eastern, I lean toward the Australian for the service return unless you can switch grips without thinking about it. For I doubt if the Australian—the newest style grip and the prevalent one among the professionals—would have been developed in the first place if many players hadn't found that the grip change took too much time against a hard server; however, it never bothered Tilden or Budge.

Is it difficult for an Eastern stroker who finds the grip change inconvenient to make the transition to Australian? As a rule, no. One thing is certain: it is far easier to make the transition from Eastern to Australian than vice versa—especially on returning serve.

This prompts the obvious question: why not use Australian on all strokes and stop worrying about grip change altogether? On the service return, the Australian grip lacks the maximum power of Eastern strokes, but this is compensated for by the time saved and an inherent deception. In backcourt exchanges, however, it is a different story. Eastern strokes have an unimpeded fluidity which maximizes power in a way neither the Continental nor the Australian can . . . all other things being equal. The ordinary player with solid Eastern strokes has a feeling of "unlimitedness"—which is invaluable —when he tees off on a backhand or forehand, especially when the stroke exchanges become a rising crescendo. Another advantage of the Eastern backhand: it is easier to impart topspin with it than with any other grip.

Jack Kramer blames the prevalence of the Australian grip for the paucity of big forehands in today's game. He has a point. I see few around as good as Gonzales, Riggs, or Trabert, not to mention Tilden, Budge, or Kramer. How about the big forehands of Connors and John Newcombe? Connors uses a form of extreme Eastern, Newcombe a type of modified Eastern.

However, on returning serve the degree of severity of the return becomes secondary; the first order of business is to get the ball back, and to this end the Australian has the advantage of letting you keep the same grip.

The Continental is also a good returning grip, but high forehands are more difficult to handle decisively with it, and it has less power than the Australian because no wrist is in back of the handle.

On receiving in the deuce court, stand two yards to the left of the singles' sideline (usually on the baseline). To receive serve in the ad court, stand on the singles' sideline (the left sideline). Most serves in the ad court are to the backhand, and by standing on the sideline you are able to get to a serve that kicks to the left (into the alley). More importantly, it allows you to take more returns on the forehand. The forehand is the better side for returning serve in either court because it is a more flexible stroke, especially on high balls. (Even Rosewall will sometimes run around his famed backhand on service return.) In the deuce court, the server may pull you way out of court if you leave too wide a space on the forehand side, but in the ad court the best he can do is try to ace you down the center line. You should stand on the baseline in the ad court as in the deuce court. (Many players prefer to stand a yard or so behind the baseline in both the ad and deuce courts. Exactly where you stand depends on your reactions and timing and how big the serve is you're trying to handle. If it's a hard flat serve, it is better to stand farther back than you would normally.)

Against left-hand servers it is better to move farther to the left—especially in the ad court where the lefty can serve wide. His serve hooks into you in the deuce court and away in the ad court.

Players will alter their receiving position depending on what they consider their strongest stroke. Running around a second serve—if your forehand is your best stroke—can often surprise your opponent and shake him up. By running around your backhand on key points you can pressure your opponent when he isn't expecting it. (Pancho Segura was a master at this, as was Kramer.) However, as with everything, it shouldn't be overdone.

A vital point on service return position: when the opponent misses his first serve move inside the baseline. It pressures him, because he knows you are in a position to take the offensive. If he serves short, then move into the net.

The best way to get a jump on the ball is to watch the direction of the server's forward swing; it also helps to keep your eye on the toss. The second you've determined where the ball is going—backhand, forehand, or directly at you—move to the best position and try to catch it, preferably on the rise, about waist high. Hit it with the racquet fully extended if you can and don't stint on the follow-through.

On the service return, the backswing may become abbreviated on both sides because of the speed of the oncoming ball, but basically you should try to make the same stroke as a regular forehand and backhand. It is fundamentally the same shot, and it is a mistake to try to return a serve with a drastic modification of your regular strokes. The great service returners—Rosewall, Tilden, Budge, Trabert, Perry, and Connors—all used their regular strokes. Any modification they were forced to make grew out of the speed or hop of the serve they were handling. It can be argued that many of the big players, such as Arthur Ashe and Rod Laver, disrupt their opponents by hitting a different shot every time they return. Laver, because of his immense talent and timing, often gets away with it; so does Ashe, especially when he's ahead. But changing your shot with every return tends to disrupt your own coordination and timing, because deciding whether to blast down-the-line or chip crosscourt involves a complicated mental process . . . not recommended when a fast serve is coming at you. Ashe pays the price for trying to keep his opponent guessing by lapses in which he misses lots of returns.

The return of serve, like all ground strokes, should be hit opposite the shoulder. How does this shot vary from regular groundstrokes? Only as to emphasis. A serve is usually a much faster shot than a groundstroke, and the shoulder reference point has to dominate the mind from the time you go into your swing. For if the ball gets past the shoulder, you'll be hitting it late and you'll probably miss or muff the return. No matter how the speed of the serve forces you to modify your swing or "deviate from form," the shoulder guideline usually allows you to keep the ball in play. Using the shoulder as a guide is the *idée fixe* of the service return—the left shoulder on the forehand and the right shoulder on the backhand. This reference point allows you to adjust your footwork and swing. It will also make you watch the ball on contact; and, just as important, your grip will tighten naturally at the moment dictated by the shoulder guideline. This gives your wrist the firmness to withstand the impact of the speeding ball and lessens the possibility of mishitting. The magic shoulder becomes the focal point of all your effort. To summarize, it assures watching the ball, the weight shift (move-on point), and a firm hit. Remember, too, that the "pressure point" on the right side of the bottom of the hand is especially vital on returning serve.

Experts agree that a low return is best. They say return deeply if the server isn't coming in, and return at the feet of an oncoming net rusher. The problem with a chip return or dip shot against a net rusher is that a hard serve is best returned with the firm wrist of a regular stroke. However a soft semiflat "dink" which just clears the net is difficult for a net rusher to volley. But you need both control over groundstrokes and touch to pull it off. Whether you should try to disrupt your opponent or vary your returns and risk disrupting your own timing depends on your personality and strokes. I'm a believer in concentrating on stroked returns and letting the server do what he can. Don't try to hit hard; just stroke easily. If your swing, footwork, and follow-through are flowing, the counterhitting of the service speed will keep your opponent on the defensive. Often you will be able to take the ball on the rise and get to the net.

There are a lot of theories about where you should hit the ball, but

I want to repeat that the main objective is: get the damned thing back. Where you return the ball is largely dictated by the position you're in when hitting it. Sometime check your own percentage of service returns; I feel your return isn't good unless 75 percent of them go in.

It is popular today to try all kinds of spins and dips on service returns. I suspect this is largely because many top-flight players aren't that confident of their strokes. A solid groundstroke catching a hard serve rarely gives the server time to attain good volleying position, so the receiver is usually the one on the offensive. Jimmy Connors is a prime example of this strategy. He doesn't need trick shots. His solid, semiflat strokes have made him the acknowledged master of the service return.

A psychological aspect of the service return I've saved till last because it is crucial. Even more than on groundstrokes the mental processes have to be automatic. As long as you know what to do . . . forget about it. On the service return you don't have time to think. I would go so far as to say that once you consciously start thinking during the course of stroke production on the service return, you're through. I'm not advocating an "inner game of tennis" approach. You definitely have to know what you're doing. This, however, is qualitatively different from consciously thinking about stroke technique. For the same reason I'm against trick shots and any kind of complicated decision making. On returning serve just keep the shoulder concept in mind and let the muscle memory take over the rest of the stroke production.

Tennis is a game of technique . . . and instinct. Consciously stressing the mental process causes an overreaction and you'll tighten up or "choke." That is why I don't emphasize watching the ball as much as most instruction books do. Yet on returning serve it is obvious that because of the serve's speed and bounce, "seeing the ball" is more important than on the ordinary groundstroke exchange. But if the mind puts too much focus on watching, the same invidious tendency appears as on the ordinary stroke trades. The ball will mesmerize you. To avoid this, all I can say is: keep the ball in mind on the service return but don't worry about it. And don't be concerned if you don't see the ball contact the strings. This suggestion is one of those wonderful ideas that sounds great when you write it in a book, but that seldom can be accomplished. If you make sure you've contacted the ball by the shoulder guideline you will have seen enough of it.

# Tactics

The words tactics and strategy are often used interchangeably, but usually strategy denotes an overall plan whereas tactics refer to specific actions employed to attain an objective, usually within the framework of a strategy. Tactics, then, are usually the way you implement a strategy. In tennis, at least, there is no way of discussing tactics without touching on strategy.

If a player is committed to taking the net in back of every serve he is a disciple of the "big game" strategy. Though the "big game" is a basic strategy most of the time, sometimes it can be a tactic. During the course of a match, if a player decides to follow in all his serves because his opponent is returning poorly, he is employing a tactic. He also uses a tactic when he changes his strategy because he is losing and starts playing the "big game." Unfortunately, most of the "big game" enthusiasts are committed to it as a strategy under all conditions, no matter who their opponent is or what he does. Suffice it to say that in my opinion the "big game" makes a better tactic than a strategy.

Tennis has been compared to athletic chess; there is the opening gambit, serve or a service return, probing for a weakness, then the attack. The analogy to chess is instructive, for to a large extent a tennis match depends on what your opponent does or can do. But there is an obvious difference. In chess, the beginner doesn't have to develop much physical skill to move the pieces around.

One obvious way of pressuring an opponent who is strong at the net is keeping him back—never give him a short ball. As long as the ball is deep it doesn't have to be hard. Gonzales and Riggs, when jerking their opponents around, often settled for soft floating depth until they had an opening for their big forehands.

Be alert to your opponent's weaknesses, for the basis of tactics is to bring your strengths to bear upon his weaknesses. You can notice

175

a wild forehand or poor backhand as early as the warm-up period. Naturally you attack what you find out is weak. If the opponent has a weak backhand, hit wide to his forehand and then to his backhand so he has to make the shot on the run. If it is his forehand that is weak, reverse the process.

The "big game" is still, after fifty years, the most popular method of putting pressure on the opponent (I was noted in the 1930s for following in my serve) and has become a way of life for most younger players. But, let me stress again, that unless you serve like Kramer or Newcombe, it often becomes a life of dissipation (of energy) and a way of putting pressure on yourself instead of your opponent.

Nonetheless, going in on your first serve can be an appropriate tactic, depending on whom you are playing and how good your serve is. It is a better tactic in the ad court than in the deuce court, for your opponent is often reaching into the alley to return a serve and you have most of the court open for the volley to his forehand side. In the deuce court, a serve to the backhand is down the middle line and the opponent is in a better position for the return. For this reason it is a good idea to change the direction of your serve more in the deuce court. If you are able to hit a wide-angled serve to your opponent's forehand, you have him out of position, even though the forehand may be his stronger side.

But no law says you should follow in a first serve, especially in the deuce court, because if you have sound groundstrokes you are usually "controlling the third shot." To go in all the time against top competition even on a first serve you need a forcing delivery . . . and a hell of a volley.

How about going in on your second serve? Taking the net on the second serve can be fruitful if the opponent returns poorly. It pressures him and makes his bad groundstrokes even worse.

Curiously enough, the greatest second serve is one hardly anybody uses anymore—the American twist. Newcombe uses it sometimes, and Tom Gorman employs it successfully, but few other top pros even attempt it. It is a difficult serve to master. It requires a pronounced bending of the back, extremely fine timing, and excellent control of the wrist. (Baron Gottfried von Cramm was the supreme artist of this delivery.) For Jack Kramer it was a potent weapon. The advantage of the American twist is that, once mastered, it is easy to control. Its slower speed gives the server time to attain the net, and the high-bounding kick to the left makes it one of the most difficult

balls for the receiver to return effectively. It is one of the strange
paradoxes of modern tennis that in the age of the "big game" the best
second serve ever devised has become almost obsolete.

In tennis your mechanical ability—the strokes themselves—is
more vital than the moves you make; this is another way of saying
that a sound game, one that "hangs together," takes precedence over
the best tactics (or strategy). However, better tactics will allow you
to defeat players of roughly comparable physical talent and stroke
equipment.

The cardinal precept of tennis is: always keep the pressure on your
opponent. And if there is one tactic I advise to implement this strategy it is: *take the net on all your opponent's short balls.* Where
should you hit this approach shot? Almost always to the opponent's
backhand. Only when his forehand is hopeless should you attack that
side: This is true even when his backhand is better. His backhand
may be steadier, but he can still do more with the forehand; it is a
more flexible shot, and its direction can be disguised and changed
later.

There are many ways of putting pressure on players, but if you are
reluctant to come in on short balls you've passed up the leading one.
For right-handers, this means hitting down-the-line with the forehand and crosscourt with the backhand—preferably on the rise—in
order to attack the opponent's backhand. And unless you have him
out of position, hit deep.

After you've made it to the net don't get so close you can't cover
a lob. Avoid volleying short unless he is out of position. The purpose
of a volley is to put your opponent on the defensive. It doesn't have
to be a putaway so long as it is penetrating. The idea is to keep him
from having time to get set for an offensive shot. As long as you are
pressing him into defense, you are in control.

The net attack on a second serve depends largely on how consistently deep you are able to hit it and who your opponent is. But for
the average second serve it is folly. This doesn't mean you shouldn't
follow the second serve in once in a while. Listen to your instincts
and forget the "big game" blueprint. Your instinct will tell you when
you're confident of your serve . . . and also when you have your
opponent on the ropes and can further fluster him by sallying forth.
Sometimes this is early in the match. If following in all serves is
working, keep it up; it is one way to end a point quickly.

When going to the net on serve stop running as your opponent makes his hit. Make a momentary pause while on your toes to see the direction of his shot. This is called a "check" or "drift." You've stopped to watch your opponent's racquet so you can move for the ball. Adjust your steps to the speed with which your opponent takes the ball. The ideal volley position is midway between the net and service line (depending on your height).

Following the line of flight of the serve in going to the net is a simple and sound guideline, and you should roughly bisect the angle of the possible return. If your opponent is hitting from near an alley you should be "off center" in that direction. There is a clever ruse to use on serves. Start as though you're going to rush the net . . . then stay back. Don't do it too often, but used once in a while it will throw your opponent's concentration off for a moment (at least), perhaps cause him to mishit the return, or return serve tentatively. But don't fool yourself! Always have your mind made up ahead of time whether or not you're going in. In tennis as in many aspects of life, he who hesitates loses.

If you wish to consider yourself an accomplished tennis player, you should get in 70 percent of your first serves. Then you won't have to worry about the risky proposition of following in the second. Getting in first serves is a sure way of keeping pressure on the opponent.

The advantage of a consistent return of serve is that it keeps the pressure on your opponent. What's the best return? Either a sharp crosscourt or down-the-line forces the server to advance further to reach the volley, which may result in an error or weak volley. This gives you more opportunity to pass him on the next shot. Always be ready to capitalize on a short volley by moving in. If you've returned a deuce court serve down-the-line and caught the server near the service line, he will be forced to make the volley from far to his left and near the ground. Anticipate a weak hit-up volley down-the-line. If he moves toward the net, dump a lob over his head or smack it right at him to draw an error.

### HANDLING A NET PLAYER

What is the best way to handle a net man in general? Good passing shots depend on your ability to force the opponent to volley short. Your position is the guide in selecting the shot to use. If you are hitting from inside the baseline you may be able to pass him with one shot. On very short balls it is often best to drive it directly at him and induce an error.

When your opponent has you pinned to the baseline, however, don't go for an outright passing shot if he is in a good volleying position. A lob is often good here to pull him off the net. In fact, when he has you "very deep" on the defensive, the lob is often your *only* tactic.

When forced to hit a very low ball and you have to "hit up," the best shot is a soft low shot down-the-line. You won't pass him but you might get another crack at it. If your opponent is smart he'll move closer to the net, as your chances of lobbing him from this position are slim. (If you are the net player, always move in close to cut off the return when you have your adversary in this position.)

When facing tall net players there is a tactic rarely mentioned in tennis books. Because he is big he'll usually crowd the net. If you hit it hard right at his middle, he often can't get out of his own way. It is also a good ploy to return his volley in the same direction from which it came. A big guy who crowds the net usually can stretch better for passing shots than he can maneuver the racquet around close to his body. When a return comes back in the same direction in which he volleyed, he has a tendency to hit it to the same spot again. This allows you to get to it fairly early. And if his volley is weaker or short he has put himself on the defensive.

There is one absolute must in handling a net player. Once you have successfully lobbed him, always go to the net to cut off his return. Also, if you've hit a good dropshot and your opponent barely gets it back while on the full run, your best shot is a lob because he'll have to reverse himself.

But whenever you face a net player, always remember this: *you win more points by making him reach than you do by attempting a clean pass.* Keep your errors on passing shots to a minimum. If you can make him volley short, you've got him on the defensive and you're on the offensive. Don't be afraid to lob, especially when you're out of position . . . and a surprise topspin lob is a great offensive weapon if you've mastered this difficult stroke. The best lob is usually to the backhand side. If you make him hit a very high backhand volley, you can usually make a return off it.

## HANDLING A DINKER

A "dinker" is a player who concentrates on soft balling an opponent to death. Dinkers' form is less than ideal, but they have a knack of getting the ball back and most of them can lob. They are the bane of orthodox players, because their "push" shots tend to throw off timing and power. They have put more smooth strokers out of tournaments in the first or second round than any other breed of player . . . and discouraged more potential talent.

Facing a dinker, you have to take points one at a time, and you've got to hold your temper or you'll blow three or four points in a row. I think the best way to handle a soft baller is: get to the net at all costs. The dinker only infrequently can muster a hard shot to pass you with, although he can return the ball all day long in backcourt exchanges. Experienced players understand this, so they attack the net at every opportunity. They know better than to fall into the trap of trying to outsteady these frustrating creatures from the baseline.

## CONTROLLING THE RALLY

There are times when playing an opponent's backhand off your forehand is a tactical mistake, at least for most players. This concerns a general strategy for baseline rallies: don't hit down-the-line, especially from the forehand corner, unless you're attacking the net or attempting a passing shot. If you hit down-the-line, you've put your opponent in the position of controlling the rally by allowing him to exploit the diagonal with a crosscourt backhand. He can (and will) run you ragged, but only if you allow him to.

An excellent illustration of what this can lead to is a forehand return on a deuce court serve when the server remains on the baseline. There is a temptation to return down-the-line because it is to your opponent's backhand. But this is the wrong shot, because it gives the opponent the opportunity to hit a natural deep crosscourt to *your* backhand. When this happens you're automatically in trouble; he is in control of the rally because he has exploited the diagonal. Because you are chasing a wide deep shot with your backhand, the natural inclination is to hit down-the-line again, at which point he'll crosscourt another long diagonal off his forehand. Again your easiest shot is down-the-line because you're on the run. Back and forth it goes . . . and you're on a string like a puppet. What would have been the best tactic here? You should have returned the serve more or less in the same direction it came over.

If no serve is involved—that is, you are involved in a baseline rally —there is less excuse to allow your opponent to exploit the diagonal. But if you've been forced to hit down-the-line, don't repeat the mistake on the next shot. When he's hit the long diagonal to your backhand, try to crosscourt—though it's a tough shot on the run. Don't attempt a winner . . . just a slow, deep crosscourt to give yourself time to regain the center of the baseline.

Avoiding deadly diagonals is connected with a basic principle of tennis strategy: try to use those tactics that keep you from running for deep backhands, high-bouncing ones in particular. In fact, as a general policy avoid high backhands as much as possible. It is one of the most difficult shots to handle offensively, especially if you have to run for it. Yet when you hit down-the-line from the forehand corner you are putting your opponent in the ideal position to execute just the shot you don't want.

If your adversary has a penchant for down-the-line shots, however, you should exploit the diagonal and put him on a perpetual motion machine with crosscourts.

Many great players have, however, hit down-the-line with impunity. Jack Kramer nearly always hit down-the-line off his forehand; he hardly ever used a crosscourt until after he turned pro. Kovacs and Segura would frequently hit down-the-line shots from the baseline.

Although it may sound contradictory, a down-the-line shot from the baseline isn't necessarily a violation of basic strategy. It depends on your weapons. Down-the-line is inherently a more forcing shot than a crosscourt simply because it has less distance to travel and gives the receiver less time to get set. When Kramer hit his famous sidespin (veering to the left) forehand to the backhand, it was very tough to return a deep crosscourt off it. The same was true with Kovacs, Tilden, Segura, and others who had big forehands. When you can really force a backhand, then you are in a different ball game.

The deep crosscourt backhand has been called the basic stroke of baseline tennis and explains why you often see a long series of backhand exchanges between backcourt stylists. Yet Don Budge wasn't averse to hitting his backhand down-the-line because his power forced the opponent into hitting short . . . if the opponent got it back at all.

But when you discuss these power strokers you are talking about another dimension of tennis. Generally speaking, the crosscourt strategy is the best for controlling the rally; such outstanding baseliners as Billy Talbert, Seymour Greenberg, Bitsy Grant, and Frank Parker adhered to it. Certain players, however, find down-the-line is their natural stroke. If you are one of these, and you have the forcing forehand of a Kramer (with a net game to back it up), then you don't have to worry. Otherwise it's advisable to learn to hit crosscourt, or else be prepared to run a lot . . . unnecessarily.

### POINTS THAT COUNT (AND GAMES THAT COUNT)

There is one yardstick that separates winners from also-rans (assuming players of relatively equal talent): the champions get the points that count. Budge Patty was able to capture Wimbledon in 1950 largely because of his ability to win the key points. There have been many stronger players than Patty but few smarter. Patty had a fine serve, forehand, and volley, but his backhand left something to be desired. He structured his games to hit as few backhands as possible and was a master at knowing what points were crucial and what to do with them. Lew Hoad in his amateur days was the opposite; he played every point in the same manner . . . just blasted away. Curiously enough, Patty was his nemesis.

Before discussing the relative merits of various points in a game, I wish to stress the importance of winning the "games that count" in a tournament. Go all out to win the first two! Push yourself to break the opponent's serve right off the bat. If he isn't a seasoned veteran, being down 2–0 may cause him to tighten up and he'll never get back in the match. If he breaks your serve, go all out to break right back.

As for points, it is amazing how even experienced players ignore the distinction between 15–40 and 40–15. (They are the ones who lose when they face someone of equal ability.) When ahead 40–15, or 30–0, you can take more chances. If they don't work, you are still in control of the game. On 40–0 is a good time to follow your second serve into the net. The pressure's on your opponent. (If you don't believe me, think back to all the 40–0 games you've lost because, with that lead, you decided to "play it safe.")

A 30-all or 30–15 situation is the worst time to gamble. Make your opponent earn the next points. In these close situations you should rely on your most consistent and valuable shot—this is called percentage tennis. If he has a dangerous shot, keep away from it. Make a special effort to get your first serve in, for if you are going to attack the net, the first is the one to do it on. Also at 30-all (or deuce) returning the serve is what separates the great players from the good ones.

If you are down 0–30 on your serve, then it's time to resort to more power. (This is why you should feel you have something in reserve on your serve—so if you really have to you can deliver it.) When you are behind two or three points is the time to come up with the big service; you are behind anyway, so it's worth a gamble to pull it up to deuce. When a server has you down 40–30, and he's ahead in the match, take a chance for a winner. If it works, you'll be back at deuce . . . and you might just shake him up.

### HANDLING LEFTIES

The tactics against left-handers naturally have to be different than for righties. Most lefties have strong forehands and weak backhands. This means your own backhands should be down-the-line, because that's where his is; a backhand crosscourt is hitting to his strength. This also requires hitting more crosscourts off your forehand to get to the defensive backhand. Thus when attacking the net, you crosscourt the forehand and down-the-line the backhand (the reverse of the usual procedure against a right-hander).

In the backcourt, however, don't be so wary of your opponent's forehand that you never hit to it, for the best way to get to a man's backhand is to hit first to the forehand and force him to uncover a lot of backhand court. Then you can attack the backhand and take the net.

Expect to get lots of topspin crosscourts from lefties, but at all costs resist the temptation to cross it back with your backhand, for you'll be playing into his strength and giving him another chance to attack your backhand with another fierce topspin. What you are trying to do is get at his vulnerable backhand, so make a special effort to go down-the-line.

When a left-hander serves into the ad court, expect to get pulled very far to the left. On your serve go for the backhand, especially in the deuce court. This will pull him out of the court and you can drive a deep return into the forehand corner.

Lob crosscourt to lefties with your forehand, and down-the-line with the backhand. This puts it over his right shoulder, a difficult position from which to smash for left-handers.

## CONSERVING ENERGY

Conserving energy is different for different players, and depends on how much of it you've got. But generally speaking if you've won two sets and you're down 5–1 in the third, it isn't particularly brilliant to kill yourself to make it 5 apiece. Save your energy for the next set; you won't be wearing yourself out against such big odds.

Once you have a service break to put you ahead in a long match, don't tire yourself by trying to break your opponent the second time. At this point, the main effort should be to hold your own serve (assuming it is reasonably good). Later when your opponent will probably be as exhausted as you are, his serve will be weakening so you will have a better opportunity to attack it. In other words, you can take more chances for outright winners. And because the pressure is on him, you are liable to make them. But at this juncture don't get trapped into long rallies, because you are going to need your energy for your own serve.

## NET ATTACK, THE TWO STRATEGIES

Throughout this book I've questioned the validity of the "big game," for a variety of reasons. Taking the net on all serves is often hazardous as well as exhausting. For a player to be successful with this strategy, it is mandatory to possess a consistent, penetrating second serve, backed by quick reflexes and an excellent volley.

However, of course I am not against getting to the net. It is the essential move whenever an offensive opportunity presents itself. My misgivings concern going to the net on the second serve . . . unless it is a deep, forcing shot. And even then it can be perilous. Attacking the net on a perfunctory delivery against stiff competition means putting yourself in a defensive position, and you'll too often end up lunging at the volley, taking the return on the half volley, or getting passed. Nevertheless, attaining the net is essential in top-flight tennis today. Even though Jimmy Connors usually doesn't adhere to the "big game," he attacks at every opportunity. The same applies to such outstanding performers as Ken Rosewall and Jan Kodes, who are sometimes mislabeled "defensive" players. Their defense consists of offensive passing shots, offensive lobs, and offensive service returns. Connors doesn't get tagged with the defensive label because of his awesome power. Yet all three of these remarkable athletes employ the same game style.

Jan Kodes, 1973 Wimbledon champion and Forest Hills finalist, offers a graphic illustration of the strategy I advocate. Kodes doesn't have an overpowering serve, so he "picks his spots" when following his delivery to the net. This is based on instinct rather than on a "big game" blueprint. An experienced player knows when he's serving well, when the opposition isn't returning well, and when the other guy's confidence is shaken. But in the backcourt it is less a matter of instinct than of deliberate pattern.

Watching the sound-stroking Kodes in action reveals he blasts off and moves to the net on *any* ball that is the least bit short. Against a right-hander his groundstrokes will invariably be a crosscourt off the backhand and down-the-line off the forehand in order to attack the opponent's backhand (although when the Czech star is taking the ball with his forehand on the left side of the court he will use a sharply angled crosscourt to the backhand corner). Kodes never hangs back, and against an equally talented groundstroker *who does*, this strategy usually spells the difference. This is the identical strategy Rosewall and Connors use (with the variation, of course, that Jimmy is a left-hander).

If you scrutinize this strategy carefully, it becomes readily apparent that it all rests on a foundation of superlative groundstrokes. As Gene Mako aptly sums it up, "There is no way of being a superstar without super groundstrokes." Yet groundstrokes aren't enough; they must be supplemented by this deliberate strategy. In world-class tennis, having a net game has become a categorical imperative to being a champion. Thus adopting the "shortball" approach, instead of the "big game" strategy, means taking the net on any shot which is even relatively short, *provided it can be handled offensively.* But an important distinction has to be made here. Strictly speaking, these tactics are not the "big game." A "big game" exponent relies primarily on his serve to gain the net, while a Kodes, Rosewall, or Connors relies primarily on his forehand and backhand. Because top professionals always seem to be at the net, this vital distinction has too often been overlooked.

The Connors-Newcombe $250,000 showdown at Caesar's Palace provided a classic example of the two different approaches. It also served to dramatize a salient tactical weakness in the "big game" method of attaining the net. Newcombe lost because he invariably followed in his second serve in the deuce court. This was the tragic flaw—in an otherwise outstanding performance—that allowed Connors to break serve and turn the tide. In fact, I think Newcombe might well have won if he had avoided this tactic; his mighty second serve could have given him the offensive jump on his first ground-stroke. As it was, he actually outsteadied Jimmy in most of their rallies. But when Newk failed to mix up his serving tactics, Jimmy could concentrate all his efforts on making an offensive passing shot.

Another drawback of the "big game" can be inferred from this match. Newk double-faulted nine times, not because he was serving badly, but because of his total commitment to the "big game." In the light of Connors' awesome ability to return, Newcombe was forced to attempt too much with his serve.

Ironically, Connors hit more aces and double-faulted only a third as much, even though Connors' delivery isn't in the same league with Newcombe's. But Jimmy had the advantage of not having to worry about following in his serve. And because he seldom took the net on service, he could relax and be content with placing it well . . . and deep. On the other hand Newcombe, who perhaps has the best second serve in the world, couldn't transcend the basic advantage a great returner has against a net attack. All I can say is, if you are one of those rare creatures blessed with a strong second serve, the "big game" can be a fine strategy against an average groundstroker. But when you face a great returner, the lesson is clear: be wary of the net on your second serve in deuce court.

A penetrating second serve is a rarity even among young professionals who devote so much time to perfecting it, and so far as I have seen young Jack Kramers are nonexistent. Nothing is easier than to oversell yourself on your serve. Because of this lack of objectivity, the difference between a good second delivery and great one can be hard to discern in a sport as ego centered as tennis. But if you are sure of your groundstrokes, you know it.

There are two more points about net strategy I'd like to make.

(1) When taking the net by hitting crosscourt on your backhand "favor coverage on a possible down-the-line return." You've attacked the (right-hand) opponent's backhand, so in order to pass you he'll

have to angle it very wide. It is tough for even good players to avoid hitting into the alley.

(2) A helpful shot for your net approach is called the "chip." It should only be attempted on short and relatively low balls. (A chip is a short swing that brings the racquet strings across the underside of the ball, with little follow-through. Quite a bit of wrist is involved on the forehand, which requires a delicate touch.) Theoretically, it allows you to play a quickly made shot, and the ball does not reach your opponent soon enough for him to pass you before you've gained the net position. (The chip tends to hold the ball in the air longer than a regular drive.) Driving the ball would take longer, and the faster drive would reach your opponent sooner. However, the chip is not a hard or deep shot and therefore rarely forcing. Bear in mind that it is no replacement for a really penetrating groundstroke. But it does make a better approach shot than a lukewarm drive.

### ONE FINAL WORD

There is a key tactical point hardly ever mentioned in tennis books. If you are caught out of court on a groundstroke be prepared to run like hell, but *don't move* until your adversary has committed himself on the return of your shot. If you dash back to the center line, he'll merely hit into the area you just vacated, forcing you into a futile attempt to reverse your direction.

# Psychology

There are two related rules which tennis champions follow religiously. "Never let the other guy get back in the match if you can help it," and "never let him off the hook." Both are basic to the psychology of winning tennis. The first isn't as obvious as it appears. There are good players who let their opponent "into the match" without knowing they're doing it. They haven't started to play badly; they've just failed to pressure the opponent sufficiently on a "point that counts."

Once he wins one of these, the tide can imperceptibly change, even though the point may not be a game-deciding one. You may have failed to move into proper net position after the first volley and he's passed you down the line. This may be enough to make him feel he has a chance. Don Budge says, "Once you let an opponent think he has a chance, it has been my experience that he does." Jack Kramer was merciless in the way he kept the pressure on from the start; he *never* let up, on any point. He would be as inexorable against an inexperienced junior as he was against Ted Schroeder or Pancho Gonzales. Once your opponent gets the impression he has a chance due to a slackness on your part, he is on his way to being back in the match. And when he's back in the match you'll know it! Suddenly from a comfortable 3–1 lead you'll find it is 3-all. You can win a first set by as little as 6–4, and yet know your opponent was never in the match. You were in control; he just managed to hold serve four times. But when he comes back from being down 3–1, that's a different matter. The psychological momentum is now with him.

"Letting him off the hook" is an allied concept, but not exactly the same. It usually refers to a point late in the match when you have an opponent all but beaten. You start admiring your own strokes (or get sloppy) and fail to press your advantage by keeping the pressure on him. It's like having a fighter on the ropes and not finishing him off.

Sammy Match—a master stylist around midcentury—was one of those magnificent strokers who would lose matches he should have won because he let his opponent off the hook. Sam would get carried away with the aesthetic feel of his own groundstrokes, instead of pressing his advantage by taking the net at every opportunity. This is a temptation when you are a beautiful stroker. Ken Rosewall is an example of a superlative stylist who never succumbs to this temptation; he always presses the net attack when he has an opening.

Another way of letting your opponent off the hook is by playing too carefully when ahead. Budge admits he lost to Jack Crawford in the 1936 Davis Cup because he became cautious when he was ahead.

Instinct will tell you when you've got your opponent "on the hook." Don't prolong it; the pressure is all on him. It is here that the two principles dovetail. If you've "let him off the hook" he may "get back in the match." Then he has the psychological momentum . . . and the pressure is on you.

How about the much repeated advice, "Forget the last point"? Good advice, but unfortunately its usefulness depends to a large extent on temperament. As a rule, tennis players are egocentric and aggressive people, so starting each point fresh is easier said than done. The best policy is to try to improve your consistency; you'll be amazed how your temper will improve. (If you've had an outburst of temper, forgive yourself and don't let it fuel another one.) But the worst course to follow is to turn anger inward into apathy. At this point, for all intents and purposes, you've quit. Getting upset won't help your game, but apathy insures defeat. Uphill tennis matches are won by "hanging tough." Keeping yourself reasonably under control, persevering, and never quitting.

One more word of advice. Don't go on the court with unfinished business. Make sure your shoes and strings are right, your glasses adjusted (and that you've gone to the bathroom). If your leather grip is slipping, get it changed beforehand; it will get worse during the match. Any problems like these will aggravate your temper. And once the match gets underway, don't let little things disturb you and upset concentration.

How about your opponent's annoying habits, often used as ploys to "outpsych" you? An opponent can't outpsych you if you don't outpsych yourself. Don't worry about what he's doing. Concern yourself with what you're doing. If he gets angry because he's playing badly, ignore it. Trying to outpsych your opponent with little gimmicks only serves to take your attention off the business at hand.

But, particularly in a tournament, don't be such a good sport you put yourself at a disadvantage. On a very close ball, don't be afraid to call it out if that's the way you saw it. If you are unduly gracious, you are liable to start mentally kicking yourself. (I'm not suggesting dishonesty, only fairness to yourself.)

In tournament competition there is an essential principle to bear in mind: never experiment with strokes while in a match. Besides being bad psychology, it's an invitation to disaster.

Another major factor in match psychology is the already mentioned necessity of going all out to capture the first couple of games. I may have termed this a "tactic," but in reality it relates more to psychology than tactics.

Getting in your first service is of underestimated psychological value, for any error in tennis is a minor psychological blow. I made this point in relation to Ken Rosewall, but it bears repeating. A fault on a serve does not lose you a point, but it is an error, nonetheless. It also brings you close to losing a point on a double-fault, with the added pressure this entails. If you do double-fault, you have suffered a mental setback, no matter what your outer calm. This is particularly true in a crucial game. I can think offhand of two players who have suffered the dire consequences of this "failing"—Dennis Ralston and Bob Hewitt. Both were considered temperamental, but I believe most players who had the expertise these two possessed would have become just as angry and disgusted if they had had the same unfortunate penchant for double-faulting on key points. Both Hewitt and Ralston might have become world champions except for this. They had everything else. Neither had any other weakness, but a double-fault of this nature is such an affront to the ego of a fine player that the resulting funk infects the rest of his game—at least temporarily. There is no possible way of "forgetting the last point" when you've just double-faulted at a critical time in a match. Just as any error is a minor psychological blow, a double-fault becomes a grievous one when an important game hinges on holding serve. It is easy to con yourself into believing that you are certain of the serve when you are not. You've got to be *sure* you can deliver when the pressure is on. It is a qualitatively different thing to double-fault once in a while because you've become sloppy than to double-fault once in a while because you've choked. The same holds true for any groundstroke, overhead, or volley. Most players don't miss setups near the net because they're sloppy, but because they're unsure of what they're doing. It's the obverse of a good player, that is, the man who rarely misses unless he's gotten sloppy.

In this regard the volley is crucial. A groundstroke can be long or netted and still be relatively sound. But unless you're lunging, a volley error is less excusable. It's a simpler shot. Psychologically a player cannot afford to muff volleys. Missing one volley shakes confidence in the next; the errors tend to run in streaks. Pretty soon you're afraid of the net. Besides encouraging an opponent, an uncertain volley blights the overall confidence you have in your game.

Tennis is a game of confidence. And confidence comes after you know what you're doing—not before—as with any other technical skill. Starting out with an ersatz confidence may temporarily relax you, but it is no substitute for knowledge. You will have confidence when you know what to do . . . and you'll know you know what to do when you can perform well on the volley and every other shot. This is the format for the kind of errorless tennis that provides a level of concentration that allows confidence to grow by what it feeds on.

If you are a quick-tempered type, improving your consistency is the best way to improve your temper. Consistency builds the confidence that allows you to take your aggressions out on the ball. Then, even if you lose, you won't mind too much because you haven't beaten yourself. If you develop really smooth strokes, then the aesthetic pleasure will provide a further outlet.

What if you have your game down pat and suddenly your confidence is shaken because you start missing? It may be due to a layoff or because you are tired or upset. My suggestion here is to avoid playing when you're physically tired or emotionally upset. If you do play when you have had a layoff or aren't feeling up to par, rally a long time prior to competition to regain your timing. By rallying you can get back into the groove. How much you have to rally is variable. But when you are "grooved" you'll know it! Your old-time confidence will have returned. Once you're set you'll feel that you can return any ball offensively.

However, let's assume that for one reason or another you do not have an opportunity to warm up and are thrust into a match. You start missing shots you ordinarily make. What to do? The answer is: Nothing—with certain qualifications.

The qualifications refer to what not to do. The worst reaction is to get upset. The next worse is to start thinking—particularly about technique. When your timing is off, the tendency is to overreact; you begin to stress one aspect of technique at the expense of the rest. Tennis technique is a unitary interdependent process; emphasis on a single component disrupts the rhythm of the interaction. It is unwise to become too conscious of the overall process. Assuming you've mastered technique, it is wise to let your game take care of you, as in any other physical skill. Let your consciousness flow—don't force it. All of which is another way of saying, "Don't think about it . . . *do* it."

All that happened when your timing went off was that your kinesthetic relationships were temporarily "out of synch." So don't panic. Just keep playing your regular game and this condition should correct itself. Overreacting emotionally or mentally can only make it worse.

Another classic situation that causes overreacting brings in an aspect of tennis psychology which is almost never mentioned. You've incorporated the "shortcuts" into your game, then encounter an outstanding "dinker"—a player adept at tantalizing soft shots—and your game collapses.

What's happened is that you've unconsciously altered the form on your forehand and backhand; in essence "you've choked." You expect the so-called easy shots to be simpler than drives to handle. The fact is that "nothing to hit" junk gives you no pace to work off, so you have to initiate all the power yourself. A soft baller tends to "break up" your game, so you don't experience the natural rhythm you have against normal drives. (In fact hitting "dink" shots is the test of sound strokes.)

The subtle psychology at work here is a blow to the ego causing loss of confidence. There's a tendency to overhit, underhit, or rush the shot, increasing the chance of error. When this happens, a mild panic sets in, with the consequent unconscious alteration in form. In short, *you* start pushing the ball back.

As pointed out earlier, your best bet is to get to the net, but this isn't easy if your approach shots are off and you lack an attacking serve. Keep your composure, and above all stick to the expertise you know. It may take patience, but if you keep your head, your form should return sufficiently to where you can force the net. Above all, don't try to beat a dinker at his own game. It usually assures defeat and violates the ultimate joy in playing tennis—that is when technique becomes an aesthetic pleasure.

# Spins

I have saved this subject for last, because it is an especially tricky topic, and I am of two minds about your using "spins" unless your game is really complete. As mentioned, topspin especially is all the rage these days, and many a class A or B player feels he hasn't had a good day on the court unless he has blasted away like Laver or Vilas, topping the ball dozens of times in a match. You need to know—and occasionally use—shots in which a spin is imparted to the ball, but if they begin to substitute for the flat or semiflat stroke, you are in trouble.

The mythology surrounding topspin is an ever growing one. To listen to certain commentators you'd imagine it was invented yesterday. As a myth, it ranks right up there with the "big game"—and is about as innovative. Tennis players have been talking about and employing topspin for seventy years.

Rod Laver has contributed more to this mystique than anyone else. It is undeniable that in his heyday in the sixties Rod was a genius with topspin. He achieved angles never seen before . . . and unlikely to be seen again. Laver's timing, strength, and superhuman wrist gave him that license that is peculiar to genius. What is easily forgotten is that genius is inimitable.

The first fact to realize about spin is that to some degree it is on every shot you hit. (For numerous great players—Don Budge for one, Tony Trabert for another—spin was just the natural outgrowth of a sound game, and rarely a conscious effort.) Even the cannonball serve—that paradigm of flatness—has a fraction of spin on it. The very action of the racquet strings coming over the ball puts a forward roll on it.

A so-called "flat" forehand or backhand drive is only comparatively flat. The racquet may meet the ball flat, but the racquet begins to rise in its forward swing before the ball has left the

193

strings; therefore a degree of forward spin is imparted.

Any forward spin is topspin. Whenever your racquet head finishes higher than the ball-contact point you are imparting forward spin. Topspin is a rotary motion of a ball such that it spins forward in addition to moving forward after impact, and the upper half of the ball bites the air first.

Topspin comes in all degrees. There is the slight forward spin of the "semiflat" drive. The "roll" which is an intentional topspin, imparted by a rotation of the wrist and forearm as the strings "feather" the back of the ball. Roll implies a certain amount of wrist and a higher finish; the degree of wrist varies with different players. Some apply topspin by lifting the elbow slightly on ball contact causing the racquet face to turn over the ball. The most common method is dropping the head of the racquet and coming up on the ball.

I'm a student of the semiflat (unintentional) topspin school. It is the alma mater of Budge, Rosewall, and Trabert—and nobody had better groundstrokes. A major difficulty with the three "intentional" topspin forehands is that they demand precise timing and aren't as easy to control as semiflat drives. The use of excessive topspin should be left to geniuses like Laver; for although it causes the ball to dip, just exactly where the ball will land rests in the lap of the gods and the force of gravity. The ball is likely to drop short and allow the opponent to come to the net; topspin is also an invitation to mishitting.

The automatic topspin of a semiflat forehand is imparted differently on certain shots. You can apply topspin by hitting slightly below the center of the ball or slightly above it. When you drive from behind the baseline, you feel you are hitting below the center and lifting on the spin. When the ball lands in the service court and bounces higher than the net, you feel you are striking the ball slightly above center and making the ball spin downward. In both cases, the forward spin of the ball is the same. When driving crosscourt you hit slightly outside the ball; this is topspin, too.

It is easy to become enchanted with intentional topspin, so that you apply it more and more. In addition to increasing the danger of mishitting, topspin entails an unnecessary expenditure of effort. Grinding out topspin is a lot of work, and the results rarely measure up to semiflat strokes.

"Thinking topspin" sidetracks you from the fundamental objective of aiming directly. Topspin brings the ball down into the court, but a true ball-control stroke allows you to drive to the spot you want.

The more spin of any type you put on the ball, topspin included, the less certain you can be of where the ball will land. I'm not saying "don't use it"; all I urge is that you don't let it mesmerize you to the detriment of an all-around solid game.

### UNDERSPIN

Underspin has been given less attention than topspin, yet a degree of it is on practically all volleys—particularly on the backhand and on low shots. The undersliced backhand is still popular, and this means underspin, or backspin as it is sometimes called.

Frank Parker was the master of the undersliced backhand, and even the famed Rosewall backhand, which looks flat, has a degree of underspin on it. Underspin is imparted by hitting the underside of the ball's surface. It differs from topspin in that the bottom of the ball bites the air first. The bottom of the ball is carried by the air underneath it and tends to fight gravity; this causes the ball to hang in the air longer than it does on a topspin shot . . . for this reason it is inadvisable for a passing shot. After striking the court, a ball hit with underspin bounces slower and usually lower than a topspin drive.

A slice differs from a chop in that it is a longer stroke. A chop is a steeply angled short stroke in which the strings are brought across the underside of the ball in a sharp downward motion—like chopping wood.

The chip is another short stroke (used mainly for net approaches), but the motion for it is less steeply angled than for a chop and more wrist is involved. Both the chip and the chop are underspin shots; but while the chop has practically disappeared from the game on the tournament level, the chip is increasing in popularity.

The chop is as old as tennis itself, whereas the chip is a relatively modern innovation, made famous by Gonzales. The chip is a better approach than the chop, because the downward motion is less accentuated, and allows you to move on the net while making the stroke. There is also a degree of sidespin on a chip which causes a skidding bounce that makes a passing shot difficult.

Sidespin is imparted on the forehand by drawing the racquet strings across the ball from right to left; on the backhand from left to right. Forehand sidespin will cause the ball to bounce away from your opponent on his backhand and toward him on the forehand. Sidespin is a form of underspin but differs from the underslice drive in that the wrist is slightly ahead of the racquet head on contact. According to Jack Kramer, the shot grows out of certain styles of semiflat strokes and is largely "accidental."

Undersliced backhands are far more common than undersliced forehands. It is difficult to escape hitting frequent undersliced backhands on the service return. Being a shorter stroke than topspin it gives you more time, especially on high balls. Also hitting topspin off topspin is easier on the forehand than topspin off topspin is on the backhand. But any underslice means a cut in power. And because underspin causes the ball to hang in the air, it makes an inferior passing shot.

How should you counter spin? The usual advice is to counter topspin with underspin and underspin with topspin. This is more useful on the backhand but even there it isn't essential. Semiflat strokes can handle any kind of spin . . . you are in a sense able to "overpower" spin.

Orthodox strokers are sometimes said to give unorthodox players the kind of shots they want and the unorthodox to give the orthodox the kind of shots they don't want. True up to a point; semiflat shots are easier for the opponent to "groove" on. However, a heavy topspin shot doesn't get to where it's going as fast or as accurately as a flatter one; it also doesn't counter speed as well. Flat shots give you the entire hitting surface for control.

But most important of all, flatter strokers can put a series together where the success of the concluding shot is inevitable . . . something heavy topspinners can rarely do. Loopers can pull off startling passing shots but generally they count on your error—not on a concluder. Nine of our First Ten had semiflat strokes; all were "concluders."

# Glossary

ACE   A service so fast or so sharply angled (or both) that the receiver cannot get his racquet on the ball.

AD COURT   The service court on the receiver's left.

ADVANTAGE OR AD   The score when one player or team has made a point after deuce. The advantage is "in" if the server wins it, "out" if the receiver wins it.

ALLEY   One of the two side lanes, each 4½ feet wide, bordering the court.

APPROACH SHOT   A drive, hit deep, that can be followed to the net.

AUSTRALIAN GRIP   A grip between Eastern forehand and Eastern backhand.

BACKCOURT   The region of the court behind the service lines.

BACKHAND   A stroke made on the left side of the body by right-handers, on the right side by left-handers.

BACKHAND COURT   Same as AD COURT.

BASELINES   The lines at each end of a tennis court.

BEVELS   The "diagonal sides" of the racquet handle.

CANNONBALL SERVE   A hard-hit flat serve.

CENTER MARK   The mark on the baseline that splits the line into equal halves to help the server establish his position.

CENTER SERVICE LINE   The line separating the two service courts on each side of the net.

CHIP   A short stroke on the underside of the ball with very little follow-through.

CHOP   A steeply angled, short chopping motion imparting under-spin.

COMPOSITE GRIP   Same as AUSTRALIAN GRIP.

CONTINENTAL GRIP   A grip in which the palm of the hand is farther over the handle than in the Eastern forehand. It is the same hand position as the Eastern backhand, except the thumb is not on a diagonal but wrapped around the handle and the "V" crease (thumb and forefinger) is on the left bevel of the handle. The wrist is almost completely in line with the top of the handle.

CROSSCOURT   A ball hit diagonally to the opposite side of the opponent's court.

DEUCE   The score when each player or team has won three points; also the score when the side with the advantage loses the next point. A set in which both sides have won at least 5 games is called a deuce set.

DEUCE COURT   The service court on the receiver's right.

DINK   A softly hit shot used by advanced players to bring an opponent toward the net and force him to hit up.

DIP SHOT   Stroke hit with excessive topspin which causes the ball to drop sharply.

DOUBLE-FAULT   Two successive service faults which cost the server the loss of the point.

DOUBLES   Tennis played with two on a side.

DOWN-THE-LINE SHOT   A ball hit roughly parallel to the sidelines.

DRIVE   A stroke hit with a full sideward swing after the ball has bounced.

DROPSHOT   A shot hit softly and with backspin—usually from the front part of the court—to make one's opponent dash quickly forward to retrieve the ball.

DROP VOLLEY   A delicately hit volley that drops the ball just over the net—used mainly by advanced players.

EASTERN BACKHAND GRIP   The most popular backhand grip. The palm of the hand is placed partly over the handle and the thumb is placed diagonally behind the handle for extra support. The "V" crease is on the left bevel of the handle.

EASTERN FOREHAND GRIP   The most popular forehand grip. The "V" between the thumb and forefinger lies in the middle of the top surface of the handle, putting the wrist behind the handle.

ERROR   An attempted return that goes out, into the net, is missed completely, or is hit after the second bounce.

FAULT   A serve that does not land in the proper service court or a serve that is illegally struck, as when a foot-fault is made.

FIRST COURT   Same as DEUCE COURT.

FLAT SERVE   A serve hit hard and with little spin.

FOOT-FAULT   A fault caused by the failure of the server to keep his feet behind the baseline before the ball is struck on the service, causing the server to be charged with a fault even if his serve lands in the proper service box.

FORCING SHOT   A hard shot that requires one's opponent to hit a fairly weak return.

FORECOURT   The region of the court between the net and the service line.

FOREHAND   A stroke made on the right side of the body by right-handers, on the left side by left-handers.

GAME   A unit of scoring. The first player to win 6 games, if his lead is 6–4 or better, wins a set. With a tie at 6-all, a tie-breaker is generally used to determine the winner.

GROUNDSTROKE   Same as DRIVE, i.e., forehand or backhand.

HALF VOLLEY   A stroke made just as the ball comes up from the court.

HEAD   The part of the racquet surrounding the strings.

LET or LET SERVE   A served ball that brushes the net and drops into the proper service court. It must be played over.

LET POINT A point that must, for one reason or another, be played over.

LOB A ball lofted high in the air.

LOVE A scoring term meaning no points. Synonymous with zero.

MATCH A competition between two or four players, usually determined by the winning of 2 out of 3 sets or, with men, sometimes 3 out of 5.

NET BALL A shot other than a serve that touches the top of the net and falls into the opponent's court. The opponent must play it as he would any shot that lands in his court.

NET GAME A style of play depending on volley and overhead hit from a position near the net.

NO-MAN'S-LAND The area between baseline and service line.

OVERHEAD Same as SMASH. A ball hit from a high position off a lob.

OVERSPIN Same as TOPSPIN.

PASSING SHOT A drive that goes past the net player.

PLACEMENT A shot that lands in the court out of reach of one's opponent, or the ability to make such shots.

PUTAWAY A shot similar to a PLACEMENT—however, this term implies that the ball has been hit very hard.

RALLY Hitting the ball back and forth in practice or during the playing of a point. A relatively long exchange of groundstrokes. Also used as a verb.

RECEIVER The player who receives the serve.

SERVICE or SERVE The stroke that puts the ball in play at the beginning of each point.

SERVICE COURT One of two courts on each side of the net into which the serve must be placed.

SERVICE LINE The line 21 feet from the net, the back boundary of the service courts.

SET At least 6 games won by the winner who must lead by at least 6–4. (See TIE-BREAKER.)

SETUP   A very easy shot—one that should be put away for the point.

SIDELINES   The lines on either side of the court that mark the playing area.

SIDESPIN   Spin imparted by bringing the racquet strings across the ball sidewise.

SINGLES   Tennis played with one player on each side.

SLICE   A stroke hit with sidespin; also a stroke hit with underspin.

SLICE SERVE   The most common serve, hit with sidespin for better control.

SMASH   A stroke in which the racquet is brought down fast and hard on a lofted ball. Same as OVERHEAD.

SUDDEN DEATH   See TIE-BREAKER.

THROAT   The part of the racquet between the head and the handle.

TIE-BREAKER   A new method of scoring in pro tennis when the score reaches 6–6. The player who wins the tie-breaker takes the set at 7–6, instead of having to be two games ahead as formerly. This crucial game is called "sudden death" and is based on a point system of 7, 9, or 12, with the participants alternating on their serves.

TOPSPIN   A forward spin on a ball, imparted by bringing the racquet strings over the top of the ball as the racquet hits "through" the ball on solidly hit groundstrokes.

TOSS   The "placing" of the ball in the air by the server before hitting the serve; or, before play, the spin of the racquet to determine choice of court or serve.

UNDERSLICE DRIVE   A long stroke in which the racquet hits slightly under the ball, imparting a certain amount of underspin.

UNDERSPIN   A backward spin on a ball.

VOLLEY   A shot in which the ball is hit before it bounces. Also used as a verb.

WESTERN GRIP   An awkward grip with much of the palm under the handle and the first and second joints of the thumb lying flat on the top surface of the handle.

WINNER   Same as PUTAWAY.